Samantha Irby

we are never meeting
in real life.

Samantha Irby writes a blog called *bitches gotta eat.*

www.bitchesgottaeat.com

ALSO BY SAMANTHA IRBY

Meaty

we are never meeting
in real life.

we are never meeting in real life.

· ·

essays

Vintage Books

A Division of Penguin Random House LLC

New York

A VINTAGE BOOKS ORIGINAL, MAY 2017

Copyright © 2017 by Samantha Irby

All rights reserved. Published in the United States by Vintage Books, a division of Penguin Random House LLC, New York, and distributed in Canada by Random House of Canada, a division of Penguin Random House Canada Limited, Toronto.

Vintage and colophon are registered trademarks of Penguin Random House LLC.

Portions of this book originally appeared, in slightly different form, on Samantha Irby's blog, *bitches gotta eat* (www.bitchesgottaeat.com).

Some names and identifying details have been changed to protect the privacy of individuals.

The Cataloging-in-Publication data is available from the Library of Congress.

Vintage Books Trade Paperback ISBN: 978-1-101-91219-5
eBook ISBN: 978-1-101-91220-1

Book design by Anna B. Knighton

www.vintagebooks.com

Printed in the United States of America
10   9

This book is dedicated to Klonopin.

contents

we are never meeting
in real life.

my bachelorette application

I am squeezed into my push-up bra and sparkly, ill-fitting dress. I've got the requisite sixteen coats of waterproof mascara, black eyeliner, and salmon-colored streaks of hastily applied self-tanner drying down the side of my neck. I'm sucking in my stomach, I've taken thirty-seven Imodium in case my irritable bowels have an adverse reaction to the bag of tacos I hid in my purse and ate in the bathroom while no one was looking, and I have been listening to Katy Perry really, really loudly in the limo on the way over here. I'm about to crush a beer can on my forehead. LET'S DO THIS, BRO.

Are you: Nominating someone [ ] or Applying yourself? [x]

Name: Samantha McKiver Irby

Age: 35ish (but I could pass for forty-seven to fifty-two, easily; sixtysomething if I stay up all night)

Gender: passably female

Height: 5'9"

Weight: Lane Bryant model? But maybe on her period week. I have significantly large ankles.

Occupation: My technical job title is client services director at the animal hospital where I've worked since early 2002, which loosely translates to "surly phone answerer and unfriendly door opener." I'm pretty lazy, although I *am* quite good at playing the race card and eating other people's lunches in the break room.

E-mail: [redacted]

What is the next big city near you and how far is it? Chicago. And it's zero miles away. I mean, I'm in it right now, doing Chicago things. You know, eating a deep-dish pizza while wearing a beat-up Urlacher jersey and sprinkling pieces of the Sears Tower (no real Chicagoan will ever call it the Willis Tower) on top and reading *Oprah* magazine. CHICAGO.

How did you hear about our search? I have a television. And I do most of my reading while waiting in line to buy diet yogurt at the grocery store.

What is your highest level of education? High school, but I took a *lot* of honors classes.

Where were you born? Evanston, Illinois. A suburb along the lake, due north of Chicago and the birthplace of hella luminaries like Marlon Brando, the Cusacks, Donald Rumsfeld (gross), Bill Murray, Becky #1 from the TV show *Roseanne*, and possibly Eddie Vedder. At least I think so? We all believe that the song "Elderly Woman in a Small Town" is about us, but we have *three* motherfucking Whole Foods. That most certainly qualifies us as a medium town, at the very least. Maybe that dude really is from someplace else.

Where did you grow up? EVANSTON. And I'm still basically there. All the time. Unlike Eddie Vedder, I can't get out. I work there, my doctor is there, and even though I technically live within the Chicago city limits, if I need to go to the supermarket or the movies, I always think of the Evanston ones first. It's a trap. No one ever leaves this place. Not kidding, I see my junior-year English teacher at Starbucks every morning, which is down the block from the bagel shop this dude I graduated with just bought. It's gross. I gotta grow the fuck up.

Do you have siblings? How old are they? When I was born my parents were almost-forty and almost-fifty, which means I have never seen either of them: chase a ball, get down on the floor to help construct a Lego set, or run along behind me as I wobbled on a two-wheeled bike. I have three sisters who are currently, brace yourself, fifty-six, fifty-four, and fifty-one years old. HILARIOUS. My sister Carmen is going to be sixty real years old in a few years and that blows my mind. Is your mom even sixty yet?! S-I-X-T-Y.

Have you ever been arrested, charged, or convicted of a crime of any type? If so, please give details: I was arrested for shoplifting once, when I was fourteen. Before you write me off as a wayward little thug, hear me out. So I have that disease that a lot of poor people who claw their way out of the miserable depths of poverty suffer from, the one that makes you want to blow your paycheck on all the special things because never before in your life could you ever have had anything even remotely fancy or expensive. But I was a teenage girl and I needed lipstick and I couldn't wait the two years it would take for me to pick up regular babysitting work, so I went to the Osco in downtown Evanston one afternoon and slipped tubes of Revlon's "Toast of New York" and "Iced Coffee" (it was the nineties, brown lips were the thing) into my coat pocket and tried to nonchalantly waltz out of the store like they hadn't had what I was looking for. I was met at the door by a stern-faced manager, an older black gentleman whose disappointment in me was palpable.

"Is this what Martin Luther King marched for?" he grumbled under his breath as he led me to the room with the mops where a handful of morose-looking degenerates were eating lunch. Pretty sure Revlon is owned by white people, but I didn't want to further piss him and the ancestors off. He sat me in a rickety office chair and I surveyed discarded Employee of the Month photos fanned like a deck of cards across the threadbare carpet while he called the police. When the portly, red-faced officer showed up, I was deep in a REM cycle, snoring hard with my head on someone's particleboard desk. As the cop escorted me to the waiting patrol car, we passed Morgan Freeman dragging a homeless-looking black dude with bottles of Tylenol and Advil spilling out of his overstuffed pockets back to the makeshift holding cell. Blood trickled from a gash on his forehead. "That guy must have some headache, eh?" The officer chuckled. What a tacky asshole.

"Arrested" might be a stretch. What happened next involved me lying as flat as humanly possible across the backseat of the police cruiser as the officer drove like he was in a fucking parade, seven miles an hour, through throngs of my recently dismissed classmates. I imagined them straining on tiptoe to see who might be in the backseat. My mildly disappointed sister met us at the curb and assured the officer it would never happen again. That is the extent of my criminal history.

Have you ever had a temporary restraining order issued against someone or had one issued against you? If so, please give details and dates: No, but when I was nineteen, I used to stalk this dude I went to high school with. I would close up the bread shop where I worked, take one of the loaves that was intended for donation to the soup kitchen, then drive my car to his parents' house and park close enough to see inside, but far enough away to be inconspicuous. Then I would sit there with the engine running, tearing off chunks of apple-cinnamon bread and listening to De La Soul while imagining our life together.

I am a deeply troubled person.

Have you ever filed for bankruptcy or Chapter 11? No, but I wish I had thought about that shit years ago before I decided to overdraw on an old bank account. DO NOT WALK AWAY FROM AN OVERDRAWN CHECKING ACCOUNT, FRIENDS. Why didn't anyone ever teach me that shit? I mean, someone should write a primer for adulthood that's just two or three sentences long:

1. WEAR CLOTHING THAT ACTUALLY FUCK-ING FITS.
2. BUY DRUGS FROM REPUTABLE DEALERS ONLY.

3. DO NOT WALK AWAY FROM AN OVER-DRAWN CHECKING ACCOUNT.

I could have been such a better human.

Have you ever auditioned for or been a performer, participant, or contestant on a reality or other TV or radio show or in a film? What are the rules as far as comedy podcasts and rudimentary videos of stage performances recorded on shitty camera phones and uploaded to YouTube by assholes? Do those count?

Do you drink alcoholic beverages? DO I.

What's your favorite drink? I don't believe in pretending to be cool anymore. If I did I would tell you that I enjoy two fingers of nicely aged bourbon, neat with a water back. In real life I drink daiquiris and Skinnygirl margaritas and shit like cupcake-flavored vodka. Also I really love beer, but not any of the impressive kinds that you order to show how exceptional you are. I basically drink like a sorority pledge.

Have you ever been married or engaged? NOPE.

Do you have any children? I'm counting the cat here. So, yes.

Are you genuinely looking to get married, and why? Honestly? I don't know, homie. Marriage seems so *hard*. I mean, even the ones on television look like they just take so much god-damned *work*. I'm lazy. Plus, getting out of one seems ridiculously expensive. And then when you get divorced, after all of the crying and draining of mutual bank accounts before your partner gets a chance to, you have to cut the children in half, which is probably very bloody and messy. You know, what I really need is someone who remembers to rotate this meaty pre-corpse toward the sun every couple of days and tries to get me to stop spending my money like a goddamn NBA lottery pick.

Why would you want to find your spouse on our TV show? Have you been to the club lately?! Shit's fucking dire, man. Also, I need someone to watch *Shark Tank* with, and I feel like that's a spousal kind of expectation. Can't just ask your casual booty call to commit to spending Friday nights indoors arguing over the valuation of some at-home mom's jelly and jam business. And I'm too poor to run multiple background checks.

Please describe your ideal mate in terms of physical attraction and in terms of personality attraction. Physical attraction? Not a real thing. If, at thirty-six years old, I'm sitting over here talking about chiseled abs and perfect teeth, then I am undeserving of genuine romantic love. I have slept with a handful of conventionally attractive humans, the prettiest of whom was this dude who worked at Best Buy and kind of resembled "So Anxious"–era Ginuwine. He was boring and lazy and totally caught off guard when I pointed those facts out to him. No one ever tells attractive children how much they suck, and then the rest of us get stuck with insufferable, narcissistic adults who can barely tie their shoes because someone else is busy either doing it for them or congratulating them on their effort. I do not have the energy to be in a relationship with someone exceptionally good-looking.

I don't know what an attractive personality is. I like charisma and charm, but what I really need to find is someone who doesn't get on my nerves but is also minimally annoyed by all the irritating things about me. That is my basic understanding of relationships at this point in my life: that it all comes down to finding someone too lazy to cheat and who doesn't want to stab her ears out every time I speak.

How many serious relationships have you been in and how long were they? If I'm being honest, the answer is probably two. And if I'm *really* being transparent, one of those was mostly sexless bullshit, and the other spent half our relationship going to Barbados with women who weren't me, so none.

What happened to end those relationships? IRRECONCIL-ABLE DIFFERENCES.

What have you not found but would like to have in a relationship? Someone who will leave me the hell alone for extended periods of time without getting all weird about it. I have a lot of audiobooks to listen to on the toilet.

What are your hobbies and interests? Hobbies: eating snacks, sleeping during the day, scrolling through Facebook quickly enough that people's stupid videos don't start playing automatically, listening to slow jams.

I pretend to be interested in a lot of things: art, theater, recycling, donating to things, expensive varietals of coffee. But mostly I just watch television and read celebrity gossip on the Internet while getting most of my important news from Twitter, which I don't even really like that much. I'm interested in animals and novels and red lipstick, but let's just say "world issues" and "social justice" so I sound kind of smart to the viewing audience.

Do you have any pets? I HAVE A CAT-CHILD NAMED HELEN KELLER; I believe we've been over this already.

What accomplishment are you most proud of? If this is in a real book that someone is actually holding between her sweaty, chocolaty paws, then *this* is my proudest achievement. Also, learning to drive stick while wearing flip-flops. You have to be kind of a genius to do that, for real.

The Bachelorette is my guilty-pleasure jam. That may come as a surprise to some of you, but you should already know that a show where a woman is surrounded by twenty-five slabs of brisket clamoring to brazenly drink her dirty bathwater and massage the corns on her toes in front of the entire country is 100 percent my kind of party. I love watching a man humiliate himself; I wish it was on every night. Particularly the introductory episode, when we get to meet all the software sales executives and tax accountants and telecommunication marketers as they line up in their finest suits, teeth flossed and smelling good, forced to do the "Hi, please date me!" tap dance women are perpetually performing. Seriously, I used to try to neatly cram everything remotely interesting about me into my "Hey, nice to meet you, I am . . ." elevator pitch. Now that I know impressing a stranger isn't worth the effort, I don't do it anymore; I just assume every man I meet is bored and hates me. I can barely be bothered to give one a high five before writing down my e-mail and saying, "Get at me if you want." So it is especially heartening to watch these smarmy, desperate clowns crawling all over one another like rats trying to get the attention of these "free spirits" and "dog lovers" who will eventually make them burst into real tears on national television.

The Bachelorette proves that men are as petty and vapid and ridiculous as women are made to seem. They're just better at hiding it, because they get to be Real Men and sulk and brood and bottle everything up. These dudes are backstabbing drama queens who are constantly cutting one another down, throwing shade all over the place, and casting more side-eyes than a Siamese cat, all for a girl who, I must remind you, could probably not do long division by hand. And why shouldn't they? Because every single one of these dudes is as boring as a glass of tap water, while the bachelorette is beautiful and friendly and forced to sit in a dress in sequins that have got to be digging uncomfortably into the backs of her thighs. I have never sat down to watch a marathon of episodes stored on my DVR and thought "Boy, does he seem interesting" about any one of the candidates up for sexlection. (Let's hit pause on the remote for a second here and say that I do pay very close attention to one or two members of the cast: the black ones clinging for dear life to the inner tubes as they drift helplessly toward the deep end of the dating pool. No, she's never going to pick Marcus or Jonathan, but she *will* keep them on life support for however many episodes it takes to satisfy the NAACP. I watch that shit like a hawk, like "This date better not include a 'fun trip' in a marsh boat on the ol' Magnolia Plantation" or "If they serve these dudes a piece of fried chicken I will throw this TV out the window.")

I usually fall off by the time they get down to the final two, because romance is a lie and true love an impossibility. Any asshole can fall in love on a private beach in a tropical locale, surrounded by lush flora and adorable fauna, shining suns and chirping birds. Give me ten uninterrupted minutes without some ding-dong demanding something or subtweeting me or making me do work and I could fall in love with my worst fucking enemy. Seriously. What's not to love about being expertly lit and drunk at two in the afternoon?

But I'm going to need you to love me on the bus, dude. And first thing in the morning. Also, when I'm drunk and refuse to shut up about getting McNuggets from the drive-thru. When I fall asleep in the middle of that movie you paid extra to see in IMAX. When I wear the flowered robe I got at Walmart and the sweatpants I made into sweatshorts to bed. When I am blasting "More and More" by Blood Sweat & Tears at seven on a Sunday morning while cleaning the kitchen and fucking up your mom's frittata recipe. When I bring a half dozen gross, mangled kittens home to foster for a few nights and they shit everywhere and pee on your side of the bed. When I go "grocery shopping" and come back with only a bag of Fritos and five pounds of pork tenderloin. When I'm sick and stumbling around the crib with half a roll of toilet paper shoved in each nostril. When I beg you fourteen times to read something I've written, then get mad when you tell me what you don't like about it and I call you an uneducated idiot piece of shit. Lovebird city.

If there was an alternate universe where I could remake this show starring myself, it would be the best dating show in history. I smell a ratings juggernaut, and it smells like cat pee unsuccessfully laundered from a fitted sheet, seared pork, and adult diapers. Fetch me a camera crew.

.   .   .

Here are my qualifications:

1. I'm fat and black.

Isn't it about time they had a bitch with a REAL 2 PERCENT LARGE COTTAGE CHEESE CURD ASS on this awkward date parade? I mean, come on. Welcome to your "after" photo, gentlemen. Prime-time television needs some real talk from a real asshole, and that asshole should be me. But they have to make sure they cast a bunch of Latinx and one white guy with dreadlocks who you can rest assured wouldn't be a real contender.

2. Instead of roses I would hand out condoms.

Because I'm not living in a house with twenty hot dudes I can't get naked with. You must be crazy. And you better believe those elimination ceremonies are taking place in the bedroom. No foreplay? NO ROSE. Keeps his socks on during? NO ROSE. Rabbit fucking? NO ROSE. Takes too long to come and starts chafing my haunches? NO ROSE. Blows air into my vagina? NO ROSE. Says dumb stuff in bed? NO ROSE. Won't let me get a good up-close look at his butthole? NO ROSE. Won't let me gag him and tie him up for fun, even though that does nothing for me sexually? NO BLEEPING ROSE. I should probably go get a robe, because my pajamas are just retired "exercise" clothes, and if I'm going to be kicking dudes out while their dicks are still sticky, I want to make sure I look as classy as possible. If the JCPenney catalog is to be believed, a bathrobe is a surefire way of achieving that.

3. I would plan realistic dates.

Do you really want to watch me giggle and squeal and pretend not to be scared out of my mind because we're going hang gliding or rock climbing or whatever other challenges these guys typically participate in? Do you really want to watch me bowling and roller skating with a group of sexy dudes? NO, YOU DO NOT. What you really want to watch is the "Can this dude pay for our meal at Alinea?" challenge and the "Can homeboy sort and wash his own laundry?" competition. Because if this show is really about marriage, my starry eyes and pinchable cheeks don't matter. That kind of thing only goes so far. I'm sure people get over my dimples easily within six fucking months. And then what? Those sharp edges I filed down in front of the cameras are back in full effect, and my real flaws are now comfortable enough to come out and leave halfway through the concert to go take a shit, so to get prepared we're going to play sexy party games like "Can you take a sarcastic joke?" and "How mad will you get if the cat pukes in your shoe?" or "Be quiet and play on the computer while Sam is sleeping" and "Please don't be salty when I put our business on the Internet."

4. The network would save so much money on production.

We're shooting it in Chicago. And I don't need a fancy wardrobe or stylist, I'd wear my own terrible clothes. That's what these brothers are going to see once they drop to one knee and ask for my paw in marriage anyway, so why front? I don't wear evening gowns and booty shorts every day. I wear daytime pajamas and orthopedic shoes, and lately I have become a big fan of the "grandpa cardigan." I shave my head, so I don't need a fancy hair person; my barber cuts my hair for twenty bucks and then I rub some African oils on it so it smells good and glistens in the sunlight. Everyone wins.

5. The winner would *totally* not be forced to propose.

If you are ready to commit the rest of your life to me after a couple of weeks of getting drunk while a camera crew follows us around, you are not a rational person who makes good choices. It would be incredibly flattering, but ill-advised nonetheless. At the end of the season I'm always surprised when the dudes actually propose, yet not surprised at all when I read in *People* magazine two weeks later that the happy couple has split because he still has feelings for his college sweetheart and the bachelorette can't leave her career as a dental hygienist in New York to move to Montana and run the family dairy farm.

The season finale will go something like this: We're sharing a postcoital can of beer and watching Jimmy Fallon. I get up (WEARING MY ROBE) to find my bra and to pee for the thirty-seventh time while he tries to wake up his erection for round two. I come back to bed with more beers, a bag of pretzels, and cold leftover pizza. I send a few text messages to other dudes; he eats all my food without offering me any while getting cheese and grease all over my remote and crumbs in my nice sheets. I pee again—I really cannot be out here risking UTIs like they don't hurt like the devil—and he takes a call that I suspect might be from another woman, because the parameters of our relationship thus far have been unclear. I can't really say anything, so I just sulk and pretend that nothing is wrong, but I'm totally ignoring him and pulling the duvet to my side as I turn on *Sex and the City* reruns (I'm a Miranda), and just to make sure he knows I'm *really* ignoring him I put on my headphones and crank up my iPod really loud and sigh a lot until he hangs up the phone and says, "What's wrong?" Then I respond, "Nothing," with a little too much aggression in my voice as I flip through the channels like a woman possessed until it dawns on him what my problem is and he exasperatedly sighs and says, "That was my *mom*," but it's too late because now he knows I'm a jealous baby and he doesn't want to be my boyfriend anymore, but maybe he'd still like to sleep with me because of that thing I do with my pinky fingers. Then we'll fall into a fitful, uncomfortable sleep, after which he'll decide that he needs to go "home" or to "the gym" or to "ESPN Zone" or wherever you penises like to hang out in your free time. I'll tell him my last name (finally), and he'll promise to get my phone number from Chris Harrison and text me when he gets home. Just like Cinderella. Or on TV.

a blues for fred

Fred and I ended our relationship on a sticky August afternoon in the summer of 2012. In the years before our introduction in the comments section on a piece I'd written about how I couldn't have sex with a man who didn't think that not having his own checking account by his thirtieth birthday was a big deal, Fred had flown to New York by himself just to see the Basquiat exhibit. For that I was grateful, as his passionate description of Basquiat's early graffiti work kept me from having to make polite conversation while huffing up the stairs at the Art Institute in the waning days of summer. I'm pretty sure there was no Instagram way back then, so I was left to my own devices and forced to look closely at Lichtenstein's brushstrokes and read descriptions as the gentle voice from the audio tour guided me from painting to painting, Fred trailing behind me taking notes in a battered Moleskine.

If you are a certain type of sap, this is one of Those Moments. You know, the ones in which you relax long enough to think that this might actually be real and cool and maybe start thinking about accidentally leaving some allergy meds and an old toothbrush in a dude's bathroom. I had already "forgotten" a lip balm and my emergency glasses on the bedside table and hidden a case of fancy bottled water in a kitchen cabinet, but visions of five inches of available space in his underwear drawer had begun dancing through my head and I could not get them to shut up. This is the shit that is exciting to you eight months into a casual-sex thing, a thing that might hopefully blossom into something less casual if maybe you play your cards right and have managed not to be too interested or available-seeming, that maybe this person who went on vacation with another woman a few months ago might give up some closet real estate so you don't have to either (1) wear pajamas on your dates, or (2) go to sleep after the dates in your clothes.

I didn't see the end coming. Which is not to say that I was surprised, because I wasn't—I just thought that I had more time. I knew that when we had Serious Grown-up Talks about our goals, and mine didn't include much more than "king-size bed and lightning-fast wireless Internet," that I was eventually in store for a heartfelt yet awkward conversation about my lack of motivation toward property ownership. And that's okay. Dating is totally weird at this age, what with all the pushy relatives and ticking clocks that people have to contend with. At twenty-four, who cares if you drink a couple of beers across from an irresponsible hipster's ironic haircut and then take him home for less-than-memorable sex; but if you wake up on your thirty-second birthday childless and untethered to a human with health benefits who has read more than one book in the previous twelve months, you have to get your ass out of bed and start Dating with Intention. And maybe people don't really say it that way, but let me clarify that that is *precisely* what "Oh, you're still dating that guy who's an iPod DJ?" really means.

Fred had a house, man. Which was like, LOLWUT. My

previous life had been filled with so many gentlemen trying to get their dicks sucked in their childhood bedrooms (complete with superhero twin bedsheets, in one unforgettable case) that the first night I walked into Fred's actual crib and met his actually spayed Rottweiler who came bounding down his actual stairs after we'd parked in his actual garage, I almost burst out laughing. I was peeking into cupboards and putting my ear against closed doors trying to determine whether anyone else lived there. That kind of shit was mind-blowing for a person who once dated a dude with six actual roommates. I was like, "How much is your seventh of the rent, thirty-seven dollars?!"

Anyway, Fred had a kitchen, and in that kitchen was a juicer and a fruit bowl that held seven perfectly ripened mangoes. I remember being struck by a half-empty bottle of Dawn propping up a sponge on the sink and thinking to myself how amazing it was that this was a dude who used dishes and then washed them. Listen, I don't want you to think I was messing around with men who couldn't tie their own shoes or whatever, but a lot of dudes in their thirties don't have proper washcloths or fresh produce, so when I crossed the threshold of this actual house and didn't immediately trip over seventeen barbells and a rat king of video game controller cords, I kind of lost my shit a little bit.

We went on a lot of Really Good Dates and he never gave me a hard time for trying to rap along with Outkast in the car or acted weird when I got all giggly and gross watching Michael Fassbender's huge dick waggle around during the movie *Shame.* Which we watched on a tall leather couch with no cracks in it, not a futon or a beanbag or his dad's recliner while he was out of town. Let's talk about the first night we had sex—no, wait, what we *really* need to get into is the morning after: I woke up in this massive California king with beams of blinding sunlight slicing through the curtains (MY MAN HAD ACTUAL CURTAINS) to warm its crispy white sheets. Dude was gone, and in his stead he'd left a couple of neatly folded fluffy towels and a brand-new bar of soap. In the shower I thought to myself, "This motherfucker has *got* to have a wife," as I blinked shampoo out of my eyes and squeezed expensive conditioner into my palm. But from the look of things he didn't, unless she used beard-sculpting pomade and wore size-thirteen work boots.

He was downstairs blasting Killer Mike and grating potatoes for homemade hash browns, and this might have been the exact moment that my brain exploded, because that kind of thing had happened to me never. Cash for a Starbucks to drink on the train going to work? Sure. Three and a half minutes to sniff at all the dried-up takeout containers in the fridge in search of something even vaguely edible before the cab pulls up? Absolutely. But from-scratch blueberry pancakes with turkey bacon, hash browns, and lukewarm mango puree courtesy of the fancy juicer on the counter? NOT EVER. And that kind of gloriousness continued throughout the course of our relationship: home-cooked meals that consisted of more than just massive blackened hunks of charred meats (seriously, it's either they cook absolutely nothing at all or pork chops the size of your head on a grill with neither sides nor condiments); thoughtful, engaging discussions about culture and news; fresh bars of soap and neatly folded towels every morning for the shower. Despite myself, I got excited. I like to be excited about stuff, and hanging with a dude I could buy a book for who would actually take the time to read it was terribly fucking exciting.

I thought Fred was my *Love Jones*, the black renaissance relationship I'd been waiting for, ever since I watched Larenz Tate chase Nia Long's NYC-bound Amtrak as it departed Chicago's Union Station, my bougie black romance set to a neo-soul soundtrack. I would be the moody, complicated writer and he the temperamental artist; ours would be a life filled with poetry readings I couldn't understand, artist lectures I would barely stay awake through, and gallery openings during which I would gracefully field questions about whether I was the inspiration for his finest works. I would write jokes about his dick, of course, but that would be offset by the afternoons spent digging through crates of old jazz records and evenings banging drums and talking about shit like the diaspora with our similarly head-wrapped, natural-haired friends. We had all the ingredients: paintbrushes, record players, notebooks, proximity to the Wild Hare. I spent an inordinate amount of time concocting our fantasy future.

I got dumped pretty much because I cannot have a baby. I could feel every bit of exposed upper arm fat catch a chill in that fancy restaurant he'd suggested, and I instinctively bent my arms and tucked my elbows into my sides for protection as Fred tried to find a nice way to tell me that his imaginary future children were more important than what I thought was a really special thing we had going. An hour before that we'd been strolling arm in arm through the Lichtenstein, and my heart was still full of all those people and colors and the fact that I was finally having sex with a person who had a membership to the goddamned Art Institute, and now I was being broken up with over a thirty-dollar pasta in A GROSSLY UNFLATTERING CAP-SLEEVED SHIRT.

I set my fork down. Halfway through, when the sad eyes and gentle tone made my mouth slick with humiliation, I attempted to defend myself. I thought it was ridiculous to talk about my gynecological history and the possibilities of adoption with a dude I met on fucking Facebook, but there I was, trying to fit the ocean into a plastic cup as it tossed and turned me in its waves. I tuned back in as he was saying, so fucking gently, ". . . can you really chase a baby around the backyard?" He didn't mean it in the mean way, I didn't think. Sometimes even when it feels mean it isn't, I reminded myself. I glanced down at my left hand, curled in a stiff black brace, my feet in their orthopedic sandals. No, I would not be chasing any of Fred's babies.

We broke up—amicably, of course, because I am not one to make a public scene—but then kept having sex for a few weeks because I am a total idiot. I remember paying the check and collecting his truck from the valet and driving back to his house as if nothing had changed, as if I wasn't feeling raw and exposed and not good enough, and then dancing in his dining room with him as Prince's "Erotic City" played on the turntable. What kind of asshole wouldn't choose this? What monster would be satisfied with some boring old broodmare when he could just stay with awesome me and get a couple of foster kids or something?! And I'm dumb, but not dumb enough to try to talk a dude out of a major life decision. I don't want to be fifty years old, married to a dude who resents me and hates our seventeen adopted children and our cats. Then I'd have to cheat on him to get some romance back in my dried-up life, and I'd inevitably be caught by a member of our child army because I'm careless and irresponsible. He'd fall into a deep depression, comforted only by the warm embrace of Crown Royal and thug passion. The care of the children would undoubtedly lapse, causing them to take to the streets, robbing old ladies and eating out of dumpsters or whatever. I can't go out like that. So instead we stopped dancing and watched twenty minutes of porn before having sweaty sex in his giant bed and wasting a tablespoon of his perfectly good semen in my useless birth canal. And then I went home and deleted his number out of my phone.

I blocked him on Facebook and unfollowed his Twitter, because the one thing I'm good at is never deluding myself that I can handle the out-of-context social media posts of someone I used to have sex with. I am not calloused in the way you need to be to gracefully handle the onslaught of confusing and hurtful images posted online by an ex. And I'm not even talking about, "Wow look at my new girlfriend our luv is 4eva!" I mean HOW COULD YOU CHECK IN AT *OLIVE GAR-DEN* WITHOUT ME, YOU SAVAGE? So he had to go. I don't know how to use apps to hide people's relationship status updates or whatever the fuck, so I wiped my Internet slate clean of him and avoided people who would ask me when I was going to get back on fucking Match.com.

In the post-Fred era of my life, here's what I would tell myself on your average Tuesday night while absentmindedly massaging some random corporeal swelling with sick-smelling medicated gel: YOU CAN JUST WAIT, YOU DUMMY. STOP TRYING TO BE HAPPY NOW, YOU CAN JUST WAIT. That I could and/or would just wait for everyone else to get old, too, that I would just smile and nod supportively while my young, healthy peers ran through exhaustive lists of their carefree romantic encounters, pretending to listen with intention, patiently waiting for the joints in their knees to erode and the discs in their backs to slip out of place so that they'd stop asking me why I didn't "put myself out there more" and maybe start to understand firsthand what it feels like to pursue someone romantically when you are thirtysomething and have a physical disability and your target is also thirty-something and does not. HOW CAN I SWIPE LEFT ON TINDER WHEN MY GNARLED AND CRIPPLED FIN-GERS CAN'T EVEN WORK THAT WAY WITHOUT A COUPLE CELEBREX?

My joints are kind of a mess. There is arthritis in the meta-tarsal joints on the tops of my feet and in my knee joints and my hand joints, and I have nerve palsy and vitamin deficiency in my sciatic nerve. (I think? Sometimes when the doctor is rattling off a list of things it all runs together.) This makes my feet tingly, and when I stand up from sitting sometimes it takes a few seconds (read: an eternity in real life when people with normal legs are already hovering awkwardly near the restaurant entrance because they had no idea that it was going to take me so long, pawing awkwardly at the ground waiting to regain the use of my foot) before I can step down on my left leg, and you should've been bored with this twenty words ago. I walk like a marionette most of the time, which, despite being kind of hilarious, is the absolute worst; because I am a human *being* and *doing* in a real world where people grimace behind their windshields and look at you funny if you take too long to uncertainly step down from a high curb when it's snowing. Hobbling clumsily around limbs akimbo is double the worst, because none of the real boys ever wants to take Pinocchio out for a glass of wine and a decent piece of meat, and what is my life if it isn't filled with breathless, passionate courtships?

I decided to wade back out into the choppy dating waters of the Internet a few weeks after Fred and I ended things, because I am not a person for whom meet-cutes naturally occur. I don't have a dog to walk through a park of available single humans, no hip Laundromat in which to conveniently forget my dryer sheets so I can ask a handsome stranger for one of his. My dating profile was pretty perfect, I thought. My friend Jill says that I joke too much, that people are scared off by someone who tries to make herself seem so clever, but I swear to God that's how I really think and not just some Internet shtick. I just can't do the requisite "I love baby animals!" and feigned interest in "trying out new cuisine!" and pretending to "live every day to its fullest!" which doesn't really even mean anything anyway. Why do people say that? What impression are they hoping to make? I watch TV all day and leave the house only for snacks: THIS IS THE FULLNESS THAT I AM LIVING. The last book I'd read at the time was *Gods Without Men* and that seemed really impressive to me, especially since I had to haul that doorstop pretentiously around on the train for a week while I finished it. Couple a handful of boring half-truths with half a dozen real pictures of my real body: weighty boobs and meaty backside and the outline of a belly in this one where I'm leaning over to blow out birthday candles on a neon-blue cake. No flattering Instagram filtration, no angled duckface surrounded by a group of my most attractive and nubile friends. The last thing I ever want to do is show up to a bar to meet a person who is expecting to meet the quarter of my sweating meatbeard I didn't crop out of the one photo I wasn't too embarrassed to post. BECAUSE POTENTIAL DATES WILL DRAG ME IN FRONT OF THE FIRING SQUAD, YES? I had read many a snarky think piece centered on blind dates derailed by the super mean lying liarface who'd broken some naive young man's heart by having the sheer audacity to arrive at the predetermined meeting place fatter than she'd advertised. I wasn't gonna be that lady.

But I *was* going to make shit awkward. I clumsily knocked a bowl of mussels into prospective boyfriend Michael's lap after wagging my tail at the bar, wildly happy that our fever dream of a courtship was starting to gel into something real despite the fact that I had worn a diaper to a De La Soul show we'd seen the week before, that I had successfully hidden most of my maladies long enough to win him over with my personality. Michael was a person who had lived in my computer for a Very Long Time before we Actually Met in Person. That kind of shit used to happen to me all the fucking time when I was trying to get the Internet to find me a goddamned boyfriend: superficial asshole with decent taste in music finds my dating profile witty yet approachable, sends me a message despite the fact that "plus-size" was the only available body-type box he hadn't checked, starts lobbying in earnest to become my new best male friend. Except who the fuck ever got on OkCupid to find another one of those? "My best guy friend" is like the fat-girl consolation prize, and if we're all being honest with ourselves, I'm not looking for another person to eat greasy cheesesteaks in my pajamas with. I have Brooke for that.

But, like the inner thighs of my most beloved dark-wash, curvy-fit, slightly flared jeans, I wore Michael down. Not through any wizardry of my own—there's just only so long you can keep having the best conversations of your life before you decide to get over your weird fear of bloated ankles and ask that fat bitch you can't stop rushing home to e-mail to meet you in a bar you know your friends won't be at so you can make each other laugh in person. And things were going okay, I think? We'd gone out a handful of times, already had a number of inside jokes, I'd given him my last two Advil when he got a headache at roller derby. Then BLAMMO! I'm wedged next to where he's sitting at the bar making jokes while he tries to figure out a way to both eat mussels and look cool, and one careless gesture later the bowl is in his lap and people on either side of us are doing that horrified jumping out of the way thing panicky people in close quarters do, like if they don't squeal and knock barstools over, the Ebola virus you just spilled is going to splash all over them. Michael didn't text me ever again after that, and I get it. He'd suffered a lapful of lukewarm beer broth in the middle of a trendy restaurant at my hand, AND I GET IT; but I was disappointed nonetheless, because he'd made me a mixtape—an *actual burned CD* with the artists and song titles printed neatly on a sheet of accompanying notebook paper. That is the kind of thing that signifies the possibility of true love. I've been accused often over the years of not being romantic, but here is where it all oozes out: a list of songs felt by you and presented to me, rendering me flushed and swooning and poring over song lyrics to determine their hidden meaning. The week I spent afterward, one when I pretended to be indifferent to the deafening silence coming from my phone, created a self-consciousness in me that couldn't be explained away by some imaginary event on his side of the universe. I had fucked that whole thing up royally. Back into my celibate cocoon I retreated. And I stayed there for two years, which, contrary to what you might think, made me realize how much sex I actually don't need.

I mourned that relationship with Fred. I mourned it hard. Wrote a eulogy, had a funeral, shed a few tears, put flowers on its grave. When you break up with an asshole, it's easy to just set fire to the shit and move on. But no one talks to you about ending a relationship that never sucked kinda amicably with your homie whom you still love to a degree and for whom you sort of want the best. No, you *actually* want him to be prosperous and happy. Not more prosperous or happy than you are, for sure, or all up in your face with it, but you aren't actively wishing for homeboy to wind up homeless or hit by a city bus. I felt robbed, cheated of my silly daydreams of scribbling manuscript notes in a Moleskine as Fred stood in front of a nearby easel painting while listening to *Kind of Blue* on vinyl, but I wasn't really mad at him. And I found myself wondering what he was doing. A lot. I'd hear a Quadron song and have to resist the urge to text him about it, or I'd throw my phone across the room like a grenade to keep from calling him to talk about a hilarious episode of *Black Dynamite*. I wanted to see Hiatus Kaiyote at the Double Door with him; I wanted to take him to this Afghani spot I had found in the suburbs with the most delicious mantoo and murgh chalau; I wanted to get his opinion on holistic remedies for my shitty, failing knees: I wanted my fucking friend back.

I dipped a toe in the water and almost got frostbite. In six months I'd gone from heartbroken baby animal to FACE-BOOK DELETER AND BLOCKER, and the response I received to my "I'm ready to be friends again!" e-mail was terse and cold and suspicious. Because, in Fred's mind, we still could've been friends all along. He didn't not love me; I didn't not love him: we just weren't each other's person. But, reasonable though it may have been, that talk had left me touchy and defensive, so I let his e-mails and texts go unanswered while I licked my "never gonna spend the morning cuddled at the Hyde Park library together" wounds. I didn't take any parting shots before quietly scrubbing that picture of us at Big Star from my timeline, no nasty voice mail warning him never to call me ever again, and I assumed that guaranteed my seamless reentry into his life when I finally got enough distance from the hurt to allow him back into mine.

I suggested Au Cheval for dinner, because that place is loud and sexy and dark and I knew that Fred would pay for however many $14 cocktails I ordered plus maybe a cheeseburger. I made sure to wear basic, dishwater-gray friendclothes and my house glasses. I probably didn't even wear deodorant. Because this was a *friend* meeting, between *friends*. When he walked in I was flooded with relief, and when he bent to wrap his arms firmly around me I nearly burst into tears. I'm not often very good at exposing my innermost feelings: I am self-deprecating; I avoid tough conversations; I joke my way through uncomfortable emotional moments. But I stood in a corner of that restaurant and poured out my soppy feelings, and I listened to Fred pour out his, and we started laying the groundwork for a friendship. And I'm not even gonna front, I have never been able to navigate a postrelationship relationship with someone whose testicles have been in my mouth, but somehow this is working. Maybe in this life you get all kinds of soulmates, multiple people who vibrate at the same level you do. I think that's what Fred is for me; I just don't get to see his penis anymore. So, no, I didn't get my happy-ending tongue kiss in the rain, but I did get my friend back. And I don't have to worry about running these busted knees around after any babies.

the miracle porker

I never even wanted a pet. I've spent the last fourteen years of my life running the reception desk at an animal hospital, and do you know what that means? It means I can give you eleventy billion real-life reasons why letting a dog or cat take up residence in the shadowy corners of your home (scratching up your children, vomiting in your shoes, caterwauling all hours of the goddamn night) is a bad fucking idea. Right now, while I'm in Detroit drinking my very first Faygo in a sunny loft overlooking the river and glaring at people enjoying themselves below, my feline companion, Helen, is in Chicago, probably definitely pressing her moist butthole against all the clean surfaces in my apartment. She is a pig demon from hell, sent to my life as payback for all the vicious thought-crimes I have committed against people who listen to music on the bus without headphones. People who keep loose change in their actual pockets. People who host sit-down dinner parties in their young, marginally-successful-person apartments.

Seven years ago, Ken, one of the vets at the animal hospital, rolled into work with a shoe box tucked under his arm. Inside was a shivering, hairy ball of mucus the size of a child's fist. It was a baby cat, crawling with fleas and too small to even really have eyes, and the high-pitched screeching sounds it was making made me want to cut my own throat. I hated it. I was standing in the kennel washing out my breakfast dishes in the dog tub and would be having no part of that mewling lump of roundworms and giardia. It was too small and slimy and gross to do anything: feed itself, pee on its own, look even remotely adorable. "Aw, it's too bad that rat is going to die," I muttered to myself as Lori, the head technician, gently placed it into an incubator. Then I went into the break room to make my oatmeal. I am not ordinarily immune to the charms of a cutie-pie kitten with its itty-bitty whiskers and teeny-tiny nose, but the minute Ken walked by, the hairs on the back of my neck stood up and told me that something was up with that repulsive thing. It had the mark of the beast.

Helen's mother was a local stray that kept averting capture and was often spotted roaming the hood with a belly full of kids. Apparently she realized that she had just given birth under a neighboring porch to an infant prince of darkness and decided to bounce, taking her healthy, non-Antichrist kittens with her to a safe house down the block. Ken's neighbor found Helen huddled near his steps, and, remembering he had a veterinarian on his street, rushed her over, wrapped in an old towel, and begged Ken to save her. Never one to panic, my man set her up in the garage away from his curious dogs and hoped she'd be alive the next morning so he could bring her into work and get her on some life support.

A week later, that disgusting garbagemonster was still hanging on. She, as we eventually discovered when her body started to take recognizable shape, was pretty resilient. She drank ravenously from her bottle before passing out milk drunk on a heating pad, KMR infant cat formula leaking from the corners of her mouth, her eyes still gooey slits too premature to open all the way. Technicians would hold her over the trash can and massage her swollen belly until urine came pouring out. They'd dab her little butthole with warm cotton balls to make her poop, then rub ointment on the crusty tumor in her ear while she napped in their cradled palms. Sounds pretty cute, right? Well, fuck that. Every time I would get close enough to watch that little succubus stumble around her cage and search blindly for some unsuspecting food source to latch on to, she would sense my presence and stop cold, turning her thimble-size head and sightless eyes in my direction before emitting a tiny hiss.

The techs and assistants named her Helen Keller because of that gnarly tumor blocking her one ear and the third eyelids that remained permanently glued over her constantly water-ing eyes (and also because, at our core, most people are ter-rible. HELEN KELLER, DUDES?! Okay, fine, whatever). That smelly little chunk probably couldn't hear and definitely couldn't see, but that didn't stop her from eating tunnels through bowls of soupy kitten slurry and taking huge (now unassisted) dumps in the makeshift litter box we fashioned out of cardboard. She still reeked of rotting garbage and had the personality of old shoes, but that little asshole just refused to die. The power of Satan or Xenu or some other diabolical deity grew stronger within her and she'd gain an ounce and an inch by the goddamned day.

One afternoon, as I was taking some samples to the lab, I tiptoed over to the cage where Helen was snoring softly atop a mound of pink towels and fluffy blankets. Just as I felt the ice around my heart begin to melt, she bolted upright out of a dead sleep, her head swiveling 180 degrees on an unmoving neck until her sightless eyes were on me and a low growl rumbled up from the pit of her distended belly. Horrified, I dropped the samples and backed slowly away from her cell, glass shattering as infected dog urine splashed on the moderately priced sensible footwear OSHA requires us to wear at all times in the hospital. I crossed myself and flicked holy water (I keep some in my pockets in case of emergency) as she levitated to the ceiling of the cage.

"I hate you," I whispered.

"Bitch, I hate you, too!" she spat back.

"Is that horrible little thing dead yet?" I asked Ken a couple of weeks later. He had Helen on the treatment table, her slimy head cupped in one gloved hand as he carefully instilled drops into her eyes. "Actually, she's thriving!" he observed, leaning down to peer through an otoscope into what were obviously ear-shaped devil horns. "Her eyes are open and appear to be fully functional."

I strained to look over his shoulder at where she'd hunkered down next to a wad of cotton bigger than her body. I picked her up—she began squeaking and yowling in protest—and cradled her in the crook of my arm. Now that the milky-white membranes that had covered her eyes for weeks had retracted, she was finally starting to look like a real cat. As she gazed up at me, blinking her eyes into focus, the corner of her lip curled into a barely perceptible sneer. "I'm underwhelmed," she sighed, visibly bored by my face. I waited for Ken to go get something from the pharmacy before squeezing her so tight her body went limp and her eyes widened in terror. "I know where they keep the euthanasia solution," I whispered into the downy fur on top of her head. A technician walked by with a load of towels fresh from the dryer and smiled. "That's so cute! You guys are bonding!"

As her eight-week birthday approached, everyone started thinking about trying to find Helen a permanent residence. Her eyes were open, the ear tumor was shrinking, and aside from a chronic upper respiratory infection (treatable with antibiotics), she was ready to start her new life in the home of some naive, benevolent stranger. There's a bulletin board across from my desk with flyers for missing dogs and sales pitches for needy kittens, and Laura, sitting at the reception desk, got to work on some prototype ads with little tear-off tabs. Should it be funny? Or maybe a serious tone would be better. Should she pull at some heartstrings? Or be straight up about what an expensive mess she was going to be? Helen's chest cavity was too small and her tiny nose was chronically stuffed with green herpes snot, not to mention that she needed eye drops every night and her crusty ear growth was still, uh, crusty, and basically what kind of assholes would we be unloading this needy medical nightmare onto some unsuspecting cat lady? ALSO HER PERSONALITY WAS TERRIBLE. THAT BITCH DIDN'T EVEN PURR. What were we, heartless monsters?! Well, I am, for sure.

"Don't disclose any of that," I snapped at Laura as she drew tiny angel wings on the cartoon rendering of Helen we were going to post on the bulletin board. "We need to make sure this bitch sounds adoptable!" I left to go to the bathroom and when I came back it had been decided: these jerks wanted me to take Helen home. The details are hazy: some bullshit about it being unfair to give her to someone knowing she'd need constant medical care, everyone had grown attached, and how would we know she was still doing okay if we gave her to a stranger, blah blah fucking blah. I didn't have any pets at home

(I am an expert at learning from other people's mistakes), and I didn't have any children (like I said, expert), so I didn't really have any excuse, or so Laura informed me. I would be taking that smelly ball of excrement and fangs to destroy the tranquility of my home, and all I would get in return were a couple of cans of cat food and a free rabies shot.

I tried to get into the whole "caring for an animal" thing, I really did. I bought a little carrier with paw prints all over it and overpriced food dishes and natural litter made from recycled newspapers. When I brought her home the day before Thanksgiving, Helen stepped tentatively out of her box, surveyed the landscape, and scoffed. "Where are we, the set of a horror movie?"

Then she smiled at me as she hopped into one of my shoes and peed in it. "I THOUGHT YOU WERE HOUSE-BROKEN!?" I screamed, racing over to dump her little ass out of my soiled New Balance. "I AM!" she shouted back.

I hate this bitch and she hates me. For seven years we've been trapped in this mutually abusive codependent relationship, tearing each other apart emotionally while booby-trapping the apartment in the hopes that this will finally be the time those scissors just *happen* to fall on the floor blades up. Helen Keller doesn't do any of that nice cat stuff you see on YouTube—no cuddling, no purring, no biscuit-making. She eats and craps and scowls at me judgmentally from her perch atop my pillow, silently critiquing my outfit choices through narrowed eyes. ("Sure, you look good in that"—she'll snarl at my elastic-waisted QVC jeans—"I mean, if *you* think so.") She doesn't play, she doesn't chase, and catnip doesn't interest her. Occasionally she'll sit on my desk, face pressed to the glass, chattering marching orders to the bird army assembled on the power lines hanging just outside the window, but other than that she doesn't really *do* anything. She brings me absolutely zero joy. Sometimes I'll wake up in the middle of the night and feel her hot body, nestled close, but never ever touching. If I move even an inch, she'll jump up and move away mumbling some shit like, "It was cold in here and I was just stealing your heat," because it would obviously kill her to admit she feels even the smallest bit of gratitude or affection toward me. I feel like I'm living with Mommie Dearest and nothing I do is ever good enough for her. More than once I have pouted and screamed, "But I'm the person!" while waiting for her to grant me access to the spot on the bed I like or clear the path between me and the bathroom. She has bitten me no fewer than 1,762 times, including once on my fucking eye while I was fucking sleeping, and another time she took an inch-long row of bites lengthwise down the inside of my wrist. (BITCH, I KNOW WHAT YOU'RE TRYING TO DO.) Every single time I get a delivery, or the laundry service comes, Helen is right up behind me in the hall when I answer the door, banging her suitcase into my ankles as she tries to slip past me to start her new life with the college kid who spends his weekends driving a busted Tercel with a Domino's light on top. And I don't care, she can GTFO. "Have fun living in a studio with six other dudes!" I said the last time she pulled that stunt, slamming the door shut in her face.

I got a Peapod delivery a couple of months ago, and she jumped into one of the cooler boxes they put all my Lean Cuisines in while I was awkwardly negotiating how best to tip the driver. Dude made it all the way downstairs in the elevator before either of us realized what she'd done. I was surprised when I heard another knock and opened the door to see your uncle Jim back in his green polo. "Oh, hi! Did you find those triple-absorbent extra-long overnight maxi pads I ordered that you thought were out of stock?" (Listen, I'm not going to rent a car to get groceries, so this is gonna have to be the way, but can we just talk about how awful it is when they go down the checklist of what you wanted that they ran out of at the warehouse and you have to pretend not to care that there aren't six cans of SpaghettiOs with franks in any of those bags?! They never run out of the spinach you ordered, just to look healthy; it's always the Popsicles or the Pizza Rolls that you have to be like "that's okay" about even though NO, SIR, THAT IS REALLY NOT OKAY. I once had to stand in the hallway and sign the form as a grown man was forced to inform my actual face that the three bags of "sweet-and-sour watermelon gummy snacks" I had paid for would be refunded because they weren't available, and I have never prayed harder to be struck dead in my entire life, can you even imagine?) Anyway, your dad's best friend rolled his eyes at me and pointed into one of the boxes where I saw eighteen pounds of misery sulking up at me. I shrugged at him, heaved her into my arms, then dumped her out into my place. "Nice try, fucker." I smirked as she immediately tried to lick my touch from her precious fur. "Too bad they didn't have those *nine* bags of tropical-flavored Jelly Bellies you ordered," she shot back. "If you need me I'll be molting black hair onto all the white shirts in your closet."

I'm tired of this thankless bullshit. I've spent seven real years letting this fool sneeze all over my stuff while bringing basically no cheer to my life and I'm done with it. I know I should feel happy that she survived her harsh early life, but I had a bad childhood, too, and no one's letting *me* sleep all day in the sun while they serve me delicious, portion-controlled meals and take all my garbage out. Could you imagine if Helen was your boyfriend? You get up at five thirty in the morning for work, tiptoe around so you don't wake up His Highness, stub your toe in the dark multiple times while hastily dressing in clothes that you won't realize don't go together until you're out in daylight waiting for the bus, and spend twelve hours slaving under a brutish dictator, only to come home and find that your companion is lying in the exact spot in which you left him. Except now that the sun is up, you see that his stinky body is curled around that sweater so new you haven't even had a chance to take the tags off it yet. And then what does he do? Get up to greet you with a kiss and a shoulder rub? No, that animal yawns in your face before taking a shit with the door open and asking how soon you can get dinner ready. This is what my life with Helen is like, except worse, because she's not even tall enough to change the battery in the smoke detector when it starts beeping. You wouldn't put up with this from a human with actual earning potential for more than a week, yet I've been suffering with this ingrate "cat" roughly the size of a human child for the bulk of my good years. Enough is enough. I've wasted all my black hair and uncreased forehead on this monster when I could've had a fish or a lizard or, better than that, NO PET AT ALL.

So I have one cat for sale. Scratch that, I'm giving her away. Free to even a marginally good home, but a terrible one is preferred. Black-and-white domestic shorthair, definitely part goblin, spayed (for the good of the species), fully vaccinated. Bites, hisses, growls when provoked, pretty malignant overall; won't destroy your furniture or living space but definitely is in regular communication with dark spirits. Neither cute nor friendly, will rebuke all attempts at cuddling. Loves eating but nothing else, except maybe mayhem, as she is clearly a disciple of the serpent of old. Pros: FAT. Cons: TRASH. Inquire within.

do you guys pay your fucking bills or what?

I have no idea how people who actually have money talk to
their children about it. But I sure as shit can tell you how poor
people do.

- "No you cannot have that."
- "The lights will come back on Tuesday when I get my
  check. Until then stop letting the cold air out of the
  freezer. I don't want that ground beef to thaw out."
- "Wash those underwear out in the sink and hang them
  up so you can wear them tomorrow."
- "Put back that box of [insert name of overpriced
  boxed breakfast cereal] and get a bag of those [fruit
  circles/oaty o's/wheaty flakes] from the bottom shelf.
  Don't you look at me like that, it's the same fucking
  thing."
- "Do you really need *every* Sweet Valley High book?
  Go back and read the ones you already goddamn have."
- *Removes package of Capri Sun pouches that the
  juice box fairy anonymously slipped into the grocery

cart and replaces them with dusty bottom-shelf boxes
of orange drink while glaring in my general direction★
"Don't try me, Samantha Irby."

- "Quit playing on my phone, you're gonna run up my
bill."
- "Who told you that you could order all these Colum-
bia House tapes?!"
- "Steer the car while I push it down the street to the gas
station."
- "DID YOU HEAR ME? PUT THAT SHIT BACK,
I SAID YOU CAN'T HAVE IT."

The only time I ever saw my mother in an actual bank was
the day my parents sat down at the kitchen table and decided,
much to the relief of every family within earshot of our snarling-
German-shepherd-chained-to-the-garage, Chevy-Caprice-on-
blocks-in-the-yellowed-front-yard suburban home, to finally
go get a goddamned divorce. After they shook hands amicably,
Mom excused herself, collected me from the bathroom where
I was trying to drown my Barbie dolls in the tub, then drove
us straight to the bank to withdraw all but one dollar from my
parents' joint account.

After moving out of my dad's house, we moved from one
cramped apartment to another, as the important business of my
early life was negotiated in currency exchanges, Social Security
offices, and food pantries run out of church basements, and
transacted in WIC vouchers, money orders, and rolls of quarters for the Laundromat. I had no idea what a credit card was;
I thought rich people just dove headfirst into the piles of gold
coins they kept in their money rooms like Scrooge McDuck
and then came up with enough stuffed in their pockets to buy
things from the comfort of their gold-plated limousines. My

only experience with credit was the dude at the corner store who would write down how many cartons of expired milk I was taking home so my mom could pay for them the third Wednesday of the month when the SSI check came.

My first jobs in high school were all babysitting gigs, and let's be 100 percent clear about what I spent that money on: many issues of *Sassy* magazine, Sarah McLachlan's *Fumbling Towards Ecstasy* and Bjork's *Post* on cassette, every brown and maroon drugstore lipstick I could get my hands on, and steel-toed Doc Martens that I would clomp around in all day every day, even during gym class. Not once did it occur to me that I should be "putting money aside" or "saving for a rainy day"; the first fifteen miserable fucking years of my life had been one great big, long-ass rainy day during which I gazed longingly at the material possessions of my classmates, scowling at their name-brand jeans and hating my broke-ass parents. As soon as I got my first envelope of twenty-dollar bills for chasing babies named Tommy and Caroline around playrooms big enough to dwarf our entire apartment, I started plotting all the dumb ways I was going to waste it, like trading my non-descript blue backpack for one from Eddie Bauer (an exercise that required two buses and much confused trudging through the "good mall") and skipping my free cafeteria hot lunch in favor of overpriced bags of carbohydrate trash from the vending machines in the student center.

I have never—and I mean ever—had a real desire to let otherwise-unaccounted-for money just chill in my bank account unmolested for more than maybe a week and a half. I barely have the willpower to leave other people's money alone for the short time it's in my custody. Money that isn't earmarked for some pressing (transportation/pharmaceutical/credit card balance) need?! Why, yes, I do need fourteen nearly identical blushes, thank you. When I got my first real pay-check, I opened an account at the bank across the street from my job at the bakery. It was the same one my bosses used, so deposits would clear the same day and that was really the only thing I cared about. I ordered some cartoony checks that the teller had to show me how to fill out so I could pay the rent in my newly leased apartment (if either of my parents ever used a checkbook I never saw it—my dad kept a fat wad of bills held together with a rubber band in his pocket), I didn't open a *savings account* or learn about *making investments*. That kind of stuff was for adults—adults who didn't have years of deprivation to undo.

So many ratty Kmart bras I needed to replace with ones that could actually hold my tits up; so many albums with actual liner notes to replace the ones my friends had dubbed for me. Finally, I could read the lyrics to all those Portishead songs I was kind of making up in my head! I wish I could say that I bought some fly shit and a fancy ride, but really I just bought a lot of Gap shirts and name-brand sodas. I'ma assume some broke people are reading this and you know what I mean. I was making it rain dollar bills as I worked my way through the aisles at the Jewel, filling my cart with grape Crush and DiGiorno pizzas and CINNAMON TOAST MOTHERFUCKING CRUNCH. I bought a lot of Converse and a genuine Sony Discman that I filled with bona fide Energizer batteries.

I was trying to fill this gaping hole inside me with "stuff I couldn't have when I was a little kid," and I assumed that one day, when I had finally bought enough magazines and name-brand snack foods to feel caught up, the feeling would go away. But it hasn't. And because I know the value of a dollar, when I get one, I want to buy the nicest thing I can with it. I'm still buying hardcover books and department-store mascara, still daydreaming about what I'm going to spend my 401(k) on when I withdraw that shit early, because who are we kidding? I'm not trying to live to sixty-five, are you nuts? Technically, I can afford it. I make good money, and I don't have any debt, because I've never owned shit and I dropped out of college. I pay for everything in cash because I don't understand APRs, and my credit file was so thin from so many years of living off the grid that when I finally got around to applying for a Discover card, Experian thought I might be dead.

Will my yawning internal pit of desire ever be full? Is there any amount of cash that's enough to fully satiate this ravenous beast?! I don't know, man. Will Céline keep making dope-ass sunglasses every season? Will Netflix and Spotify and HBO ever stop providing me with unlimited access to hours upon hours of entertainment to distract me from the ennui that awaits in real life? Will the ghost of Steve Jobs keep putting out next-generation iPhones with that *one* new feature I absolutely must have no matter how many of my firstborn sons I gotta give to Sprint to get one? How many lipsticks is too many? Is a daily Starbucks run really that big a deal? Why do they keep making new shampoos if you're not supposed to immediately toss the half-full one you've been using just fine for months and get the shiny new one advertised in one of the many magazines you're always "wasting" five dollars on? (Side note: I spend a lot of time anxi-sizing [anxiety fantasizing] about jobs I would never be able to do, and number one on that list is definitely "inventor of new cosmetics," because how many different eye shadow kinds can there even be, how many kinds of lip pencil have yet to be thought of?)

If scientists could just cool out for a minute on the whole manufacturing of hot shit I will surely die without, I might be able to set aside some money for stocks or whatever, but I can't right now, because did you know that for a scant $7.99 surcharge during off-peak hours, you can get Whole Foods precut watermelon pints and gluten-free vegan pizzas delivered right to your door by a dude named Jared driving a Smart car? That is if you don't want to take an Uber there and back because fuck the train, a bitch just got paid!

Do I need to cancel my Hulu subscription? And if I do, can I wait until this season of *The Voice* is over? I don't want to suffer through the indignity of commercials!

Ugh, I was feeling bad about my shoes at this fancy "cocktail lounge" the other night with this bitch I don't like that much who I know for a fact is greater-than-slash-equal to me in levels of poverty, and she made an elaborate show of heaving her giant designer purse onto the bar so she could dig through it to find the laundry money she was going to use to pay for her Sazerac. "That's a really nice bag," I said genuinely, taking a sip of my light bill. "Did you recently receive a settlement of some kind?" She laughed heartily and poured her Obamacare deductible down her throat in one long swallow. "Girl, nah, I bought this with money I should've spent on my car payment." I clinked the ice in my checking account overdraft fees and nodded solemnly in agreement.

A lot of us are living like this, right? Taking cabs and ordering takeout Thai on payday, then walking the three blocks to work from the train with a bologna sandwich in our bags a week or so later? How does anyone do anything? Or, better than that, how does anyone do both the shit they *want* to do with their money at the same time they're doing the shit they *need* to? Example from my own dumb life: I need to buy a plane ticket to LA on some last-minute shit. If I buy it now, I'ma probably have to pay my rent late. If I wait, chances are I'm gonna have to fly out at 10:30 p.m. and pay $1,200 for a center seat or some equally undesirable thing. Every time I pay an overdue bill from a doctor visit so long ago I can't even remember what was wrong with me at the time (WTF is the point of this insurance if it doesn't cover anything?), I shed a tear for the half dozen quirkily adorable T-shirts I could be ordering from ModCloth instead. I want to be one of those people who feels satisfied when I pay my bills rather than cheated out of whatever frivolity was sacrificed in their place.

The other day, while I was trying to figure out how I could work fewer hours yet still have enough money to buy something at CB2 called an alpine gunmetal bed (yes, I need that), a thought came to me: I SHOULD MAKE A GODDAMNED BUDGET.

Then I thought, Fuck a budget. I grew up poor and now I have money, so I'm going to spend it on Chanel nail polishes. I don't know how you can possibly have joy in your life when you do shit like "balance your checkbook" or "pay your minimum balance on time," and if doing those awful-sounding things means I can't see four movies in one weekend, then I don't ever want to do them. I can't go to the *library*. I mean, first of all, what if someone else checked out the book I want? I'm not the only one reading the book reviews in the *Times*, so now I gotta put my name on a list after your aunt Karen and my elementary school principal, then just, like, wait for them to be finished? I would rather be dead.

But at some point you have to start thinking about saving up for something other than a lobster dinner, so I caved and read all the brochures in the after-hours ATM lobby while trying to loiter nonthreateningly behind a lady depositing what had to be 437 individual checks (hurry up) and tried to make a budget for myself, but it was as trash as you'd expect. I bought a Suze Orman book and remembered that I'd signed up for Mint

.com in 2013, but I stopped using it because I felt too judged by all the expense categorizing (90 percent of the things I spent money on qualified as "amusement.") Then I just googled "how to make a budget." Essentially: At the beginning of the month, you make a plan for how you are going to spend your money that month. Then you write down what you think you will earn and spend. All month long you have to write down everything you spend, no cheating. At the end of the month, see if you spent what you planned.

I made it through two days before quitting because it was too embarrassing. I don't like knowing how much of my rent money I've spent downloading children's games to play on my phone. If my plan is to die peacefully in my sleep before my hip inevitably slips out of place, do I even need to worry about a retirement plan? Do any of you guys think about that shit? Wait, don't tell me. No, I mean, only tell me if the amount of money you've spent on bottled water this month is more than you set aside for your savings. I prefer to admit my inadequacies to assholes who can relate. So after I burned the notebook I had halfheartedly dedicated to my frivolous daily expenditures I googled "money-saving tips." Oh, don't worry, I HATE MYSELF, TOO.

Pack a lunch!
House lunch is so boring, though. Also, packing it the night before feels gross, and the prospect of making it in the morning before I leave feels impossible. Sometimes, if I cook too much dinner for one person, instead of trying to cram the excess down my throat so I don't have to rifle through all the mismatched plastic containers in my cabinets to find a top that fits with a corresponding bottom, I will wrap those leftovers in

foil or toss them in a ziplock bag and vow to myself to take it with me for lunch the next day. But the next day that Bomb-ass Dinner just looks like Half-a–Sad Lunch and will inevitably need to be supplemented by a few stolen bites of Someone Else's Break Room Sandwich. And then you're *that* person.

Save your loose change!

Can we have a serious, vulnerable, heart-to-heart talk for a minute? So I have very few phobias. Like, almost none. Clowns, spiders, flying, public speaking, balloons, needles: NO PROBLEM. But if you try to give me a handful of coins, I will literally burst into tears. (Cue strangers throwing nick-els upon recognizing me on the street.) I cannot stand any little metal thing, especially if it's clinking together and making noise, and touching disgusting change makes me want to peel the skin from my hands like an orange and then soak them in bleach. The thought of a piggy bank sitting on my dresser makes me want to cry. Once, my boss put a swear jar on my desk, and because I never have change in my pockets, I had to pay a dollar every time I cursed. I lost twenty-seven mother-fucking dollars the first son-of-a-bitching day.

Use coupons and take advantage of discounts!

Oh no, this makes me so sad. And is it even possible if I have Cody from Instacart doing all my grocery shopping?!

Buy items in bulk!

A few years ago I went to Sam's Club with my friend's mom. I am not capable of things like "having memberships to places," and also, it was maybe the dumbest thing I've ever done in my life, so I will never be going there again.

(1) All of the produce—and I mean all of it—rotted before I could even make a dent. I am one person who lives with one salty garbagecat, and the two of us have pretty much zero use for four real pounds of spinach. Even now that I've traded in rib tips for fennel bulbs, I can't use that much fucking spinach. WHAT AM I GOING TO DO WITH SEVENTEEN APPLES, SAM WALTON?

(2) I am an obsessive bathroom cleaner, so imagine my joy when I happened upon a six-pack of Clorox toilet bowl cleaner just chilling there all shrink-wrapped and begging to live under my kitchen sink! I still have one of those bottles. Years later. Under my sink. Because I am one person with one ass and one toilet and buying things in bulk is for people with guest bathrooms who are responsible for snack day at the elementary school. What was I even thinking? Also, I'm pretty sure it took me six months, minimum, to recycle the boxes they make you take your stuff home in.

Take fewer cab rides!

Uber is going to bankrupt me. Did you know that for sevenish dollars, you can ride to work in the luxury and comfort of the backseat of a 2009 Toyota Camry driven by a bored old guy who will ask way too many questions and will safely deposit you right at the door of your destination without your having to dodge a single double-wide stroller or knife-wielding bum? Compared to the threeish dollars it's going to cost you to run-walk—a backpack full of three-for-$10 frozen dinners and the (now soggy) library book you're going to read in the closet you eat lunch in jostling against your shoulder blades—through pouring rain to the unpredictably late or early elevated train. You will ruin your top with anxiety sweat, the expensive cotton of your best work shirt clinging wetly to the hairs at the small of your back, as an increasingly angry rush-hour mob forms behind you and your ineffective swiping of the Ventra Card you put twenty bucks on last night. The train rumbles into the station overhead, and you step in what you're pretty sure is liquid human waste as you hustle up the stairs, only to have the doors clamp shut just as you reach them. Yes, that woman in the fur coat pushing a grocery cart heard your strained pleading for her to hold the door as you limped across the platform, and, yes, she absolutely chose to ignore you. So now you're shivering, soaking wet, and you can't sit down because someone left a soiled baby diaper next to a dirty hypodermic needle on the bench. The announcer just informed everyone that the next six trains are running express past your stop, so, yeah, maybe it's a better idea to just jump onto the tracks in front of one rather than continue with this miserable day. I lost a perfectly good hat one winter as I walked from the brown line to Union Station when a 75 mph blast of arctic wind blew it off my head and across three lanes of traffic. Standing impotent on the corner as icicles hung from my lashes, I watched a grimy cab squash it into a pothole thick with muddy slush and whispered softly into my scarf, "Man, *fuck* the train."

Socialize at potluck meals instead of at restaurants!
WHAT DO THESE WORDS EVEN MEAN? You know how I know my friends love me? Because they've never asked to come over to my apartment. Going to other people's houses is terrible. What if the food they made from one of those

thirty-second instructional videos is gross? What if their dog is super annoying? What if you have to poop and the bathroom opens into the room you guys are all chilling in, so you're basically shitting with an audience? You can't just subject innocent people to your butt! The real problem with going over to Craig's Saturday night for a little get-together is that there is no way for you to leave without looking and feeling like an asshole. You wouldn't have to worry about holding in a turd all night if your homie would just let you bounce after dessert (i.e., a half-eaten box of Girl Scout cookies he found in the freezer, because people our age never remember to buy a fucking pie when they invite you over). But noooooooooo, he just set his projector up and you have to watch a movie on the living room wall and I'm sorry you hated that movie but don't leave yet! We haven't even played Cards Against Humanity!!!

I just want to go down to the bar, listen to three beers' worth of your problems, then claim that my stomach hurts so I can leave and get in bed before nine. And, yeah, we could probably get a case of home beers for the price of the ones I'm tipping two dollars apiece on, but then I'd have to sit in your house for the time it takes to drink all those beers. The cost-benefit analysis of brunch versus trying to find a polite way to tell you I'm about to fall asleep on your couch has shown that twelve-dollar eggs win every single time.

Clearly, what I need to be is rich. I need to invent something rad or get hit by a city bus so I can get enough zeros in my bank account to ensure that I will never have to touch any icky loose change. I gotta start playing the lottery. Except if I win, I definitely need a trustee or Britney Spears's dad to get me some municipal bonds and dispense a weekly allowance, because I am not to be trusted. I would buy half a dozen pairs of glasses and legally download a bunch of movies I don't even *like* before the check even cleared. I would buy that Rainbow Brite doll I never got Christmas 1986 and drive her around in my new car full of gasoline with my windows electronically rolled down and the air conditioner blasting, eating fistfuls of Life cereal and sipping a motherfucking Capri Sun.

you don't have to be grateful for sex

I saw my first adult human penis when I was thirteen years old. My mom had been gone for approximately thirty-seven seconds, and I heard a lilting patois call from the bathroom: "Sweetheart, come in here and give me a hand. I want to show you something."

This maintenance guy had been working in our apartment all morning; his work boots thundering down our hallways, his aggressive stench filling my nostrils every time he swaggered past the bedroom where I sat, blissfully ignorant, in a backward Kansas City Chiefs cap with a library book held an inch from my face. Even though I was five-foot-eight and had my motherfucking *period* already, I was not allowed outside without adult supervision, and the multiple sclerosis that my mom was diagnosed with before I was born left her too disabled and too tired to properly supervise. I spent my summers indoors on hot, musty days like these, watching Cubs games on WGN and earnestly singing "More Than Words" along with the Top 9 at Nine countdown on the radio every night.

I carefully folded a corner of the page and slid off my bed. I am not, by any stretch of the imagination, *handy*. I cannot:

Fix a flat tire.
Change the battery in my smoke detector.
Correctly hang a picture on a wall.
Tell you which cord goes into its corresponding hole on
    the back of my television.

I am also not sexy. At least not in the traditional sense, not in the way that makes erections jump to attention the moment I walk into a room. I feel like my sexiness is a thing that creeps up on you, like mold on a loaf of corner-store bread you thought you'd get three more days out of. One day you're slapping me on the back like I just pitched the shit out of a Little League game, then the next you're like, "Holy shit, this lumbering laundry bag full of damp tennis balls actually has reproductive parts, and, boy, do I want to touch them."

Which is why the dick thing was so weird. We'd had a passing introduction when I walked past the door as my mom was letting him in, certainly nowhere near long enough for him to graduate from slyly convincing me to write his social studies paper to awkwardly putting his hand up my shirt in the far corner of the playground. But when I rounded the corner to see what he needed, dude was just standing there with the damp slug of his thick penis stretched across his palm, a smug, satisfied smile plastered across his face. He'd obviously been peeing in the toilet he'd just fixed.

A champion masturbator by that point, I recognized what I used to think of as "the sparkle feeling" stirring to life in my flooded basement as I studied it from root to tip: tufts of dark curly hair nestling a ridged, veiny shaft that curved to a pale, smooth tip, still glistening with drops of urine. My immediate reaction was a desire to stroke it with my fingertips before gently taking it into my mouth, but other than a limited knowledge of some of the dirtier passages in an illicit copy of *Wifey* obtained from the library down the street, I didn't know anything about sex or men or where a penis goes in your actual acne-studded, oily T-zoned body.

Theoretical television penises slip painlessly into women as they moan and writhe in ecstasy beneath someone they obviously love very deeply, but I had read enough magazines to know that it can be bloody and clumsy and embarrassing in real life. Also heterosexual intercourse definitely leads to fertilized eggs, and my mom and I were still sharing a bed, so where the fuck would we even put a baby? And while it might be good to have a baby with a skilled laborer who could stop leaks and put up drywall and apparently come to work in a freshly ironed shirt, I had gotten a B minus in science at the end of the school year. I was a thirteen-year-old who still sucked her thumb and was definitely not ready to be anyone's mother.

"You wanna touch it?" he offered hopefully.

"Oh, no, thank you!" I replied with a forced cheerfulness, like I was at a friend's house turning down his mom's offer of a second helping of peas. (JUST GET TO THE DESSERT, DIANE.)

"No? Really?!" he asked in disbelief. "Not even a chubby girl like you?"

What does that even mean? It's not like he was standing there holding a warm loaf of banana bread—I might have taken him up on that. But it was just an old, semi-flaccid pervert penis: What the fuck did my chubby have to do with his chubby?!

I stood on the threshold of the bathroom, trying to gauge how mad I should be at his insult. Why was he so shocked by my refusal—do fat girls like sex more than skinny ones? Does touching a penis lower your blood pressure or lessen your risk of developing type 2 diabetes? As a fat, gawky adolescent who was surely destined to live the rest of her life as a fat, gawky adult, would this be my last chance at sex? SHOULD I JUST TAKE WHAT I COULD GET?

As one of the few early possessors of breasts, I had certainly had them furtively felt up in various dark hallways and unmonitored bedrooms, but I wasn't interested in racking up more physical conquests. I used to read a lot of dreamy romance novels, and so who cares about touching a cock if the person attached to it wasn't going to fall madly in love with the beautiful princess buried under these unlovable layers of processed foods and self-loathing? Years of watching shows like *Degrassi* and *Fifteen* alone in my bedroom while my friends were trying out for the cross-country team taught me that it was okay to keep eating Cheetos for dinner because, one day, some hot young man would transfer to our school, and I'd trip adorably in front of him. I'd drop my adorably unorganized books and papers on his socially acceptable footwear, our eyes would meet as he crouched to help me pick them up, and he'd realize he should take me to prom and love me for the rest of my life. I spent the entirety of 1993 to 1997 biding my time waiting for Drake to get out of that wheelchair, slide my glasses off, and see the real me.

A semi-detailed manifest of a few smoking-hot dudes I've banged who thought I should have thanked them for the pleasure:

1.

"You really don't know how lucky you are to be with me." M was talking to me from the bathroom doorway, pulling his dick and balls taut so he wouldn't nick them as he attended to his pubic hair with an electric beard trimmer.

I took a bite of my night doughnut, pensive. "Why, because you have six percent body fat?"

He laughed, which made his pecs flex, causing me to feel sorry for us both. "Man, kind of? I'm just, like, a really good catch."

"But you wax your eyebrows. And you work at Best Buy."

I'm not shitting on people who work in mass-market consumer electronics, because I have an hourly job, too, but dude, you were wearing a shirt with your name on it when you met me. What is all this "you should be grateful" bullshit? Also, you are the type of person who doesn't understand that artfully styling one's pubes is a shameful thing that should be done in private.

I've had sex with a lot of hot dudes—*surprisingly* hot dudes. And I'm sure you're all, "Yeah, but they were pity bangs," and maybe? I mean, probably?! But there have been so many! They all couldn't have been trying to star in the John Hughes movie of my life! The first time I got a super-ripped bonehead naked in my bed I couldn't believe my luck—I thought my life was going to completely change the second he wedged his rubbery penis into my vagina. Because I watch a lot of TV, and if nothing else, TV has taught me that if you are a positive person who is kind to the tiny woodland creatures who burst through your open window to help you clean your room and make up your bed, then one day the hottest prince in the kingdom, the one with a foot fetish, will find you after that house party you had to bail on early and fall madly in love with you.

So that first time: I lifted up his Sean John polo and used my tongue to trace every single groove in the unyielding ice cube tray of his abdomen while waiting to feel a change in my outlook and/or social status. After I sucked his dick, I reached over his taut, glistening body and dug through the crumpled parking tickets and past-due ComEd bills and fished out my wallet, surprised to find that hundreds of dollars hadn't miraculously materialized within. Earlier in the evening, while we'd been making googly eyes at each other over dinner, my granddaughter had shyly approached our corner table with her hand extended, smiling at M. I'm pretty daft sometimes, and also there was a cheese plate involved, so I didn't pay her any mind. It took a couple of minutes to realize that she was hitting on a dude I was on an actual date with—not asking what time it was, or if he had any quarters for the parking meter. HILARI-OUS. He gestured to me as he informed her that what she was interrupting wasn't a meeting between a troubled young man and his dowdy social worker, but that we were, in fact, eating a meal of a romantic variety. Her disbelief was palpable. And I just sat there with an exploded cracker in my hand because the goat cheese was too cold to work with but I kept trying anyway. I sat there with pieces of shattered cracker down the front of my sweater registering this beautiful woman's unbridled shock while the wheels turned in my brain to come up with a suitable explanation for our inconceivable pairing. "Lucky lady," she said as she walked away.

OKAY, SURE. But why, though? It's not like he'd made

her laugh or rescued her cat out of a tree. He just had glorious cheekbones and a magnificently crafted beard. Lucky people win the lottery. Or fly to California with no one sitting in the seat next to them on the plane. Or get the movie theater to themselves. What did she know about my luck? Was I going to wake up a millionaire after I had sex with M?! I flagged the waiter to bring us another bottle of expensive wine.

2.

H had a job—I'm not exactly sure what it was, though—and this beautiful apartment in Hyde Park that I only ever saw at night. It had high ceilings and massive windows big enough to curl up in with a book, but since he didn't seem to read a whole lot, he must use it for something else. The first time I ever heard him sing, we'd just had sex, and I was lying in bed watching thunder and lightning rage outside while holding my asshole tightly closed because I knew I would have to shit soon and was going to try to make it home to avoid a clumsy "what's that smell?" type of situation. Suddenly H slid out of bed and into a pair of gauzy white lounge pants, padding across the room to where a couple of guitars and a keyboard stood sentry in the shadows.

I pulled the blanket up to my chin and watched his skin glow deep purple in the moonlight, his biceps rippling beneath the surface as he tuned the strings of his guitar. I closed my eyes as his rich baritone filled the room, momentarily forgetting that I really needed to get a move on if I was going to get out of his place before the 6 bus stopped running. But his voice was so beautiful, and lying there smelling his lingering scent in the sheets while he sang one of Usher's slow jams was an intoxicating mix, what with the steady rain and flashes of lightning, and yeah, I totally missed that bus and ended up running the shower so I could take a dump without his listening to my farts.

H also had a for-show girlfriend and a for-after-the-show girlfriend, and I'll let you guess (A) which one I was, and (B) just how humiliated I felt when I figured it out. No, it wasn't at his daughter's fourth birthday party, where I stood awkwardly on the perimeter of the festivities sipping sun-warmed prosecco out of a child-size paper cup, the stranger whose inexplicable presence justified relegating her to super-vision of the craft table. "I don't know who that woman is, so let's put her in charge of the pipe cleaners and the paste." It also wasn't during his mom's annual July Fourth cookout, which I'd grudgingly attended even though I don't like eating corn on the cob in public. That day, after I'd hauled bags of ice to a beachfront park under the punishing summer sun, I was rewarded with heaps of fawning praise from all the aunts and cousins who'd gathered round to poke at me with kebab skew-ers, inspecting my tender meat. I was approved!

For a giant slothperson, I am always amazed at how many rooms I can slip into unnoticed; I attribute this to the force field of negativity I project at all times. So when no one spotted me in the back of the café on "Undiscovered Soul" night, it was fine, because I could just chill in the shadows and not distract H from that song I'd heard him rehearsing when he thought I was asleep. He was performing in front of approximately seven people, five of whom were visibly irri-tated that their free Wi-Fi was being interrupted by a dude super-earnestly singing Donell Jones's "U Know What's Up." At the end of his set I went to the stage to congratulate him and was intercepted by a woman who introduced herself as his girlfriend, a speed bump I hit going too fast but pumped the brakes fast enough to ensure a smooth landing. She'd heard of me, you see, his good friend the writer, and she wanted me to know that she enjoyed my work. As I was thanking her, H broke away from a crowd of admirers and said "Oh! Hello!" too enthusiastically, swiftly ushering me to the other end of the café, where I put on my I COULDN'T CARE LESS ABOUT THIS PERCEIVED SLIGHT AGAINST ME satisfied smirk mask and waited for his explanation, which sounded like, "Words words words words words"—deep breath—"words words words words words." In that moment I wished that I'd ordered a coffee so at least I would have something to do with my hands. ". . . value our time together," he continued. "It's just that with this whole music thing she just fits my, you know, my *image* better." And I do know. Which is why I gracefully stepped aside so he could pursue his dream of singing outdated urban contemporary hits in empty coffee shops for people who don't care. And it's a good thing I'm so selfless and full of gratitude, because if I wasn't, the universe would never have been introduced to the modern hero also known as D'Angelo.

LOL JK, THAT DUDE WORKS AT A GROCERY STORE NOW.

3.

I was standing in my tiny bathroom, waiting for the poisonous-smelling Veet I had dripped all over the floor to eat through the hair on my legs, when my phone rang. I was using it as a timer so that toxic slime wouldn't burn through the top two layers of my skin and start incinerating vital organs, and, because I was in a charitable mood, I answered. It was J, and he immediately launched into a long, convoluted story about a whole bunch of shit I didn't give a shit about. No one ever tells good-looking dudes when they talk too fucking much, which is why I always end up looking like a bitch when it happens to me. "I have to remove my leg hair," I interrupted. "This is why I never answer the phone when you call." And just as I was about to hang up on him, he asked, "Would you go to a Weight Watchers meeting with me today?"

Despite the fact that I could feel the thioglycolic acid starting to cook the tender meat on the back of my calf, I hesitated, then said, "Weight Watchers is for quitters who are in denial about how good ribs taste." At that moment, smelling my seared leg flesh, Helen Keller slipped into the bathroom brandishing a knife and fork.

I'm not sure what compelled me to eventually go, other than my bubbling undercurrent of self-hatred and fear of further alienating myself from a sanctimonious vegetarian who believed I had a greater appreciation for jazz than I actually do, but twenty minutes later, my chemically smoothed legs and I were watching him fasten his seat belt snugly over a nonexistent belly. I looked down at where my left thigh spread a little bit over my seat, coming perilously close to grazing the gearshift.

I'm not friends with the kind of people who suggest going to dinner and then agonize over whether to get a little oil in addition to the lemon juice on their vegetable-only salads; my friends get the chips. And the queso. And the tacos. Unless I'd begged for an assisted suicide, no one I know in real life would ever propose to me an hour of horrified weight checks and guilt-ridden calorie tabulation disguised as social activity. "Is this because I got bacon on my burger the other night?" I demanded of the sleek, hardened profile, its darkness standing out in sharp relief against the blazing sunshine outside the car window.

"Of course not!" he lied unconvincingly.

"Mm-hmm. I saw you give the waiter a look when I asked him if the restaurant had a set of defibrillator paddles."

"SAM, THERE WERE THREE DIFFERENT PRO-TEINS ON YOUR PLATE."

Aha! There it was: BACON SHAME. From someone with a preternaturally high metabolism who looked very good in the inappropriately tight turtlenecks he was fond of wearing. I should have never given my number to a man I'd watched writing his name on the clipboard for open mic at a poetry reading, but I was momentarily dazzled by the perfectly aligned, piano-key teeth revealed when he smiled and pointed at the book I was reading (*The Devil Finds Work*) and proclaimed it his favorite Baldwin. I should've rolled my eyes and told him to keep it moving because that is *no one's* favorite Baldwin, but this is the beauty of being beautiful: people just let your dumb shit rock. So, ignoring the inner voice screaming at the sight of his scribbled-in notebook full of Deep and Meaningful future song lyrics, I heaved my backpack off the seat next to me and let this walking stereotype talk to me about Fela Kuti.

"How many points are in an entire pizza?" I stage-whispered to J halfway through the meeting. All 1,287 chins in the room turned to glare at me. "You know, what happens if I just can't stop and I eat the whole thing? Do I just add up twelve pizza-slice points and not eat for three weeks?"

THAT IS A REAL QUESTION, OKAY. If you can have one square of triple-thin-crust pizza and happily close the top of the box and put it in your refrigerator until the next day and not wake up periodically throughout the night asking yourself whether or not you made a huge mistake, then maybe this is not the book for you. BITCHES GOTTA EAT. J was hoping that the riveting world of calorie counting and cheat meals would spark a desire to get with his version of healthy so that we could, in his words, "be a better match." And I kept a notebook so full of formulas and calculations that it looked like Good Will Hunting wrote that shit. I was crabby and terrible and went to sleep dreaming about pudding every night, but I lost ten pounds. J was happy; I was hungry: all was right in the world. Until I asked him if he was ever going to not have three roommates and maybe get a checking account. You know, so we could be a better match. Then it was over.

I know a lot of hot, unconventionally beautiful ladies who kick ass and have sex with rock-star dudes and aren't sorry about it at all. I need to say this loud for the girls in the back of the class: if a dude doesn't want to have to use both hands to grab your ass that's totally cool; it's his choice. But that doesn't make you a piece of shit. You hoist up your saddlebags and go find some dude who thinks you're rad and doesn't mind wiping the sweat off your bottom stomach when you switch sex positions. Don't be all down in the dumps (like a truck truck truck) and let opportunists and perverts take advantage of some low self-esteem you're absolutely too awesome to have. When I couldn't catch a goddamned cold for two-plus years after Fred and I broke up I DID NOT GIVE A SHIT, because I vowed to stop fucking around with people who hate me or don't laugh at my jokes or want me to be thankful for the opportunity to split a lunch check on a Tuesday with a man who was in *one* motherfucking Old Navy shorts ad in the summer of 2009. He was sexy and everything, but, I mean, he didn't even know how to CC an e-mail to multiple recipients. I don't have to be grateful for shit.

a christmas carol

My freshman year of college I accidentally became best friends with a couple of grade-A douchebags. I didn't even want to go to college. But I couldn't fix cars, and I couldn't do hair, and I hadn't had a baby sophomore year, so an accredited university was the next best choice. What I *really* wanted to do was pull a blanket over my head and listen to Pearl Jam's *No Code* on repeat while eating snacks and pretending to be searching for myself all day (fuck, that's all I want to fucking do *now*), but I couldn't find anyone willing to pay for that shit. The state, however, was offering me $15,000 to sleep through English 102 and watch *The Young and the Restless*. HOW COULD I REFUSE?

The bro was called Adam and his brah went by John, and it was my first experience with the species inside its natural habitat, a medium-size state school with a, uh, flexible GPA admissions requirement. I ran into them, literally, while getting off the elevator on the sticky-hot freshman move-in day. Adam reached for my large cardboard box full of grunge CDs and an economy-size bottle of Head & Shoulders, while John grabbed the small television tucked under my arm, and they marveled at my minimalist approach to dormitory life. "You don't know any poor people!?" I asked as I struggled to keep up, the back-pack stuffed with my two good pairs of jeans and a handful of T-shirts shifting uncomfortably across my spine. They were seniors, John told me over his shoulder as we pushed past the crying parents and exasperated teenagers dotting the hallway, and had been roommates for all three years prior. He was inor-dinately proud of their novelty disco ball and "fridge full of brews" and promised to show me their room later.

Adam, though Jewish, was from the north side of Chicago and considered himself a homie, as was evidenced by his low-slung baggy jeans and the insertion of out-of-context Snoop Dogg lyrics into almost every conversation. (I hate the fucking word "wigger" more than I hate anything else on earth, but if I'm being totally honest, that's exactly what this dude was even though it grosses me out to say so.) He had large, sleepy brown eyes and a slow smile and was the kind of guy who hit on black girls by demonstrating his encyclopedic knowledge of Luster's Pink oil hair lotion and BET prime-time program-ming. John was your typical west suburban, chest-thumping meatbag, with a body built for date rape and a giant shellacked auburn head that remained defiantly empty, save for a handful of professional baseball statistics and whatever Greek letters you need to learn to pledge the fraternity with the most lenient academic prerequisite. John was the kind of dude who already looked like someone's dad; you know what I mean? Like, the kind of dude in mirrored shades who chews bubble gum really hard with his arms crossed over his chest, the kind of per-petually tan, leathery-skin motherfucker who always looks like he's standing on a sideline somewhere. The kind of asshole you are continually surprised to find without a whistle around

his neck; a gentleman who should be shouting red-faced into a Bluetooth or standing on a deck he proudly built flipping burgers on a grill he got on sale at Lowe's.

They weren't bad dudes, though John's slicked-back hair and unironic gold chains *sometimes* made me want to punch him in the dick. I kind of felt bad that these dinosaurs were still working on BAs in communications and eating cafeteria lunch with eighteen-year-olds despite their visibly graying beards. Over time the three of us became friends because, in exchange for my discounted tuition, I had to post up at the overnight desk in the lobby of our dorm as part of my work-study package, checking IDs while trying not to fall asleep or get vomited on. It was not glamorous work, and I was not very good at it. Mostly my job was blocking drunk dudes from entering a dorm they didn't live in and keeping the Papa John's guy company as he waited for girls in topknots and printed pajama bottoms to come down and collect their cheese-only pizzas. John and Adam loved what little nightlife DeKalb, Illinois, had to offer, and after several nights of staggering in at 2:00 a.m. totally shithoused and with no identification, they started to recognize me on our floor and would call out, "Hey! Amanda!" every time I walked past their open door with a giant bag of Doritos on my way to watch *Jerry Springer* in the communal lounge, because I would risk the tenuous grasp I had on that job to give them a pass.

I was having a hard time finding my groove. I had a handful of friends to eat dinner and go to the movies with, but I grew up with nice kids in a nice town that had a nice school with a college-and-career center filled to overflowing with brochures from idyllic liberal arts college campuses across the country. I was dumb enough to be hopeful that something nice would finally happen for *me*. The earlier part of my lackluster senior year had been filled with daydreams of escape and reinvention: my cool New York feminist Sarah Lawrence–self or my crunchy/artsy Bennington-self or my sexually free Oberlin-self. I could see the sprawling lawns and smell the libraries full of old books. I had pored over all of the hip college guides, the ones that skipped all the percentages and statistics in favor of "real talk" about what kind of jeans to wear to class and the best local bars at which to test out your fake ID. I wrote thoughtful, honest essays trying to explain how a person with a 1520 on the SAT was also the same person who never took physics (or trig, for that matter) and hadn't bothered with any AP courses and had just barely held on to a 3.2 GPA because they let me take Spanish and choir for honors credit. I went through my sweaters and boots looking for ones that might work in New England in the fall. I filled page after page with my handwritten good intentions, exchanged my saved baby-sitting cash for money orders to have those applications processed, then enclosed them in fat, creamy envelopes and sent them off just before the deadline to lovely sounding places like Williamstown and Northfield and Gambier and Claremont.

Months later, as names like Stanford and Wesleyan and Princeton bounced excitedly off the walls of the student center, I was coming home every afternoon to skinny rejection letters mixed in with my sister's subscriptions to *Essence* and *Cooking Light*. My counselor skimmed my list of colleges over her reading glasses while I thumbed through one of the many astrology books lining her shelves. She reassured me that there were colleges out there that would look past the C-minus in Latin American history and into the core of who I really was as a sensitive, creative air sign, but she suggested I probably should add a couple of safety schools to my list so that I definitely had somewhere to enroll come the following autumn. This is the problem with neither applying oneself nor working up to one's potential, these moments when you are reduced to a bunch of abstract letters and numbers whose unflattering reflection cannot be charmed or joked aside. On paper, I am an asshole: a National Merit Scholar who barely passed chemistry and had to take three different gym classes senior year because I failed one freshman year and dropped out of the summer-school makeup class. Three summers in a row. I led an insurrection of my classmates and refused to read *The Grapes of Wrath,* for which I should have been expelled. The schools I daydreamed about going to? You know, the ones with the lawns and the sweaters? They were looking for girls who got As and volunteered at homeless shelters after school; I got mostly Bs and a lot of Cs and spent my afternoons watching *Ricki Lake* and sleeping until dinner. My acceptance letter from Northern Illinois University, NIU, received two weeks before graduation, basically read, "Our condolences. Here's where you pick up your books."

"What's my name, fool?" Adam said, letting himself into my room without knocking. Because I had let that dummy cheat off my biology final, he'd offered to drive me back to Evanston for the two-week winter break, where I was going to grudgingly listen to people I passive-aggressively hated whining about how oppressive their course loads were at Harvard and pretending I hadn't just taken a 300-level math class at Northern in which the professor had used rhymes to teach trig. My roommate, Cara, had already gone home for the holidays, and Adam made himself comfortable on her bed, his long legs dangling off the XL twin mattress as they'd done dozens of times before. We'd spent many nights just like this, in beds opposite each other as we shoveled Chinese food into our mouths from cardboard containers and watched trash TV or listened to records with a bag of greasy Taco Bell. College was surprisingly lonely. It turns out that I am not very good at making friends unless I am already trapped in an insufferable hellscape with someone who doesn't mind my cracking a few inappropriate jokes as we circle life's drain. I kept being introduced to people who didn't know any black people or, more often than not, any black people like *me*. Which they exclaimed while taking me in with eyes widened to the size of dinner plates, as if I'd just hopped off a motherfucking spaceship with my cheesy black-light posters and newfound interest in sexual experimentation.

I found myself surrounded on all sides by the kind of dudes who wore shorts in the winter and blasted Tim McGraw while tucking in their polo shirts and putting on belts to go party on a Saturday night. And, surprise, surprise, I kind of liked these jagoffs. I liked watching wrestling and would never mind going in on the delicious party sampler to eat in front of *Monday Night Football*. (Hot wings! Onion rings! Egg rolls! Pizza bites! Corn dogs! Jumbo mozzarella sticks! Heart disease.) I'm not a "just one of the guys" kind of person—I fucking hate men— but I love eating and marathon television watching and I never met any girls in DeKalb willing to endure six hours on a busted couch with cold cheese fries and reruns of *Mystery Science Theater 3000*. John could eat seventeen ground beef tacos in one sitting and once watched *From Dusk till Dawn* three consecutive times on a Tuesday morning before class. Swoon.

Adam was convinced that the later we left, the quicker the drive home would be, so we laid in bed all morning watching corny Lifetime Christmas movies and listening to our floormates leaving for home. I was feeling strangely conflicted, anxious to get back to gossiping in my friends' cozy bedrooms yet apprehensive about what, if anything, I could contribute to the discussion. I hadn't gone to homecoming and I didn't have a crush on anyone and I couldn't remember how to get into my e-mail; what was I going to talk about? I got the same activity books everyone else did, and the one time I ventured out to one of the vaguely interesting events (to the Movie Club, which turned out to be me and three other weirdos watching *Pulp Fiction* in an empty classroom at night with no snacks) I was disappointed and vowed to never try any new things ever again. Except for that one time John dragged me to a Young Republicans meeting. Oh, and Bible Club.

My winter break would consist almost entirely of coffee shop gatherings during which I'd sit silently listening to the kinds of sugarcoated fables of idyllic college life that I didn't have to offer: lush, sprawling lawns and picnic lunches on the quad, and sororities chosen and pledged. I hated these get-togethers. First of all, I didn't know how to order coffee. I still goddamn don't, because it is gross and unnecessarily fussy and I am a grown woman who really cannot tell a cup of bad coffee from a good one. I will drink coffee if it has a pint of cream, nine hundred packets of real sugar, and comes with a shot of insulin. Which is why I don't drink coffee. So I'd be sitting there in the same hoodies and gym shoes I'd worn in high school, feeling like an asshole because I ordered a hot chocolate while everyone else was drinking complicated lattes, bored and mute because the most exciting thing I'd discovered in the months prior was that if I showed my student ID at McDonald's they would take 10 percent off my fries.

These bitches were at Brown and Harvard and Georgetown, driving their parents' old BMWs to parties around campus while once a week I waited two hours sometimes for the local Sycamore bus to drop me off to buy Pop-Tarts and maxi pads at Walmart. NO, I WAS NOT GOING TO VOLUNTARILY

TALK ABOUT MY COLLEGE EXPERIENCE. So many expectant eyes, peering at me from under so many shiny blunt-cut bangs. What could I tell these girls that would satisfy their curiosity? That college, at best, had been a lateral move I hadn't really wanted to make? That I *really* should have learned how to sew in a weave or take apart a carburetor, because school never really has been my thing and there is no shame in being an hourly working person? I couldn't tell them that all I did was constantly call my friend Anna in Rhode Island and anxiously wait for her monthly care packages (Portishead's second album, various SARK books, etc.). That my very first ATM PIN was Matt Shaffer's birthday even though he was halfway across the country playing rugby at Dartmouth and probably didn't even remember who I was anymore. That's the kind of gross creepy weird I am, the "your birthday is my PIN number" weird. In my mind I poured hot chocolate down the front of the ringleader's silly Fair Isle sweater and bounced the empty paper cup off the top of her head. In real life I told them about the used record store I hung out in pretending to be Janeane Garofalo in *Reality Bites*. They remained unimpressed. It was a long afternoon.

Adam and I were the last ones out of the dorm. Adam hauled the luggage through the hushed, darkened hallways while John carried what was left of a Budweiser-fueled McDonald's run the week before: a crumpled bag filled with slimy old nuggets and cheeseburgers that he had reheated in the tiny communal kitchen on our floor and cleaned of bits of mold. The three of us slipped and fell across the parking lot toward one of two remaining cars while sideways winds blew snow directly into our faces. While John wedged his oversize frame horizontally into the backseat, and I struggled to breathe under the weight of what I can only assume were suitcases full of mesh tank tops and Cubs jerseys in the front, Adam uneasily piloted his tiny car through the blizzard and out of the student lot.

I shouldn't eat old McDonald's. An hour on the road and we were still only ten miles outside of campus. As holiday traffic inched imperceptibly along, John snored peacefully in the backseat and I squinted at the radio dial and tried to pick up a signal from DeKalb's one decent radio station. Suddenly, I felt something strike a match in the pit of my stomach. I ignored it, continuing to search vainly for strains of that one Third Eye Blind song everybody knows by heart and hates. What I found instead was droning conservative talk radio, artificially cheerful Christmas carols, the play-by-play of some football game being held in the middle of a cornfield, and fuck there it was again, except this time it was slick, boiling oil churning through my large intestine at breakneck speed. "I need a bathroom," I blurted at Adam, my armpits suddenly damp. "I NEED A BATHROOM RIGHT NOW."

Adam threw up his hands, helpless inside his toy car, gesticulating wildly toward the stretch of motionless cars in the icy tundra before us and, I don't know, bleating like a teenage girl about how far the nearest exit was. I tried to distract myself from the reality that I was trapped in a metal box with two spray-tanned pieces of beef jerky by returning my attention to the useless radio in front of me. An eerie calm washed over me as I felt another wave of molten lava break gently against my intestinal wall. I bolted upright. "I am going to shit in your car," I announced, surrendering to the inevitable. John awoke with a grunt, jumping out of the backseat as Adam desperately yanked the car out of traffic and onto the shoulder. I kicked out of my reasonably priced new Walmart winter boots. John snatched my door open, threw the suitcase I was holding into a snowbank with one hand, and held the empty cheeseburger bag out to me with the other. "IN HERE," he commanded. OKAY. SURE, BRO. Leaning with my right side against the open car and my left arm wrapped around John's leg for balance, I squatted, hopeful and relieved, my eyes trained on the bead of sweat trickling slowly down Adam's temple.

When I first moved into the dorm I didn't shit for three days. The morning after move-in, I got up at dawn and eased out of my room in my freshly purchased pajamas into the dimly lit corridor. I had everything the Bed Bath & Beyond ad suggested a young woman headed off to college would need: a large shower caddy with multiple compartments to carry things from my room to whatever shower stall I could claw a bitch's eyes out to get into so I wouldn't be late for Biology 101, bacteria-resistant flip-flops to protect me from other people's periods, and a towel big enough to protect my boobs from the prying eyes of girls who had never seen their moms' grown-up, veiny breasts before.

I tiptoed into the bathroom, glancing under the stalls for tiny manicured feet. When I saw none I slipped into the closest stall and waited a few seconds before letting out the loudest, grossest fart any non–zoo animal had ever emitted and taking the biggest shit ever. Like, the fattiest, fast-food-iest dump any human had ever taken. I emerged from the stall several minutes later, light as air, my butthole singing, and ran smack into a trio of girls responsibly washing their faces over the sink, eyes aghast behind the thin layer of Clinique mild cleanser they passed between them. I avoided eye contact in the mirror while washing my hands, then spent the rest of the semester sneakily shitting at 2:00 p.m. in the crumbling library in the center of campus.

Now: I shit all over my jeans, legs, hand, and that greasy, disintegrating bag, as good Christian people in Ford Tauruses pretended they weren't trying to figure out what was happening on the other side of Adam's car. After the first wave, I kicked out of my jeans entirely, held my butthole closed as tightly as I could against the cold, wet air, and started digging a toilet hole in the snow. "YOU ARE A GODDAMN GENIUS," John boomed proudly next to me, swirling snowflakes getting caught in his beard. I crouched again as another forest fire raced through my guts. Under ordinary circumstances I would be totally fucking humiliated, demanding that these dudes turn away from the embarrassment of my thighs, but when you are shitting yourself in public in broad daylight, the last thing you worry about is some drunk kid from Schaumburg seeing how long your pubic hair is. "Atta girl!" Coach John shouted encouragingly over the dull roar of the howling winter wind, awkwardly patting the top of my head as I was, once again, clinging miserably to his knees while evacuating my bowels onto the side of the road. "You're doing so good!" An odd surge of pride rushed through me.

Adam, absolutely horrified, tossed me an NIU T-shirt he'd yanked from his gym bag. I fashioned it into a make-shift washcloth—GO HUSKIES—and then used mittenfuls of melting snow to clean out the diarrhea that had splashed into my vagina. John kicked fresh snow into my shit hole as Adam hyperventilated inside the car, punching buttons and twisting knobs like a man possessed as he tried valiantly to not look at my shame. The radio finally caught a spark, that "Bittersweet Symphony" song that was *everywhere* in 1997 suddenly crackling out of the tinny speakers. And then the car died.

happy birthday

Thursday, February 12, 1998, was the day before my eighteenth birthday. Some girls on our floor had papered the hallway with pink and red construction-paper hearts in anticipation of Valentine's Day, and it was a source of constant annoyance to me. No one at NIU wanted to have sex with me, and that was fine, but I didn't need a visual reminder that I was hideous and unloved every time I dragged my pore-unclogging face wash to the goddamned bathroom. I had a break after my English class and came back to the dorm to drink imitation Cokes and watch MTV while ignoring the mountain of homework I'd accumulated since the beginning of the semester. The phone on the wall rang as soon as I unlocked the door and I paused to figure out whether it was for me. Two rings for Cara, one long ring for Sam. Or maybe it was the other way around. The phone was for me.

On the other end of the line was a detective from the Evanston Police Department, and I knew, because he was using his gentlest inside voice, two things: (1) someone had made sure to tell him that I was seventeen years old, and (2) my father was probably dead.

At this point in the heartrending after-school special of my life, there would be a flashback to the week before, when I'd received another startling and unexpected phone call. But first, a little bit of background: Samuel Bishop Irby was the kind of alcoholic who made grain alcohol in our bathtub and sold what he didn't drink in SunnyD bottles to the local degenerates in his crew. Samuel Bishop Irby was the kind of alcoholic who would drink three bottles of NyQuil if my mother forbade his going to the liquor store and hid his car keys where he was too drunk to think of looking for them. Samuel Bishop Irby was the kind of alcoholic who, when desperate for a fix and home alone with his preadolescent daughter and an empty liquor cabinet, would soak a loaf of bread with shoe polish and drink whatever he could filter through the loaf into a glass. SB, as his friends called him, was handsome and charming and affable, and he had the greatest laugh you've ever heard. But SB was also broken, just totally broken. And I couldn't grow up around him. It wasn't safe.

After my mom and I moved out when I was four, SB's life underwent a series of changes, most of which I have no real idea about. He'd move away, get his life together, come back, destroy it again. I saw him randomly, in fits and starts, and always on the upswing. Always with a healthy glow and toothy grin, singing a new song about how he really was going to get his shit together this time. I'd like to think that eventually he pulled it together for me, that when he'd gotten word I was suffering, some paternal urge deep within him willed him clean and sober and back in town, superhero cape affixed firmly to his collar. The part of me that needs to believe my life was important to a person who created it clings to that, but I am logical, realistic. I know otherwise. At that point I was worth little more than the five-hundred-dollar-or-so monthly Social Security check that followed me like a dowry to who-ever was willing to take me in. When he caught wind that this money was up for grabs, he was back in town in an instant, back in his chauffeur uniform and cap, buying me a futon and a tiny television set.

But SB had his eyes on a bigger prize. The state was paying my mother's nursing home rent to the tune of nine hundred dollars a month, and my dad figured that if he could somehow get her into his household, that money could be his. "This is not a good idea," I whispered into her ear as my father laid out his plan, fast-talking like a used-car salesman as he spread papers of zero consequence, full of calculations that she could barely understand, across the cafeteria table. I glared at him, my chubby fingers laced through her skeletal ones, my eyes shin-ing with tears. She was nodding excitedly. "You need a nurse," I murmured, my heart fracturing, incrementally, as I watched her excitement build. "This house doesn't even have a ramp. How are we going to get your wheelchair inside?"

She didn't want to hear me. She had been locked away in this place for three years already, waiting to die, and now she could have what she always wanted: her husband and her kid and a home. Together. I tried to hide how much I was crying as two techs and my father loaded her into the car, my father sweating and cursing as he folded her wheelchair and shoved it awkwardly in the trunk. It took half an hour for us to get her inside the house, me tilting her wheelchair backward up the concrete steps as SB grimaced under the weight of her bal-anced on his shoulder. I read the lists of her medications and the instructions that the Patient Care Technician had scribbled on a notepad over and over as she beamed up at me from the couch. As much as I wanted my mom back, this wasn't the way to do it, with no nurse and no real money and a man with a hair-trigger temper sleeping in the next room.

I have to stop and tell you that this is not a place I revisit often in my mind. Of everything, of all the sad things and disappointing things and hurtful things, this is the place in my head that it hurts most to go to. This part, where my mom, my *baby*, has such a monumental insult added to injury—it makes my heart die a little to even think about it. She was so hopeful, man. So happy. Like a kid finally being adopted after having been passed over in the orphanage dozens of previous times. And all we had to offer her was a couch. A television with all the cable channels on it. Diapers she was too humiliated to wear in front of a man who had chosen the bottle over her love, and pills I had to put in applesauce so she could swallow them because she couldn't really swallow anymore. She needed a nurse. She needed a bed that she could raise and lower. She needed a feeding tube. She needed a call button and a daily doctor visit and occupational therapy because she couldn't remember how to use her hands anymore and, for the nine hundred dollars my father had already gambled away on the lottery, she didn't have any of those things.

You also should know that I was fifteen when this experiment took place, and lest you start to cast me in some sort of saintly light, I was still wholly consumed with fifteen-year-old things: Spanish tests and boys and Tori Amos and *things*. I was anxious and stressed out and, most of all, resentful. Resentful that, as I'd suspected, all of the caretaking would again fall to me. I had played this game before. Years before my mother had even gone into the nursing home, I had done the "pretend you can have a real life while inadequately caring for this terminally ill person" charade. I felt like my time had already been served, that the payoff was a normal curfew and shoulders that weren't hunched beneath the weight of adult responsibility.

Mom would sleep sitting up, bolstered on either side by shapeless pillows on a couch salvaged from some rich person's trash and from which she was rarely moved. She watched TV, ate her meals, took her medicine, and decomposed a little bit more every day. The three of us were such a goddamned nightmare. When she went back to the nursing home, it came as no surprise to any of us; the ambulance slid away from our rented house with her tucked safely inside, malnourished and fragile, deflated by this most recent disappointment. Her meager belongings bounced in the small suitcase balanced across my knees as SB and I silently followed behind them in the Cadillac, his face grim.

Now I stood facing the corner near our dorm room's door, nose almost touching the wall, because I could feel Cara's concerned eyes searching my back for a clue. The phone felt hot and slippery against my ear. "Your father is missing, Samantha," the detective said. "He's been gone for over twenty-four hours and no one has any idea where he is." I let silence fill the empty space between us. After thirty seconds he cleared his throat. "We will be in touch with you as things develop, okay? We're doing everything we can to find him."

Finally, I whispered, "I'm turning eighteen tomorrow."

"Oh. I'm sorry. Happy birthday."

This is a tiny little love story.

My mom had three little girls, born when she was sixteen, eighteen, and twenty-one. She raised them on her own and was often seen around town with the three of them trailing behind her, all ribbons and bows and shiny patent leather. She was an emergency-room nurse who mostly worked nights so that she could be home with her children during the day. SB drove a bus for the now-defunct Evanston Bus Company. My striking mother (six feet tall with hair, lips, and talon-length nails all a shocking red) would line up her three little girls a few afternoons a week and wait at the corner of Main and Elmwood for the bus to take them downtown. And WOW-O-WOW MY PARENTS MET ON A BUS, but here's the thing: every day the four of them, pretty as a picture, would get on my dad's bus, and every day he would cover the coin slot and refuse to let my mother pay. Fuck, I don't know what's sexy anymore. But it's probably a sign that I am a grown-up for real that the idea of someone saving my weekly bus money is, like, totally hot. THAT IS ROMANCE.

So this cat-and-mouse game continued for a while (my dad covering up the fare box, my mom smiling coyly while taking her seat and never speaking to him), then it took a turn toward next level when my mom decided to repay this charming bus driver's kindness with an invitation to dinner. When I heard this story as a kid, the thought of inviting some strange dude over to my house to eat dinner with my kids made me go, "Gross, weird," but it was the 1960s and my mom had three little girls, and driving a bus for a failing suburban bus company was as good a job as any.

They dated for eleven years before getting legally married, which, for those of you who don't know any black people, is just the way we do things. I guess it takes a while to know what you really want. Carol, the youngest of my sisters, was fifteen by the time I came along to usurp the affections of the only father she'd known, and she expressed her displeasure by immediately trying to suffocate me in my crib. My mom and sisters had been living on the second floor of a duplex where my skinny, mean grandmother fried sardines downstairs while SB lived in a shag-carpeted bachelor pad across town. As a wedding present, my dad conned the bank out of a loan to buy them a large Victorian in a decent black neighborhood not far from where two of my sisters were finishing high school.

There is nothing better than being the product of a late-in-life pregnancy, at least until the shriveling invalids pushing their walkers around your tenth birthday party begin their rapid decline before you even get hair on your privates. But before that? IT'S ALL GRAVY. Before their eventual divorce I was spoiled and coddled and feted and fed Frosted Flakes in front of the television like King Shit of Fuck Mountain. My sisters had grown up sharing clothes and crammed into one tiny bedroom while my mom slept on the pullout couch; I, on the other hand, had a room to myself just off the dining room, with a desk and a television and a little rug for our collie, Trudy, to sleep on. I had every doll imaginable, every Cabbage Patch and Monchhichi and Strawberry Shortcake doll; a toy box stuffed full of Lite-Brites and Hungry Hungry Hippos and Connect Fours; a little record player on which I listened to "Here Come the Smurfs" ad nauseam. I was their opportunity to Do Things Right This Time. There were no missed parent-teacher conferences, no preschool talent shows left unrecorded.

The thing about fucking dirtbags is that no matter how much cologne you splash on them, they're always going to be fucking dirtbags. My father, ever the entrepreneur, decided that it wasn't enough to work all day and pay for this prize of a house. He decided to build rooms (read: erect shoddily constructed clapboard cubicles) in the basement of our house (read: where his three nubile stepdaughters and tiny infant baby lived) and rent them out to his friends (read: winos). So yes, I had the limited-edition Strawberry Shortcake doll whose shiny plastic skin actually *smelled like actual strawberries* (TECHNOLOGY HOORAY), but I *also* watched my dad hit a dude in his head with a hammer on our front porch in an argument over a dice game. It was like a seedy men's hotel, except (1) illegal, and (2) IN THE BASEMENT OF OUR HOUSE. Some dude died down there! It never struck me as strange because that is how my life had always been: school bus pulling up to take me to day care at the YWCA while some junkie was passed out asleep on our front lawn. Normal: sitting on my dad's lap while he cut up my dinner and spoon-fed it to me despite the fact that I was old enough to use words like "tolerate." Also normal: accompanying my father to throw a wrench through the windshield of his mortal enemy's car in the middle of the afternoon.

Two days after I turned eighteen there was a card in the mail from my mother. It was a generic birthday card, one I'm sure the nursing home had boxes of tucked away for residents to use. The lettering on the outside of the envelope had been carefully printed, nothing like my mom's usual artsy loops and curls. The inside read, in the same steady hand, "Dear Samantha. I am very proud of you for being at college. It was so nice to see you at Christmas. I can't wait to see you again. Love, Mom." In the bottom right corner there was a series of unintelligible dots and squiggles. A piece of paper had fluttered to the ground when I opened the card, and I picked it up. It was a note from my mom's hospice nurse, apologizing for the formality and explaining that her condition had deteriorated to the point that she could no longer use a pen without help. "Grace is a real nice lady. She is having a lot of trouble speaking lately. I tried to figure out what she wanted me to say as best I could. I hope you have a good birthday." This is a luxury, you know, being spared the day-to-day deterioration of someone you love. I really wish I could've hugged that nurse.

My aunt called. My father had had two heart attacks and a stroke. Or two strokes and a heart attack. Fuck, these are the kinds of details that blur. I can tell you with near certainty that I was wearing an oatmeal-colored knit turtleneck sweater, but not the ratio of heart attacks to strokes my dad had at the end of his life. He'd been living in a halfway house in Memphis since the failed attempt to reconstruct our ailing family. After we put my mother back into the nursing home, I spent my junior year of high school tiptoeing around his rules and his rage, with mostly successful results. He slapped me a few times, and, once, he punched me in the eye. We ate a lot of navy beans on hot-water cornbread and vegetable soup made with V8 juice and frozen vegetables because, besides hard-boiled eggs, those were the only things I could cook at the time. It was okay. Somehow I managed to get a really high score on the ACT.

His heart had always been bad. Multiple heart attacks and surgeries, that kind of thing. I remember coming home from school one day that winter to find a note that he was going into the hospital, written in his shaky, girlish hand. He said that he hadn't been feeling well and that Dr. Weiss wanted to admit him for observation. I immediately kicked off my snowy boots in the middle of the living room (not allowed), grabbed a bottle of Baileys from where he'd hidden it (under the sink), and cuddled on the couch under a blanket in front of the television (definitely not allowed). I called myself in sick the next few days, leaving the house only to walk to the corner store for cans of soup and to play the lottery numbers my dad would leave on the answering machine every afternoon with the money he'd hidden for such emergencies in a shoe box in his closet. I shoveled the sidewalks so no one would suspect anything, but other than that, I watched *My So-Called Life* repeats and slept the dreamless sleep of the relieved. When SB finally came home, he did so with a long scar snaking across his chest.

"It's called a defibrillator," he said, tapping the tender flesh over his heart as I tried not to vomit. "It sends a little electrical shock through my heart whenever it stops beating." He explained the differences between the exciting new technological advancement that had been installed in his shiny new Frankenchest and the average, run-of-the-mill pacemaker inserted into other septuagenarians ("You see, the pacemaker regulates the heart constantly but this guy only gives me a little shock when I need it and that's pretty cool, right?") while proudly brandishing a card that he had to carry with him to keep him out of jail in case he set off a metal detector at court or in an airport. He looked gaunt and skinny, even though he'd been gone only a little over a week and had been on solid food for at least five days. My glasses were still taped across the bridge from when he'd broken them with his fist months before, the bones beneath them, though healed, still slightly shifted off track. I remember thinking how big he'd seemed that day as I stood bleeding uncontrollably into the kitchen sink from my broken nose, my vision blurred. This dude here looked like a guy I could take in a fight. He commented on how clean the house looked, but my stomach churned as he surveyed the room, hoping he wouldn't notice the dust on the piano that I hadn't practiced on even once while he'd been in the hospital.

I have never owned a microwave. I have lived on my own since I was eighteen years old, and every time I've eaten a Lean Cuisine in my pajamas at eight thirty on a Friday night, I have waited forty-five goddamn minutes for that motherfucker to cook in the oven before doing so. Sam Irby had a thing about microwave ovens. "Those silly machines destroy all the nutrients in your food," he would grunt, shuffling away from the freezer case where I stared longingly at all of the Hot Pockets and Pizza Rolls. "Just get a pack of hot dogs and meet me in the car." My dad resented that no one had ever taught me how to do "women's work"; he was disgusted that I had spent fifteen years on his earth without learning how to buff a linoleum floor to a mirror shine or make a proper casserole. It was beneath him to fold his own boxers.

I didn't know shit about keeping a house. I didn't know that mini blinds need to be dusted and rugs dragged out in the yard and beaten clean. No one ever taught me how to defrost a freezer or scrub a dirty oven without setting my hair on fire. My dad wanted a perfect 1950s TV housewife, while all I wanted was a perfect 1980s TV dad. Steven Keaton never punched his kids over a frying pan, and Phillip Drummond never kicked a hole through Arnold's bedroom door because his pants hadn't been perfectly pleated. But I'm a quick study. You have to pile all of the dirty dinner dishes atop my snoring body only one motherfucking time for me to understand never to go to bed without cleaning the kitchen first, no matter how tired I am.

Dan Conner was the kind of dad who might let you get away with nuking a can of Beefaroni and serving it to him for dinner, but Samuel Bishop Irby wouldn't stand for any of that. Especially not with his new mechanical heart. The night he came home, he peered at me over his reading glasses with the ICD user manual balanced on his lap. "No magnets, and no microwaves, EVER," he said authoritatively, tapping the page. "My heart could explode."

The afternoon of the detective's call, Cara and I had been studying for a biology test. I had a huge crush on our professor, this swaggering Brit who would roar up to the science building on his Harley-Davidson and never took off his leather vest, not once the entire semester, while teaching us about eukaryotes and recombinant DNA. It was a lecture course that took place in this massive auditorium, which meant that we spent most of our afternoons fighting sleep in the nosebleeds while trying to discern scientific terms through a thick English accent. I was listening to Ani DiFranco (of course) on my headphones because Cara didn't like to study with noise, but I couldn't stay the hell awake unless I paired bio vocabulary with lyrics from "Hour Follows Hour." Cara's notes were better than mine, but I was better at drawing and labeling, so we often studied this way, back-to-back at our opposite desks, trading sheets of graph paper every few minutes. Cara tapped me gently on the shoulder and pointed toward the phone. I snatched my headphones off and ran to pick it up. It was Dr. Weiss.

Ira Weiss is an angel. I'm sure there are times he doesn't put the cap back on the toothpaste or leaves only an inch of orange juice in the carton, but as far as real-life patron saints are concerned, that kind, soft-spoken gentleman was my father's. Dr. Weiss had been SB's cardiologist since the first of many heart attacks, in 1984. And my father, ravenous consumer of

potted meat and salt pork, dormant volcanic mountain bubbling with an undercurrent of molten rage, enthusiastic guzzler
of the corner store's finest four-dollar champagnes, kept that
dude in practice. You know what that asshole was doing when
he lectured me about how my desire to enjoy a bag of micro-
waved popcorn was going to cause his heart to burst forth from
his chest? EATING A POLISH SAUSAGE WHILE HIGH
ON COCAINE. 147 arterial blockages (give or take) and my
dude would still be like, "WHAT IS THIS? LETTUCE?" if I
deigned to serve a salad alongside our grilled Spam in Tampico
punch reduction or whatever slave food we used to eat every
night.

Dr. Weiss is an orthodox Jew who keeps kosher and rides a
bicycle everywhere he goes, and no matter how many times
my father jumped gleefully from the wagon into a waist-deep
river of cheap brandy and two-dollar steaks, Dr. Weiss would
take him back, crack open his ribs, and scrape some more cor-
rosion off the rotting meatfist in the center of his chest. The
last time I had seen my father was the final day of my junior
year of high school, when he moved me into the spare bedroom in the back of my sister Jane's apartment. "Who's gonna
fold your sheets?" I called after him as he hobbled down the
stairs. "Who's gonna fry your smelts?!" He waved at me over
his shoulder without looking back and disappeared. A few
weeks later at church, I saw his old boss, the man who owned
both the house we rented and the limousine SB leased to drive
for work. I had never liked James; he laughed too loud and
talked too much and dropped by our house unannounced too
often. I do not like conspicuous men. And there he was, prais-

ing the Lord at the top of his lungs, shaking hands with people as they entered the vestibule. A sickening, oily smile spread across his face as he intercepted me. "Your father stole a lot of money from me before he left town, darling," he growled through a phony smile. "A *lot* of money," he reiterated, squeezing my shoulder as if a twenty-dollar bill was going to shoot out of it. Bile rose in my throat as I pulled away and slunk to a pew in the back of the church. I remembered running across a large plastic bottle, the kind used in an office water cooler, in the basement of the house one afternoon. It was filled with change, mostly quarters and dimes, and sometimes while cowering in the closet as Tropical Storm Samuel roared outside my bedroom, I daydreamed about rolling that thing to the bank and trading that laundry fortune for a train ticket to freedom. Of course he took it, I thought. I imagined him in the rickety Cadillac he'd bought before he left, bouncing down the highway back to Tennessee in a car filled with nickels.

Dr. Weiss informed me that after SB had suffered two heart attacks and a stroke (or two strokes and a heart attack), he had spent his own money to send for my father so he could be under his local care. He told me that things weren't looking good, that my father (born in 1933 in Tunica, Mississippi) had survived poverty in the South and war in Korea and alcoholism in suburbia, yet refused to give his body a break for even a minute. He was drinking again and fighting again and not taking his prescribed medications again. I listened to the doctor, his voice soothing and calm, waiting anxiously for him to tell me what was going to happen next. And then my father was on the line, cheerful and gruff. He told me that he was feeling great, that Dr. Weiss had taken him on a skateboard tour of the morgue, and that everything inside was painted in psychedelic colors—it didn't look anything like the cold, refrigerated vaults you see on television! Samantha, I am having so much fun! I didn't cry, even though I felt like I should. "My father has gone crazy," I mouthed across the room to Cara as I waited for the doctor to get back on the line. "You rode a skateboard through a room full of dead bodies?" I asked skeptically when Dr. Weiss finally returned to the phone. "Of course we didn't. I'm afraid your father hasn't recovered this time as well as we'd hoped he would."

The evening of my birthday, I had gone down to dinner with some guy friends from my floor at five, but they both had girlfriends so there was no watching *Braveheart* on a continuous loop the way we usually spent our Saturday nights. Cara had gone home for the weekend. I had a stack of *Jane* magazines and a handful of birthday cards that needed responses, but then my sisters called, two of them on one line, and I braced myself for an explosion of off-key birthday singing. "SB is dead," Janie said. "They found him in someone's yard earlier today. I'm so sorry, pumpkin."

Here are the things that I know:

1. My father was placed in a nursing home a couple of days after I spoke to him. Coincidentally, his nursing home was down the street from the one my mother was in.

2. On February 12, 1998, he decided to go for a walk. Without a coat or socks, and several days after surviving some ratio of heart attacks to strokes that I am still not clear on because sometimes the details just get away from you.

3. SB visited my mom and swindled $10 from her room-mate. He'd always had a way with the ladies. Even half-dead, he was totally charming.
4. He was missing for two days.
5. They found him three miles from the nursing home. Cause of death: hypothermia.

Dr. Weiss was on my father's emergency call list. He rode his bicycle through the streets of Chicago and Evanston all day and all night for two days, calling my father's name to no avail. No one comes to a junkie wino's funeral. Cara came, and I was so humiliated that we couldn't even have it in a church. Men like my father aren't eulogized by the well-respected ministers in their communities, and now she would know that about me when I'd tried so hard to construct this new self away from home. No one sent flowers. No one stood up to say a few kind words. There were drunks and hobos crowded around the entrance of the funeral home, a cloud of E&J brandy hanging over them as they tipped concealed pints of liquor out onto the sidewalk for their fallen brother. Dr. Weiss shyly introduced himself and I felt another pang of embarrassment knife through my chest. Seeing him in that tiny red room in his bulky safety helmet, imagining him awkwardly questioning the dirtbags who hung out in the parking lots my father frequented and knocking on the doors of houses of ill repute, looking for this dude who kept letting him down again and again so that he could save his life one more time, made my chest constrict with longing. He said a few kind words about his old friend, and then, in a lilting and beautiful tenor, he sang the Lord's Prayer in Hebrew over my father's lifeless body. The room fell silent. I hadn't cried before then. I was too tired, too angry, too overwhelmed by what it meant now to have a Dead Parent, like the exotic new character introduced midseason on a TV show. Dr. Weiss was singing with his eyes closed, and I felt my eyes flood with tears. For myself, for my mother, for Dr. Weiss. Sometimes I feel like I haven't stopped crying since.

SB's ashes are tucked away in a box in a Gap bag inside my hall closet. The sheets and duvets within are decidedly unfolded.

a case for remaining indoors

Wouldn't you rather be dead than hot? I am 100 percent over people pretending that open-mouth breathing in 1,000 percent humidity while being burned to a crisp by the sun is the jam. I prefer winter, when everyone has to be bundled beyond recognition to survive. Or fall, when you can wear something nice without sweating it sheer in the punishing heat. Too bad I can't afford to pack my one bag and move to the Arctic, because the minute I start seeing bare arms and booty shorts my *sad* kicks in and my *happy* doesn't return until late in September when, thank goodness, I can cover it up with a scarf. You dudes frying under the sun at the beach can't really expect the rest of us to believe that you enjoy painfully peeling your seared flesh from plastic chairs while everyone in the restaurant is staring at the armpit stubble revealed by your tank tops, can you? I'm not hating, it's just that I'm baffled when these hot-weather enthusiasts try to convince you how totally awesome it is to be standing around outside in air that's as thick as soup while trying to pick the char off smoldering ribs and hot dogs. While gingerly clutching a beer that won't stay cold. Would it be so bad if we ate this inside? At a table that is sturdy? Where no flies can vomit on my plate while I'm trying to balance it on my knees?!

It is a cloudless seventy-two degrees in Chicago today. The sun is blazing in the sky (I closed the blinds when I finally woke up around one thirty in the afternoon), birds are chirping sweetly in the trees (I shut the windows), and people are crowding the streets in droves celebrating this long-awaited break in the dreary gray spring weather (I assume—like I said, I shut the goddamned windows and blinds). I'm going to take a shower and order a grocery delivery, then maybe stare at the wall until it's time to go back to bed.

If I went outside, I could:

- Walk down the street to the beach, stroll along the lake path, and get bit by a dog.
- Suffer through an awkward conversation with someone who lives in this neighborhood, someone I will now be forced to avoid until the end of time.
- Watch children beating each other with sticks while enjoying the fresh air.
- Soak up some vitamin D and also harmful UVA and UVB rays.
- Get the perfectly-acceptable-to-wear-again-tomorrow clothes I'm wearing all sweaty and gross.

On the flip side, in my apartment I can:

- Eat the rest of this box of cereal, dry, by the fistful.
- Look at people outside without having to smell them or listen to their opinions.

- Organize my ketchups.
- Write song lyrics for my easy-listening band, Queasy Listening.

Words like "outdoor music festival" are why I am so glad summer in Chicago lasts approximately seven minutes. I nearly wept tears of seasonal affective disordered joy as I pulled out my North Face boots at the end of last November. As good as the warm air feels on my immobile joints, I can't help but love winter and fall. Mostly fall, because fuck snow, and that hawk blowing off the lake is enough to make your teeth drop right out of your skull, but winter can be kind of okay if it doesn't snow a whole lot and no one asks me to go sledding or do some other Hallmark-movie nonsense. The more sweaters and scarves I can wrap around my head the better. Summer can be an exercise in torture (but not an exercise in actual exercise, duh, it's too humid) if you don't want to do crazy shit like "wear sleeveless shirts" or "enjoy close proximity to actively sweating strangers." One summer, I walked by these dirty hipsters at Division Fest—the kind of outdoor food and music festival that sounds like fun in theory until you actually get there and find yourself eating an overcooked hot dog while standing in a curdled pool of someone else's puke—dancing in a large gray puddle of used tampons and diarrhea and thought miserably, "I hope you guys catch something incurable." I was instantly burning with hatred for those people, dancing *with their mouths open* in a shallow pool of urban toxic waste. And the band they were dancing to wasn't even that jamming. I never have to go outside again because:

1. My boyfriend, the television, is inside.

Have you heard of those thunder shirts for dogs to help them stay calm during loud storms? They should be made for people, to help us stay calm in situations when we have to listen to someone explain at great length why they are too busy to own a TV set. Picture it: you're chilling in the corner at a party full of people you've never met before and hated on sight, humming the lyrics to a Coldplay song to yourself to drown out the Swedish death metal the hostess put on to prop up her apparition of coolness, then here comes some asshole who makes her own yogurt and just discovered Ta-Nehisi Coates condescending at you about how damaging reality shows are to impressionable youth. MAN, I FUCKING LOVE TV. And I don't mean educational programming on PBS or crackly documentaries about important historical figures. I mean I know all of the cast members of *The Real Housewives of Atlanta*, past and present, and all of their children, pets, and significant others by name. I once walked blindly past my own sister on a sparsely populated train platform on a Saturday afternoon, but I could tell you who won *Survivor* the last few seasons without even having to google it. Television has forever been my unwavering companion and trusted friend. Every bad day, every breakup, every inexplicable 2:00 a.m. awakening: television has been there for me through all of them. I would trade every deadly hornet sting and itchy eye-causing spring bloom, without hesitation, for the warm glow of my Samsung for the rest of my life.

2. Are there enough blazers in my closet?

Years ago I decided that I was going to be a jacket person. I'm not sure it was a conscious decision—like, I didn't just wake up one day and throw out all my long-sleeved shirts, but I remember finding this insanely well-cut cropped denim jacket with a military collar and cinched waist and the first time I wore it I didn't take it off for the entire day. At some point the next morning, stumbling around hungover and bleary-eyed trying to get my shit together for work, it dawned on me that I could just wear that jacket again. I already knew it looked good and anyone paying close attention would just assume I'd changed the T-shirt I had worn underneath, so why the fuck not? I put that damn jacket on every single day; if Michael Kors could wear the same uniform every day, why not Samantha Irby? Now I have all kinds of jackets: leather ones, tweed ones, twill ones, the works. And you would not believe how many pajama pants you can get away with wearing to nice places if you just slap a sharply cut blazer on top of them. I went to a party recently at the Museum of Contemporary Art, and I almost took an anxiety shit in the charcoal Spalding Women's Boot-Leg Yoga Pant I'd just ripped out of the plastic Amazon packaging after gazing at all the angular haircuts and avant-garde outfits teetering around on sky-high heels, their delicate ankles bound by complicated-looking straps. I was wearing a baggy V-neck, riddled with holes from moths and actual wear and tear, but I had gotten my nicest blazer from the dry cleaner. So even though I felt wildly out of place between the blush I'd put on in the cab and the jacket my dry cleaner starched the shit out of, I felt okay enough to hang out for an hour before demanding my homeboy drive me home.

Home, where I can gaze lovingly at my closet and organize my jackets. By color, by material, by the likelihood they will ever see the outside world. I'm sitting in my crib right now, listening to this Gretchen Parlato record from three years ago, ripping sheets of toilet paper off the roll I keep on my desk because buying boxes of Kleenex feels like a waste when allergy season is about to destroy my life anyway, and I am wearing a jacket. A black pleather motorcycle jacket I got for sale at ASOS that has a little fringe on it but not so much that I look like I'm going to an Aerosmith cover band audition later. That's the thing about being an inside person who enjoys the occasional wardrobe splurge; you gotta be cool with modeling it for the cat and hoping the delivery dude from Apart Pizza Company assumes you just got home from work. You were so busy writing checks and taking important calls that you hadn't had time to shrug it off before opening the door for your pizza, even though you both know deep down that you haven't left the apartment all day and only put the jacket on because it's a shame to let an eighty-dollar coat go unworn.

3. Food just tastes better inside.

White people love picnics. So much, in fact, that they'll stop just about anywhere to have one. Why? Everywhere you look someone has turned a bus bench or statue or filthy curb into an outdoor café. You dudes just stop and bust out your wicker baskets anywhere, hmm? I know my people love a summertime cookout as much as anyone, but we don't just set up a three-legged grill in the alley next to the dumpster as soon as the winter snow melts and throw our chicken on it. We organize, we plan. First of all, we need to know who is going to be responsible for the potato salad. You can't just let that one lady from work you invited to be nice bring hers—it has to be known potato salad, from a vetted and reliable source.

I can't even commit to going to a white person's house for dinner in the summer unless we have specific plans to do something that requires four walls and a roof while I pretend to be picking at their homemade tabouleh. Because guaranteed I am going to walk into the house and be greeted with, "Hey, let's eat this out on the patio!" And by "patio" they mean "that little scrap of cement at the base of my back stairs that holds only one chair and is right next to the trash." LOL FUCK THAT. And I try to avoid restaurants with outdoor seating at all costs, especially with my non-melanotic friends, because when your Uber driver makes a wrong turn and they beat you to the place by a hair, they always do some slick shit like put your name in for an outside table. I don't care how long the wait is, I'd rather wait an hour for a table that won't get covered in pigeon shit and the airborne pathogens expelled from the mouths of curious passersby.

4. You can daydream about things in catalogs you are never going to buy.
Without fail I get the IKEA catalog every single year. Let me remind you that I currently live in a space that contains this many things:

- a full-size bed
- a television on top of a television stand
- a stack of magazines next to the bed that used to hold a small fan and my BiPAP machine because finding a bedside table seemed like too much work
- a desk whose resale value I just today discovered I ruined with a broken bottle of nail polish
- a large air conditioner currently sitting on the floor beneath the window
- a table my friend's dad made that I keep in the dining room to hold wine bottles and plants

- a stainless steel shelving unit that serves as an "open-air concept pantry" ★eye roll★
- a dresser whose bottom two drawers I am terrified to open
- a bookshelf I have inexplicably moved six mother-fucking times
- one chair

There's other shit in here (laptop, house phone I no longer remember the number to, prosperity candles from the occult bookstore) but it doesn't count, since those are things that go on top of other things. Suffice it to say, I have no reason what-soever to be comparing backsplashes. I have been a renter my entire life; my home-improvement joy is firmly grounded in novelty items like matching clothes hangers and interesting dish towels, affordable splashes of color and beauty that can liven up this space that's crumbling at the corners and painted like a prison cell. The idea of owning a home feels stressful to me. Like, if the toilet breaks and it's not my paycheck week, am I really going to have to shit at the gas station for nine days until my direct deposit clears? YES. Also I don't under-stand how mortgages work other than a handful of scenes I can remember from *The Big Short*, and don't quote me on this, but I'm pretty sure Steve Carell told me the dumbest thing I could ever do is sink my regular-person money into any type of real estate. Let someone else take the risk, and I can relax and waste the money I should be putting into a savings account on deco-rative pillows and champagne flutes I'll never use.

But catalogs are a miracle, because you can design your very own dream house with none of the risk or expense. I'm like a little girl with my Post-it notes and red Sharpie: "I want the farmhouse sink and these marble countertops and a butcher block island in the center of the kitchen. These brass sconces would look good in the master bathroom, and definitely some track lighting in the family room, and ooh wouldn't this leather sofa look amazing in the den?!" I could spend an entire week-end locked in a five-hundred-square-foot studio apartment circling armoires in the Crate and Barrel catalog that will never see the inside of any place other than my brain. I like to pull all the Bed Bath & Beyond coupons out of the Sunday paper and stick them in a drawer for the day I decide to stop living like a trash person and buy sheets with an impressive thread count. One of these days I'm going to move to a place in which a footstool might not look out of place, and I am going to need that 20 percent off, okay?

5. Your space, your rules.

Now, this is assuming that you haven't made the fatal mis-take of trying to be inside at someplace other than the one in which you live. People who don't understand that my writing ~process~ consists of staring sullenly at my computer waiting for the jokes to come while willing myself not to get up to reexamine the contents of the almost-bare refrigerator I just took stock of ten minutes ago often ask if I like to write in coffee shops. I used to, especially before I caved and got a high-speed Internet hookup in my casa. Sometimes I'd roll down to the Heartland to pick at a bowl of vegan chili and soak up their Internet, but then my favorite bartender quit and they took the black bean nachos off the menu so BYE. There are a handful of coffee shops in Edgewater that feel cozy and relaxing, but the problem with that is I am never cozy or relaxed. Even with headphones on, I could never get over the idea that someone was watching me, that they knew I had a deadline or a draft due and noticed that instead of putting my head down and working, I'd spent the entire time glancing around wondering what everyone else was working on. And I live near Loyola University, so the answer was probably definitely "a term paper for Indigenous and Settler Colonialism," but still I'd sit there with my laptop open to a blank page waiting to be filled with at least forty-five hundred words on the scintillating topic of my anus, wondering what the girl with the blue hair and hand tattoos had picked as her major. I would pack up my computer and the book I liked to carry in case I got frustrated with the writing and grumble as I banged out the door, take the train a few stops to a place with quality scones and iced tea, then sit there for hours paralyzed with fear that if I drank too much I would have to go to the bathroom and be faced with the dilemma of whether someone would steal a computer cheaper and more busted than theirs for the three minutes I was gone.

I am unfamiliar with coffee shop etiquette. Since I let the dude texting across from me hog the outlet, is he morally obligated to make sure no one runs off with my wallet while I'm in the can? If I take my wallet, will he keep an eye on my laptop? And what about my bag?! I am anxious, and I don't trust anyone and would also never want to burden a stranger with my literal shit, but I had to buy a drink to get the Wi-Fi password and didn't want to look like a cheapskate, so I got the big one, and a doughnut, and now I have to pee but I'm not ready to leave and Jesus God what can I do?! So I would take everything in with me, a mess of tangled cords spilling from my shoulder bag, my unfinished teacup balanced precariously in the hand not fumbling for my phone. I usually could manage to pee without letting my cup touch any contaminated surfaces, and when I emerged from the bathroom someone new would inevitably be sitting in my seat, unsheathing her gleaming

MacBook Pro from its protective case, nodding with a smile at the outlet hog as he unplugged so she could use it. Defeated and deflated after multiple days sulking home with my work undone, I finally called RCN to come connect whatever wires I needed to get the fastest possible mature lesbian porn on my phone. I can make my own tea. Better yet, I can smoke a bowl, and drink an entire pitcher of Crystal Light, and finish that butthole essay in my nicest house jacket and take as many breaks as I want, and no one is going to steal my seat when I get up for a cookie refill or cause me to break out in a sweat when my battery is at 7 percent and the nearest outlet is in use. I won't get sucked into watching a young man artfully arrange his latte and muffin just so for the gram, no eavesdropping on conversations about bands I've never heard of and am too uncool to understand, no nervously asking an irritated barista what "sumatra" means: just me and the cat and the bags of Lipton I shoved in my pocket at work because buying an actual box of tea in real life feels like a ridiculous, unnecessary thing. It's fucking perfect. BRB, gotta go pee.

a total attack of the heart

The first time I had the kind of anxiety attack that makes you feel like you're going to die, I was standing next to a friend's car in the parking lot of a combination gas station and Subway. I tossed my sandwich onto the passenger seat and pawed at my chest while trying to catch my breath. What a fucking terrible place to die, I thought, surrounded by cabdrivers shouting unintelligibly into Bluetooth headsets and people in wheelchairs from the nursing home down the street rolling up to buy candy bars and beer.

I assumed I was having a heart attack because I had been in line at Subway behind three of my people, each of whom had a long list of complicated instructions for the sandwich artist tasked with preparing his evening meal. Since we can't get reparations, we will make it up in toppings. "I want provolone cheese and cucumbers and spinach and lettuce and red onions and tomatoes, olives and banana peppers and giardiniera. I need the chipotle southwest sauce and the ranch, and extra meat, but I don't want you to charge me for it. Also, let me get the green bell peppers and the herbs and spices, oil and vinegar, too, on the Italian herbs and cheese bread, then I want you to toast that shit but don't, like, *toast it* toast it." It's nerve-racking—please just let me get my plain scoops of tuna on wheat bread before I sweat through my clothes with anxiety over this transaction not turning out the way you intended because most of those things don't even go with meatballs but what the fuck do I know God just let me leave.

It took less than two minutes to get to my place and I spent the entire car ride wondering whether my outfit looked good enough for my ghost to float around in for an eternity. I got off the elevator in my building and stood in place, gasping like I'd just run a marathon, and I felt this weird pain radiating from my left shoulder down my arm and into my hand and the crushing realization that now I was going to die in a hallway that doesn't get vacuumed often enough before the next *Game of Thrones* book comes out made me dizzy with rage. After struggling to get the key into the lock, I finally stumbled into my apartment and collapsed on the bed, gulping air and wondering if the paramedics would keep my dying with a footlong tuna sub crammed into my mouth a secret. Seriously, I for real thought I was having a motherfucking heart attack, and while balanced precariously on the precipice of death, my biggest concern wasn't life insurance or whether my toilet had been bleached or if I had time to write a list of who would get my worthless belongings, it was SHOULD I TAKE A BITE OF THESE TUNA FISHES BEFORE THEY GET SLIMY OR NAH?

I spend an inordinate amount of time fantasizing about death. Not normal shit, like wondering if heaven is real (no) and if my parents have reunited there to continue that one argument from 1983 over the light bill (probably), but about how and when and what I'm going to be wearing when it finally comes for me. You would think that someone this pre-occupied with dying would take better care of her plants and apartment, but nope. I prefer instead to lie awake, petrified that I'm not going to wake up and that whoever finds the stinking meatsuit rotting away in my two-week-old sheets is going to know I was too lazy to wash off my mascara before I went to sleep. Sometimes I feel ready to die. Like when I have to sit through the painful drunken rambling toasts at a wedding, or when a stranger accidentally grazes my skin with his visibly dirty, overgrown fingernails. But other times I think I need to stick around longer, because I haven't gotten to see Ben Affleck as Batman yet or had a really good pineapple upside-down cake since the ones my mom used to make.

I really do think about dying every day, though. Sometimes I think about what would happen if the electricity in my brain just suddenly shut off, like a light switch. Like what if I was just sitting there watching that same Mike Epps comedy special I always watch (does Netflix track that? Is someone in a windowless Silicon Valley office counting that I have watched *Mike Epps: Under Rated & Never Faded* 237 real times?!) while unbeknownst to me a giant clot was creeping its way from behind my knee up to my lungs? Somebody from work, pissed off that I've missed so many shifts, is gonna find my dead body next to a pile of dried-up baked beans I had been eating in the dark out of the can. In a robe I didn't even bother to cinch shut because who the fuck is even here. I would be dead in my fancy black robe, tits splayed, tomato sauce congealed in the corners of my mouth as Netflix asks judgmentally, "Are you still watching this?" If you are the person who happens to find me, please at least switch the television to something educational before you call the police.

I turned on *Family Feud* (if I gotta die I want to be watching something wholesome in case I'm wrong about the heaven thing) and called my number one call-in-an-emergency-especially-if-I-think-I'm-dying friend, Carl, who is a total idiot in most instances, but dude has been a paramedic supervisor for ten-plus years, so I figured I could defer to his judgment. He'd talked me through a couple of bug bites and mysterious rashes previously with mostly satisfactory results. Before I even finished describing my symptoms, he was like, "Call an ambulance." Slow down, homie. Having an ambulance come to rescue me from the warm embrace of death is my biggest fear other than whether the people who deliver my takeout are secretly judging how many quarts of soup I order every week. I assume that everyone is as simple as I am, and if I were an EMT, while my main objective would be to save a dying person's life, I would definitely notice the overflowing cat box in the corner of your bathroom as you writhed on the carpet clutching at your throat while trying not to die. Sure, I'd put out the grease fire threatening to engulf your whole kitchen, but only after Firefighter Sam paused for a second to check out the spines on those haphazardly arranged books on your shelf. I might need a suggestion for book club.

I glanced at the pile of Lands' End catalogs I'd tossed into the laundry basket full of balled-up socks and possibly an empty McDonald's bag. "Not doing that," I gasped into the phone, feeling the cold grip of death wrapped around my lungs grow tighter. I texted my sister Carmen, and after she picked me up, I instructed her to please drive me to the good emergency room. I'm not kidding. If I gotta die, that's fine—it just has to be at a hospital with individual rooms and satellite television. So we left the car with the valet (I told you guys this place was dope) and checked in at the desk, where they pulled my chart up instantly. "It's not my intestines this time, I am definitely dying," I wheezed at the receptionist. "Do you still have United HealthCare?" she asked drily, never once glancing away from the computer screen, and I tried to explain with my eyes that I, too, know the agony of manning a desk where I am expected to facilitate care for inconsiderate jerks. I nodded and slid the flimsy plastic card across to her with the hand that wasn't clutching the invisible knife wounds in my chest. She pointed to a chair in the waiting room and told me to wait for triage.

"Aren't you having a heart attack?" Carmen asked, looking up from a magazine as I approached. I shrugged and slumped in a chair next to her while apologizing to the air for those Little Debbie oatmeal pies I stole from the corner store when I was a kid. WHAT IF THERE IS A HELL, OKAY?

A dude with a black eye and severed thumb he held against his hand with a dish towel sat down across from us. My heart was seconds away from stopping and homeboy's thumb was indisputably detached from his hand, and they had us just sitting out here with all the stomachaches and bee stings?! A tech came to get me, guiding me through a crowd of influenza and broken arms to a small room in back. He explained that the hospital was undergoing some construction and that he'd be administering my echocardiogram in this closet while I sat in a recliner. There were no ill-fitting gowns, no drawers full of gauze, no dispenser full of crinkly blue vomit bags. I took off my shirt so he could try to affix electrodes under my sweaty boobs, then sat in the recliner and closed my eyes while trying to picture something relaxing. The tech suggested a beach, in Tahiti. But I hate the beach, that dirty sand getting in all your moist cracks and bugs feasting on your sunburned skin, so instead I focused on something that would actually calm me: one of my enemies choking on a salad.

Twenty minutes later I was in a real room with a bed, my sister Jane, who'd met us in the waiting room, next to me yammering into her phone. The doctor pulled back the curtain and gave me one of those condescending sad smiles. The kind you give a child who says 2 + 2 = 7 and believes it. Apparently, I hadn't had a heart attack. No, instead of "life-threatening cardiac event" the reading on the EKG came out "not right emotionally." Not kidding, all those lines and squiggles on that mile-long piece of tape spelled out the words "MENTALLY ILL" like an electric Ouija board. Did you know that a panic attack can feel just like a heart attack? I didn't, but I learned that shit quick as the phlebotomist jammed an IV into my arm and the doctor loaded a big dose of Ativan into my veins and knit his eyebrows together with concern while batting around words like "therapy" and "anxiety."

When I have a panic attack, my throat closes up like someone has a big, meaty hand clasped around it, and my chest hurts and I can't breathe and I become 100 percent certain that I am going to wither and die right then and there. I know when you feel it coming on, you're supposed to relax and do the breathing exercises your very sensible doctor taught you, but it feels like if I lie down or close my eyes for even a second, I will never open them again. And most of the time I'm down with that, but this shit always happens when my sheets need changing or my garbage can is full of freezer-burned Hot Pockets I tried to salvage, and I get even more stressed out at the thought of whoever finds my corpse discovering the last thing I googled was "Shark Tank bonus clips."

Not being able to deal with your life is humiliating. It makes you feel weak. And if you're African-American and female, not only are you expected to be resilient enough to just take the hits and keep going, but if you can't, you're a Black Bitch with an Attitude. You're not mentally ill; you're ghetto. Sitting in that hospital bed, talking with a dude who was fresh out of medical school and looked like he was playing doctor with his father's stethoscope looped around his neck, I was so fucking embarrassed, ashamed to be talking to him about being so mad and so sad most of the time. Letting Rosa Parks and Harriet Tubman down by talking about my silly little feelings.

I was born to one of those mythical black hero women, a single mother who somehow managed to graduate both high school and a nursing program despite having had her first child at sixteen, a woman I never saw pop a pill or take a drink or bury her head under a pillow for three days at a time. Every single time I just can't . . . get . . . up I beat myself up a little, because it's not like I have children or a job I hate and there's probably nothing the matter with me other than laziness. When I was growing up, no one in my house was talking about depression. That's something that happened to white people on television, not a thing that could take down a Strong Black Woman. Which also destroyed me on the "Why are you listening to Smashing Pumpkins instead of [insert name of popular early nineties R & B artist]? Are you even black?!" level.

So I was (1) super fucking depressed, (2) super fucking depressed with no one to talk to about it who wasn't going to immediately suggest child services remove me from my home, and (3) super fucking depressed while clocking in on the low end of my skinfolk's negrometers because I identified hard with Courtney Love and read *Sassy* magazine because *Essence* wasn't really speaking to me yet, so wasn't this whole thing yet another way I was desperately trying to be white?!

When I was young I was frequently described as "moody." Or dismissed as "angry." According to the social worker who routinely pulled me out of class, I was intellectually bright but "quietly hostile." Never mind that I was basically living in squalor with my mother's half-dead corpse, subsisting on the kind of cereal that comes in a five-pound bag and whatever nutrient-rich meals were being served for free hot lunch; I was diagnosed as having "an attitude problem." The Black Girl curse. So I rocked with that. When you're a kid it's sometimes just easier to go along with other people's definitions of who you are. They're adults, right? So they're smarter? I would listen to this Faith No More tape on my Walkman (DO YOUNG PEOPLE UNDERSTAND WHAT THOSE WORDS EVEN MEAN) over and over while sulking and looking morose or whatever it is poor kids get to do when we have no access to semiautomatic firearms or prescription drugs. It was the only thing I could do to make it to the next goddamned day.

I tried to take my own life in 1993, and the general response when it failed was basically LOL TOUGHEN UP. My first-semester freshman report card:

English: C
History: C
Gym: D
Band: B+
Algebra: A (Because Kate Lewis helped me do my
    homework. I love you, Kate.)
Suicide: F

I just slept straight through the rest of the weekend and went back to school the next Monday. I kept doing the same shit I'd always been doing and figured that if I wanted to try again, I needed to wait until I was old enough to get a car and drive it off one of suburban Chicagoland's many cliffs. I think my mom started watching me a little more closely? But what was she really going to do? She was severely disabled. My being hopeless all the time was trumped by "You know I can't walk, right?" and I get that. I was a kid, and it was my job to go to school, so I did my job. I would deal with it when I was off Medicare and making enough money to pay for cognitive therapy myself. BAHAHAHAHAHA *choke sob* AHAHA-HAHAHA!

Even when my fucking parents died in 1998 and I had an actual thing I could point to as a source of my unrelenting depression, a cause to substantiate the effect of my simmering hatred, I played it off. I don't know if it feels like this for anyone else, but I definitely come from the kind of people whose response to "Hey, man, I'm pretty bummed out" is "Shut up, there's nothing wrong with you." Or how about "You just sleep all the time because you're lazy." Like, if it isn't broken or hemorrhaging, you need to bury it under these dollar-store snack foods and work it out by your fucking self. OH, OKAY, COOL. So then I developed very glamorous coping mechanisms like covering myself with grisly death tattoos and eating food out of the trash. And then, because I wasn't actively trying to kill myself and could keep a job and make friends and pay my rent and not do heroin, I made peace with it. This is just how I am. I'M FINE. For as long as I can remember, I've had this undercurrent of sadness that, if I'm being honest, I don't totally mind. It was easy to ignore because it doesn't bother me that much. And I don't want to be some shiny, happy idiot. This is gritty; this is real.

One of my most favorite extracurricular activities these days is taking a Klonopin. But not just taking it—also making a big production of getting up to get the water, then swallowing it and looking up potential side effects that I really don't give a shit about yet am mildly terrified might actually occur. I would like to meet the person who gets a medication to fix a for-real fucking problem and is like, "Hold up, appetite changes?! Unacceptable, doctor dude." And then, like, dramatically flushes all the pills down the toilet before collapsing into an anxiety-ridden stress puddle. I will take anything, at any time, if a doctor tells me it will repair whatever is wrong with me in that instant. Maybe I'll read about it if I have to spend a little extra time on the toilet, but that definitely happens after I've already swallowed the pills dry and set a timer to see how quickly they start working. I will also take any combination of NyQuil, antihistamines, nonsteroidal anti-inflammatories, vitamins, and assorted syrups at the first sign of a weepy eye or scratchy throat. To hell with my liver: FIX THIS.

I am just an old garbage bag full of blood patiently waiting for death to rescue me, but sometimes when I tell people that, their immediate response is HOW CAN YOU BE SAD, YOU'RE HILARIOUS!!!!! and then for five seconds I'm like, "This person who has never met me before is correct. I'm so funny I should stop thinking life is a trash can." But five seconds after that, some human roadkill yells at the grocery store bagger or pulls his scrotum out on the train, and I get the insatiable urge to peel my skin off like the layers of an onion and jam my thumbs into my eye sockets, just hoping that I'll disappear down the garbage disposal of human existence straight into hell. Then it's easy to just write the depression off as an irritation at the dummies I have the misfortune of sharing the planet with. "I'm not depressed, dudes who ride unicycles in rush-hour traffic are fucking idiots," or "Nothing is wrong with me, the *real* problem is all these people mindlessly texting while their dogs shit in the middle of the goddamn sidewalk."

Two things happened that forced me to finally have the "sometimes I have a disproportionately rage-filled response to otherwise harmless shit" talk with my doctor. (1) I was at work and the worst person in the world came in to buy dog food. This is the kind of person who asks an unending stream of questions that I, as an unfamiliar customer-service representative, couldn't possibly answer as she empties the entire contents of her handbag onto the counter in front of me. I hate that, the "Please don't write a negative Yelp review of this business" trap that requires my standing there trying to look engaged while this woman uses me as a sounding board for questions like, "Is [redacted] going to eat three cans, or should I just get one?" She's not asking me, but she's not *not* asking me. I mean, we're making eye contact and everything but how could I know?! And I had to wait there held hostage because one of these questions pouring like vomit from her toothless maw might be one I can actually answer. I felt the familiar rageheat claw its way slowly up my neck and into my jaw before finally scratching at the backs of my eyeballs. And as she kept rambling nonsensically to herself while pretending she needed my help for five minutes in real time, I calmly raised my hands to my ears and used my forefingers to hold them closed and said, "You have to get the fuck out of here or I will destroy you." So much for that stellar Yelp review.

My panic attacks usually don't have any obvious triggers. The last time I was hospitalized for a bad one I'd had a surprisingly good day: brunch with a friend at m.henry, a field trip to the metaphysical bookstore for smudge sticks and oils, back home in bed watching eyeliner tutorials on YouTube for the rest of the afternoon. Bills paid, snacks in the fridge, clean clothes folded and put away and then bang: pain I couldn't ignore snaking up my left arm before encircling my heart and squeezing it so hard I thought I was going to faint. I remember thinking to myself, "CHILL OUT, BITCH, YOU KNOW WHAT THIS IS," but you know how that goes. I just freaked out harder and tried to breathe and get my shoes on, but every breath felt like an ice pick to the center of my chest and I couldn't lace them up. I called an Uber, then sat in my lobby wearing headphones and disgusting Crocs, and when the car arrived I tried to say hello as cheerfully as possible, so I wouldn't tip the driver off. The emergency room was slow that night and they saw me right away and talked to me in their most soothing voices. I got some X-rays and a CAT scan and when the doctor came in to tell me my heart was enlarged, I asked, "Is it because I love too much?" and we both had a hearty laugh before he was like, "STOP EATING MEAT" and put through the order for me to be admitted and hooked up to a ventilator for two days.

All this might be easier if I could punch something, but I'm not a punch-something person. I'm a "sit in the dark in the bathroom with a package of sharp cheddar cheese slices" person. Except I don't even really eat cheese anymore. Plus I can't fight. I'm soft, man. And I don't have any answers. The world is scary and terrible and people out here don't want Obamacare to fix a paper cut let alone offer some discounted mental health care, so what is left for us to do? Talk about it? Stop being afraid of it? Shut down those who want to dismiss us as fragile or crazy?! I went on Lexapro, but after three weeks

I had stopped sleeping and fuck that. Maybe it doesn't work that way for everyone, but I'd rather be angry and well rested than tired and happy. Or "happy," I guess. I have pills that make me sleepy instead of panicky, and I learned how to do this four-seven-eight breathing technique that's supposed to switch your body from fight-or-flight to a passive response, but come on. Seriously, the only time it even occurs to me to do it is when I'm already sweating and trying to dry swallow some of these benzos. Do black girls even get to be depressed? If I ever have more than $37 in my pocket I'm going to open a school for girls with bad attitudes where we basically talk to therapists all day while wearing soft pants and occasionally taking a field trip to the nearest elote cart. And if that doesn't work, I'll just tell some more stupid jokes. Good thing I'm hilarious.

a civil union

I witnessed a Civil War reenactment once. And that is a straight-up miracle, considering I had absolutely no idea that people in the North even participated in that kind of thing. Having grown up in this liberal North Shore enclave where no one blinks an eye at your Liberal Gay Blackness, I sometimes forget that the minute you jump on 355 heading west, Illinois becomes an entirely different place. A place where mullets are still fashionable and fanny packs are considered an acceptable accessory.

My homie was getting married on a gorgeous Saturday afternoon in Naperville, because that is where he is from and that is where his parents still live and would it kill one of my idiot friends to marry some asshole who could afford to throw a wedding downtown? But I love him, so I had to go. After waking up at noon and dragging myself out of bed, the first thing I thought was "Shit, I totally forgot to buy nude panty hose. I am going to look so out of place around these sensibly shoed people."

Deciding who to drag with you to a wedding when you're unattached is a tenth-circle-of-hell situation for real. Especially if it's a church wedding and you have the type of friends who might burst into flames upon entry. I made my friend Amy go with me, promising that I would sit through her traveling folk metal band's next show in Chicago but secretly hoping I would die before the time came to make good on that promise. When I went downstairs to meet her, carrying my reusable grocery bag with nice shoes, makeup, and one of those inner-thigh chafe sticks in it, I stopped cold. Amy, my beloved tomboy, typically clad in trucker hats and fitted tank tops and baggy ripped jeans from the boys' section at Target, was wearing a dress. My sweet, sweet Amy, five feet tall and built like a Lego, was wearing daytime sequins. It looked like someone had stretched an ice-skating costume over a refrigerator box. I gasped. She put the cigarette she was smoking out between her fingers and tried to twirl her sparse mustache, the octopus tattooed on her partially shaved scalp shining in the sunshine. "My tux is at the dry cleaner's so I'm wearing my old prom dress," she said by way of explanation, and I put my head down to keep from laughing as I went to toss my stuff in the backseat. "This was the only nice thing I had!" she wailed, and I basically almost choked.

As Amy's grumbling, oversize truck belched a steady stream of greasy blue-gray smoke from its exhaust, she took my hand to help hoist me up, then climbed over me like a toddler to get into the driver's seat. We peeled out with a screech, Ice Cube bumping from the brand-new speakers she'd proudly installed herself. Naperville is a relatively wealthy and predominantly Republican suburb a little over an hour outside of Chicago, and I knew I was in trouble the minute I saw how many churches we were driving past as we exited the tollway. Seriously, it was like church, church, Burger King that whole families actually sit down and eat dinner in, church, church, Walmart, church. We saw at least 137 churches in a two-mile stretch, and that was only after I'd actually started counting them.

Despite having stayed at least ten miles over the speed limit the entire trip, we arrived late to the ceremony. Blame CVS for not having any good wedding cards and for putting the generic Aleve too far from the Doritos and snacks we needed for the road. Blame all of the semis that kept trapping us between them, condensing the prolonged horror show that is my life into an incomprehensible flash before my eyes. Please also blame my closet for being disorganized and not having any fancy clothes in it. They were already at the altar reciting their vows as we snuck into the back of the church, Amy in the gym shoes she hadn't thought to bring (or didn't own) an alternate for, and me in bare feet so my heels wouldn't click on the hard-wood floors, and while that definitely made me feel like a jerk, I was also kind of relieved and hoping that we'd missed some of the boring "what is the meaning of love?" parts.

Anyway, I tried to inconspicuously scan the room to see if any black people other than myself were in attendance—defense mechanism! we all do it!—and my eyes locked instantly with those of a black woman a few pews over from ours. And she was glaring at me like I'd stolen her fucking bike. I was all ready to breathe a sigh of relief, and homegirl over here was scowling like I'd taken the last piece of chicken off the buffet. Can you even believe that bullshit? Doesn't she know the unspoken rule that all black people have to stick together within large white gatherings? You never know when a lynch mob might be forming next to the cupcake table!

Maybe it was because I was wearing sunglasses indoors, or maybe she's a real stickler for punctuality, but rather than give her the benefit of the doubt, I instead hissed and bared my fangs, which is International Black Code for "I would never light your path to the underground railroad."

I let her stare a hole into the side of my face as I shifted my attention to the bridesmaids, who looked absolutely perfect. Combed and sprayed and cinched and plucked, and no unlucky fat friend ruining the uniformity of the bridesmaid roster. Man, I have been that bitch before and I hate it and it sucks. Can't I just sit in the last pew and undo the top button on my expensive outside pants and make eyes at all the bride's single uncles? Why you gotta shove me into this tight and shiny shit? You knew I wasn't going to lose fifty pounds, you asshole, especially because your incessant calling and e-mailing me all hours of the day about the florist and the caterer and the dressmaker caused me to stress eat like you would not fucking believe. Would it have killed you to pick a nice jersey or cotton-poly blend? My *eyelashes* are sweating in this cheap-ass dress, and my tits are exploding out of the top like biscuit dough from a can. I was in a wedding once in which every other bridesmaid was five-foot-two and approximately thirty-two pounds, and they all looked gorgeous and toned and please keep in mind that I do not shave my armpits. I only went because the bride had a cousin I was interested in, but I ended up looking like some sort of mythical creature, all giant and hunched over and tucking my T. rex arms into my sides so I wouldn't mess up the pictures with my mossy pits. It was a fail, believe me. After the humiliating amateur photo shoot ("On the count of three, everybody jump!"), I threw my Spanx in a trash can at the hotel, put on a hoodie, and took off my pinching shoes before they had even served the salad course.

The service was lovely and brief, praises be to the most high God, and the only blemish on the whole thing was that the minister spaced on the words to the Lord's Prayer as she was reciting it. Holy crap! I'm the biggest sodomite this side of Gomorrah, and even I know all the words to the Apostles' Creed, the Twenty-third Psalm, and the Lord's Prayer. Don't they teach you that on the first day of Ministry 101?! Lesson one: skimming the collection plate. Lesson two: Our father, who art in heaven, hallowed be thy name. Thy kingdom come, thy will be done, on earth as it is in heaven. Blah blah daily bread, blah blah trespasses, AMEN. I was saying it along in my head with her, feeling pure and clean and washed in the blood of the lamb, and when she flubbed the line my first thought was, "Well, Sam, it's obvious you're the devil and that Jesus really was watching when you let that kid finger you in the laundry room of his apartment building freshman year. Give it up, dummy." But then I realized that *she* was the wrong one, and now I've found the loophole through which I'm going to slip into heaven come Judgment Day. Like God is Judge Mathis.

The wedding was at four and the reception at six thirty, and the minute we walked outside to stand broiling under the summer sun and wave ribbons at the happy couple as they descended the steps of the church, I turned to Amy and was like, "Dude, we have two hours to kill in the [redacted] suburbs." Now, if Janessa hadn't been turning her nose up at me in the church I would've asked her and Marquise if they wanted to team up and find someplace to day drink, but by the time I took my ass off my shoulders and thought about inviting them along on whatever adventure we were about to get into, they were already getting into his grandmother's Buick Regal. So I did the next best thing: I unbuttoned my pants and decided to take a driving tour of the western suburbs. And that, my little pumpkins, is how a dude in a dress and a runaway slave happened upon Civil War Days.

When we initially drove past the field full of tents and camp-fires in the middle of downtown, my first thought was "White people will go camping *anywhere*." Then, spying the hoop skirts and Confederate flags peppering the crowd, I told Amy to turn the truck around. Right. Now. As we drove past the second time, two young soldiers in homemade Union uniforms were walking down the sidewalk, rifles slung low across their backs. We obviously needed to park the truck. I started humming "Lift Every Voice and Sing" as I got a couple of bottles of water out of her trunk and Amy readied her camera for our long journey back to 1862.

Being away from the city is terrifying to me. I am not com-fortable being around people who homeschool their children and sew their own clothing, and I am never doing that ever again. I was for real afraid for my life. I also really don't under-stand this fascination some people have with going back in time. Why in the world would I want to sit around in nine layers of dark wool on an eighty-degree day, sweating into my beard as I pretend to be Robert E. Lee at Antietam, when in the present there are iPhones and air-conditioning? (Well, I guess sometimes you just want to call a woman a nigger in the middle of Main Street, but that's just you.) You'll never catch me spending a week in the wilderness trying to "get back to nature" or whatever, especially not when I have an apartment and a bed and a refrigerator. (AND MY FREEDOM.) There's nothing glamorous to me about sleeping outside or drink-ing from a different water fountain, particularly when circum-stances don't require it. Seriously, do you Starbucks-drinking people know a single person who cures his own meats?! No, you don't. Because in this day and age that shit is not necessary. What is this thing people have with pretending they want to go back to when doctors did surgery with two sticks and a roll of jute? I like technology! I love medical advancements! I would rather be dead than dress up like Little Bo Peep on a Saturday afternoon to chase diaper-clad babies named Malachai and cook food over a trash barrel that has been fashioned into some sort of old-timey grill by putting a Bunsen burner inside.

We walked up and down this stretch of sidewalk for half an hour, gawking through the chain-link fence at your grandfather and the rest of the infantry getting their musketoons and artillery swords ready for the next battle, all while trying to inconspicuously take their photographs. They caught me looking every single time, and I had to pin my freedom papers to my shirt just to keep them from tackling me at the waist and forcing me to braid their children's hair. Amy and I were making fun of a life-size rendering of Abraham Lincoln made out of mayonnaise (pretty sure) when someone straight out of an episode of *Little House on the Prairie* appeared from out of nowhere and stood there scrutinizing us. She was wearing a long-sleeved plaid dress with a pinafore, a petticoat, a bonnet, leather, and held a woven basket with both arms. I waited for her to appraise the width of my hips and ask if she could get a look at my teeth, but she didn't. Instead, she said, "Your necklace is pretty intense." I was wearing this necklace I got on Etsy, a coyote mandible hanging from a chain that I only wear when I need to feel edgy and cool. And while she might have had a point, this broad was dressed like fucking Florence Nightingale. I was like, "Honey, you are wearing a hoop skirt in 2013." She stormed off, probably to soak a pig carcass in saltpeter or make coffee out of okra seeds.

Amy and I drove through the rest of downtown, which pretty much looks like downtown everywhere else: a Gap and a Talbots and lots of little adorable places for your mother to put antique sugar bowls on her house charge and eat overpriced crab salads. From there we drove out through a bunch of subdivisions and new developments, and it was so insanely *Children of the Corn*–y that I was almost afraid to ride with the windows down for fear someone would reach in with a scythe and slice me to death. So many churches. So many blank blue eyes drinking in our close-cropped city hair and head-to-toe black outfits in disbelief. I was exhausted by the time we got to the reception, which was at this beautiful restaurant that had been dressed up like the ballroom in *Cinderella*. And even though we'd fought the Battle of Vicksburg and survived, we somehow were still too early and had to stand in the parking lot waiting for the only people of color other than me and Stinkeye to open the doors. (We didn't really have to stand outside, I guess, but I hate to be the first big bitch in a room full of food, so hovering awkwardly near Amy's truck was what it was gonna be. I am not going to be the asshole who has a bib tucked into her shirt and is pulling a chair up to the hors d'oeuvres while people are wandering in looking for the gift table with their starter glasses of champagne.)

Whenever I walk into a room like that I think, "I'm going to ruin this tablecloth or break this chair" before I even get a chance to set my purse down. It took us approximately an hour and a half to find the little placard with my name stenciled on it, and I said a silent prayer to Horus that this dude hadn't messed up and sat me with his parents' ancient golf buddies or something. (I already almost got called a nigger once that day, no need to tempt fate). Since we were among the first people in, we were the absolute first people in line at the bar, and the cocktail-hour sangria was flowing. The bartender handed me a plastic cup full of green apple chunks and I paused, paralyzed by the memory of my sister's wedding with its "either buy drink tickets or suck down tap water all night" theme, then Amy elbowed me in the ribs to get me moving. "It's free!" she whispered, balancing three cups in one hand and pulling my shirt with the other. Everywhere we turned, someone was shoving a tray loaded with crostini and olive tapenade or bacon-wrapped dates in our faces. I hate olives but I love fancy wedding food, so between the two of us we probably consumed an entire pig and wiped out every olive in the Mediterranean. Seriously, I had toothpicks sticking out of all my pockets. I had to hide them under my chair before anyone noticed the amount of food we'd eaten was greater than what I'd spent on the gift I'd purchased from the low end of their registry.

I had bet Amy at the church (is "thou shalt not make pointless wagers" one of the Commandments?) that we'd be at the same table as the other black people at the party, but they were seated at the table across from ours, just close enough that I could barely make out the bulging vein in Brenda's forehead as she glared at me in the romantic candlelight. I wanted to shout, "Look, I just survived typhoid pneumonia and the Battle of Gettysburg to be here and eat these tapas, lay the fuck off," but my mouth was way too full of manchego cheese. Amy and I got put at the "fun table," the one full of hip single people who did not speak to us save for this trio of drunk bachelors who were hilarious and asking questions, all except "Are you guys a couple?" because, duh, they are polite and have manners, but you know that's the only question they really wanted to ask.

Dinner was equally delicious: a bunch of really good hot and cold dishes that they served family style, which caused me a great deal of agita, but what can you do? People waiting for me to serve myself from a communal food dish stresses me out. I took a quarter of what I'd normally eat, then watched wistfully as the platters circled the table. You could tell how much the bride's parents loved her by the quality of the food. Seriously, as we passed all of the gleaming fresh seafood trays and steaming bowls of chicken with artichokes I couldn't help but think, "I bet she got really good grades in high school." Plus, we were sitting so close to the top-shelf open bar that I could pretty much serve myself.

At one point my boy came over to thank us for wolfing down his free food while making fun of his friends, and I was like, "Way to have only three black people at the party, David Duke." He laughed and said, "I almost put you guys at the same table, but I thought it would have been too obvious." It was a good thing he didn't, because at that exact moment I glanced over to where ol' girl and her man were waiting in the cake line and she glowered at me once again. I was like, "Who is that lady and what is her deal? Is this about her man? Because I can just go over there right now and tell her that I'm not feeling dude and she can keep her dirty looks to herself." The last thing I ever want is a dude who is some other woman's problem, because (1) I'm not a hater, and (2) I don't need a bitch playing on my phone all night. Can't we all just get along?!

The big band in the corner started playing "Cheek to Cheek" and I took that as our cue to leave. We gave daps to the frat brothers at our table and took our customized cupcakes to go. People were lingering on the lawn outside the ballroom, chatting amiably about travel hockey and hating vaccines and other white things. We made our way to the parking lot, where men with stock portfolios clapped one another on the back and compared BMW interiors. It wasn't even dark yet, but Amy pulled her dress over her head, showering the gravel below with sequins from 1995. She shimmied into her cargo pants and a plaid shirt as I painstakingly rolled my damp, expensive shapewear down over my lumps and bumps. I tossed it on the dashboard to dry out during the ride home and was circling around to the trunk to get my flip-flops to relieve my smashed toes when I saw it: a faded Bush-Cheney sticker on the back of Jerome's grandma's Buick. I hobbled over and cupped my hands to peer in the window in the fading daylight. A Walgreens bag with Flamin' Hots and a can of Olive Oil Sheen Spray sat on the back seat: HELLO, NEMESIS.

"I get it now!" I called out to Amy, who was sitting on her bumper packing a bowl for the ride home. "They're Republicans! They hate us queers!" I wondered what the two of them had done during our intermission—enacted some legislation against impoverished children or maybe stripped some black people of their right to vote? It's too bad they'd gotten away from us; I would have died to see their reactions back at Fort Sumter.

Amy's engine roared to life behind me and she tapped the horn twice. "Come on, hoss! Let's go find you a drive-thru!" I took one last look inside the car (a Tim McGraw CD, really?!) and patted the hood. I climbed awkwardly into the truck and tried to find something good on the radio. Amy placed a cigarette between her teeth and passed the bowl across the seat to me. "Should I ram it?" she nodded toward their car. I shook my head and cranked up the music, remembering a quote from fake Abraham Lincoln on this old episode of *Star Trek*, marathons of which I used to watch on channel nine in the summer when I was little because I didn't have any friends and I never went outside: "There's no honorable way to kill, no gentle way to destroy. There's nothing good in war except its ending."

mavis

I had ripped the tender flesh on my finger trying to open a piece of mail that wasn't even fucking mine, a fancy wedding invitation on creamy heavyweight card stock intended for some girl named Alicia who lived downstairs in apartment 209. Blood splattered across the velvety envelope while I raced frantically around my kitchen, sucking my finger and snatching open drawers in search of your grandma's favorite adhesive bandages, the thick stretchy fabric kind that conform to every wrinkly crevice.

I am not OCD. I'm really not. Like, if I buy peaches? It is almost 100 percent guaranteed that a week later my kitchen will be humming with the low drone of ten thousand fruit flies. I bought this adorable fruit bowl and I put peaches in it because I like peaches, but then I probably got distracted by a gyro or some old chili and before you know it, a plague of tiny bugs is feasting on my rotten $7.98/pound Whole Foods white peaches. That would not happen to a meticulous person. I mean, really, sometimes I don't even wipe that good. But if I have a bandage on my finger and am forced by crushing poverty and ever-mounting debt out into the real world to earn a living, I become fixated on it, watching its crisp, pristine edges wilt and dampen throughout the day, holding back vomit while handling customer credit cards and loose change speckled with influenza. I watch it grow loose and dirty throughout the day even though I changed it four times before lunch, repulsed by its fraying edge as I raise my hands to mock some dumb asshole with a well-timed air quote. It's fucking disgusting.

My and Mavis's modern romance had begun the same way as so many passionate love affairs before it: ON FUCKING TWITTER. Her initial tweet to me had read something like this: "reading your book and never wanna stop," which is incredibly humbling and flattering and all those silly blush words. And who knows, I probably sent back a bunch of heart-with-the-arrow-through-it emojis or something. She responded, and our fledgling courtship took off, two modern girls falling in lust (or something?) one trending favorite at a time.

We moved the conversation to DM, and I really need you guys to know that it physically pains me to both have participated in something called a DM and to recount what happened in one for you now. Don't get me wrong, I love giant computer phones and talking cars and vaccines, but hashtagging and RTs make me motherfucking #crazy. I can't follow that shit. Dude, I still have a house phone. And one of those old-timey answering machines that goes gurgle-scramble-gargle as you rewind the tape after listening to the customer service representative at ComEd, whose tone suggests that the $42.73 I am past due came from her account personally, express her shock and disbelief that I have an actual answering machine. Mavis and I talked about dresses and my favorite brand of matte lip stains, and when I asked for book recommendations, she sent me nineteen, give or take a few. (*The Book of Unknown Americans* was really good, by the way.) Then she asked me to mail her a letter.

When we first met in person I knew immediately that she wanted to slurp me up like the finest cup of cold-brewed, pour-over Ethiopian coffee nine dollars could buy. I'm not sure exactly when things changed. We sent a handful of cards back and forth (mine handmade and purchased from Etsy because I'm twee like that), our texts shifted from informational to conversational to something bordering on intimate, and then there she was, lithe and lean and carrying a baby cactus to meet me for a bumbling and awkward first lunch. A lunch during which she housed a giant plate of huevos rancheros and pota-toes and sausages in a matter of seconds. I mean, she wolfed down her food with such ferocity that I felt my pants go damp. I LOVE PEOPLE WHO LOVE EATING. Mavis was tall and skinny and I could tell at a glance that she's the do-gooder kind of white people: vegan earth shoes and woven Mayan handbag and the kind of hair you get from using natural products. She listens to Black Star and Public Enemy and eats yard tomatoes that grow behind her house and bakes from-scratch pies and buys multicultural reading material for her children. I am very familiar with this varietal of grape.

A few weeks later Mavis came back to town and got us a room at the Acme Hotel. I don't know, man, I just didn't want our first time to be in my little apartment, pushing the cat off the bed and trying to ignore the drunk college kids puk-ing in the hallway outside my door. Better instead to get busy in a sterile hotel room downtown that looked like something out of a *Real World* house: trompe l'oeil paint on the walls, iPhone chargers in the outlets, a glowing red neon lip print on the bathroom mirror in lieu of a night-light. We drank French 75's, the ingredients for which she'd thoughtfully packed in a cooler; I sipped mine nervously on the far side of the bed, flipping maniacally through the television channels and thinking about how I am never that prepared, for anything, ever. I knew her well enough to know that she is not a Television Person. A Multiple-Section Reader of the Sunday *Times*? A Listener to Public Radio in her Bumper-Stickered Volvo? A Learned Individual Courtesy of the BBC or Al-Jazeera or Some Other Unbiased Non-American and Therefore Inherently Superior News Source? DUH. ALL OF THOSE THINGS. But a Consumer of Daylong Pantsless *Top Chef* Marathons? I'm no expert, but I don't think a bitch who makes her own kombucha is the same bitch sitting around in her house bra for hours on end watching old episodes of *Roseanne*. Because I am that bitch, and kombucha is disgusting.

Those people, the "No TV, Eat at the Dinner Table, Get Your News from a Reputable Source Other Than Facebook" people, are terrifying to me. I have a subscription to *BUST* and I read Matt Taibbi's articles in *Rolling Stone* sometimes, but those people always want to talk about world events and I'm like, "Yo, my dude. I don't know shit about Russia. Let's go get some chicken." I don't know anything about the economy; I can barely keep track of who my elected officials are; I hate learning things; why can't everyone just watch *The Voice* so we can all have something exciting to talk about?! God, I love those battle rounds. So I sat there and watched Middle Eastern explosions on CNN while Mavis busied herself making cocktails and chirping about smart shit.

It wasn't until I felt her definitely female fingers fumbling awkwardly with the zipper of my hoodie in that hotel room downtown that it dawned on me: I don't really know how to fuck a lady. My stomach dropped as I tried to recall every article I'd ever read about G-spots and nipple sensitivity, my arms stiffening at my sides as she bent down and pressed her lips into my neck. I assumed it was up to me to do the man stuff because I have a fantasy football team and can grow a full beard, so I just lay there while she did stuff to me, waiting for her to yell at me because I hadn't taken the garbage out. THAT'S HOW THIS WORKS, RIGHT? I expertly slid my female hand under her bra and unhooked it with the flick of a wrist in one smooth, effortless motion. JK, FOLKS. I wrestled with that clasp like an alligator, finally resorting to the use of a chain saw and my teeth.

"Do some nipple stuff," offered my dumb brain, and I did while peeking at her face to make sure I was getting it right. I don't know, man. I mean, she didn't recoil or punch me in the side of the head, so I figured I was doing pretty okay? But then I remembered she said her boobs were desensitized from years of having nursed two children and I promptly removed my mouth because BABIES. I tried to think of the worst thing boyfriends past had done in bed with me and actively tried to avoid doing any of that. I peeled off my socks (I hate when dudes wear socks in bed) and asked Mavis if there were any feelings she wanted to talk about before we really got started. "Has anyone in the patriarchy oppressed you lately?" I asked attentively. "Wanna read some stuff on *Jezebel*?" She launched herself at me, pinning my arms down as she scaled my body like the face of a mountain.

I reached for the waistband of her jeans and there it was, in the flickering blue light of the flat-screen hanging across from the bed: that old grimy, tattered Band-Aid loosely affixed to my wounded forefinger.

I don't really know all the rules yet, but I am pretty sure you aren't allowed to finger a woman while wearing a wilted, unraveling, dirty-ass Band-Aid. I tried to create enough friction between my sensible yoga pants and the scratchy duvet to slide it off without either tipping her off or starting a brush fire, but that stupid thing wouldn't loosen up. The more furiously I worked at it, the more it wouldn't budge. "Do we really need this on?" she asked, nodding at the television. Even though I wouldn't have minded the dulcet tones of Anderson Cooper serving as the soundtrack to our first, officially official coitus—maybe I could learn something about midterm elections through osmosis?—I seized the opportunity. Plunged suddenly into darkness, I used my teeth to scrape that nasty Band-Aid from my finger and tucked it out of sight under my pillow. Then I slid my pale, wrinkled finger inside her vagina, rooting around in there for the rough and spongy G spot, just like all those magazines had taught me.

Vagina Dentata

MY MOTHERFUCKING TEETH. MY SIXTEEN-THOUSAND-DOLLAR SON-OF-A-BITCHING TEETH. That is what I was thinking about when my head moved between Mavis's thighs, pretending to know what I was about to start doing. The carefully sculpted, realistic-looking crowns affixed to the dead stumps of hollowed-out bone jutting raggedly from the receding gum tissue inside my head; the hours and hours and hours spent horizontal beneath blinding lights as the dentist jammed a pickax between my pulsating molars and went after my eyeteeth with an old-timey saw; the ten-inch needles piercing through my skull, crammed into my sinus cavity, wedged into softened, bloody tissue already vibrant with excruciating pain. *Ugh this is fucking Coldplay,* I think as I try to figure out a sexy way to tell her to scoot her butt forward so that she's positioned right under my chin without dislocating my goddamned elbow in the process. *Now this hoe knows I have embarrassingly mainstream taste in sex music.* "Inch your butt up, sister," I say, patting her haunch like a horse. "Just like at the gyne."

Eating pussy is easier than you'd think. I learned on the job and I am really quite good at it. Sometimes my disabled ass gets the angle wrong and I'm, like, sucking on a wet dreadlock or whatever, but for the most part I just sort of put my face where it feels like it should go and let my tongue do what comes naturally. It's sort of like licking the inside of someone's mouth? Except there's hair and no teeth and you have to be really careful not to disembowel your girl with your wanton incisors. The first time was in daylight, and I really inspected everything up close, but in a sexy way so she wouldn't feel like her labia were in a petri dish or something. And then, I don't know, I just licked it like you would an ice-cream cone. A soft-serve one, though. Because sometimes you gotta get a little rough with the regular kind and use your teeth on the chunks or use your lips really hard to mold it into a lickable shape. Sometimes I use my nose or my chin and really I don't think she can tell the motherfucking difference. The fingering was easy to master, because I basically just do what I do to myself when the vibrator is out of batteries while intermittently trying to feel what she had for breakfast from the inside. That part is easy; I was doing the Jay Z "brush your shoulders off" dance by the third time we got busy as Mavis was seeing stars and catching the holy ghost while having orgasm after orgasm. I thought it might take some time for me to get good at cunnilingus, but nah, I just get a supportive pillow for my neck (I'm old) and get all up in that soft-serve.

I have always been above average at sucking a d, probably because I am the kind of person who excels at alone tasks rather than thriving in a group project. Like, I just want to make the diorama the way I want to make it, okay, Ms. Mitman? Then I know the shit will be right. So when I'm down there, face-to–open-faced medium-rare roast beef sandwich (picture it), it's important for me to do a good job. I never much enjoyed being eaten out by dudes. One would slowly make his way down there, burdened by obligation, and I would literally clam up: I'm smelly; I'm hairy; I've got enough yeast in there to make dinner rolls; just stick it in my butthole and hurry up so we won't miss our dinner reservation. But Mavis understands that my nose-searing musk is nature's self-cleaning oven just handling her business. And that that coarse mouthful of hair I'm serving is payback for never having received my reparations when Obama was elected.

$149.95

The year I turned thirty-four, I decided to buy my vagina her first grown-up-lady sex toy. A Lelo Mona 2, from the Pleasure Chest, more expensive than the most expensive thing in my closet. It's the Cadillac of vibrators, with its velvety silicone curved for the G-spot and its multitude of settings and speeds. And worth every penny, as one time I had Mavis lying on her side and was banging her with it and she was caterwauling like a crazy person then squirted for the first time ever, so hard and so much that it splashed on the goddamned cat. THAT IS FUCKING AMAZING.

I always thought I would eventually end up with a woman. Men are too taxing, too mischievous, too restless, too naughty, and I don't want to spend my Chico's years with my stomach tied in an anxiety knot waiting for a dude to leave me for someone younger. The idea of spending my Social Security checks fussing over some goddamned man has never appealed to me; I want afternoons spent shouting at the television set with my best friend in our matching house sweaters and magnifying readers from Costco. I have always been sexually attracted to both men and women, although the sex part is more of an afterthought for me. My compatibility checklist is full of very important qualifications, like:

- leaves me alone while I watch my shows
- doesn't leave globs of toothpaste in the sink
- would never finish the ice cream without checking with me first
- understands that I don't like to touch while sleeping
- isn't an asshole to the cat

And so on. I understand my limits, and my deficits, and I know that to get through life with some relative degree of happiness, we have to find someone who can figure out the taxes or make the lunches or whatever it is we aren't good at doing. I don't need a charming person with a good sense of humor who specializes in getting extensions on the cable bill, I got that covered; I need someone who balances a checkbook and remembers when her last tetanus shot was.

I get tired. I work fifty hours a week, man. I wear compression stockings and orthopedic shoes, and most nights I fall asleep in the middle of my dinner. So when Mavis is nudging me in the ribs at 9:00 p.m., elbowing me in the kidneys to get me out of my end-of-day coma, it makes me feel like an ass-hole. My body wants to say, "LOOK, BITCH, I AM TIRED" but my brain is all, "Be grateful someone wants to see a body with this many varicose veins naked." And my brain is right—I *do* have a lot of weird moles and shit. Halfway into the kissing, I usually realize that I've made the wrong decision, that I just should've stayed asleep and woken her up at three in the morn-ing with twenty passionate minutes of finger sex, but then I remember the Lelo. Sure, it feels like cheating, reaching for that smooth piece of silicone on the charger next to the bed. But then, as I am the drooling, semiunconscious big spoon working my multispeed robot penis while little spoon is none the wiser, I think to myself, "Worth every goddamned cent." ZzZZZzzZz

This Is What Wearing a Harness Is Like.

I felt like to really commit to the lesbian thing we had to get ourselves a strap-on, that it wouldn't be really real until I'd awkwardly tried to have hands-free penis sex. So I did some research (meaning I read two short articles on the Internet), then decided to make a purchase.

First of all, I had to go into Early to Bed and ask for the plus-size kind, which was weird because I made it weird, not because they did. The woman at the counter handed me a plastic bag filled with what looked like a tangled mess of black jump ropes. She asked me if I wanted to try it on, and I just stood there, dumbfounded, flushing scarlet as I imagined this young woman helping me navigate all those hooks and pulleys, trying to get my angry joints through the right holes. Also, it was like three in the afternoon and I'm not sure what my baby parts smelled like, and please just give it to me in an unmarked plastic bag, okay? I chose a large lavender penis, smooth silicone with a curved tip and a couple of soft ridges, paid for it and the harness, then promptly hid them in my closet for three months.

Mostly because I'm lazy. And everything I read on the Internet about fucking someone with a strap-on said I would need to practice while also subtly hinting that I could probably stand to be in better shape to provide the most fulfilling sexual experience. What would Helen Keller be doing while I was tiptoeing around my apartment with my big plastic penis waggling between my legs? Or worse, while I was simulating doggy style on a pillow while standing next to the bed?! The one time I took everything out of the packaging to practice assembling it, I walked out of the room for half a second and came back to find the goddamned cat hugging and kicking the dildo while gnawing on its head. "Put my dick down!" I yelled, swatting at her with the edge of a blanket as she continued scratching up my new penis. "Put my motherfucking dick down!"

I've watched enough porn to know how to do it. At least in theory. I was especially anxious to try that move where you mount the lady from behind and push her head down so she won't notice you're reaching for that last piece of bed pie you left on the nightstand for a snack. I wasn't so sure about the other positions:

Missionary: BORING. Also, I am a heavy person who has a very real fear of collapsing a skinny person's lungs beneath the weight of my tits or whatever. Also also, the idea that I would have to do something with my face other than grimace in excruciating pain is the worst.

Girl on top: Fine, but again, I would be thinking a lot about what's happening on my face, which would be a direct reflection of what was happening with my strapped-on member. So, mostly nothing.

Spooning: Well now, this sounds lovely and nice. Like cuddling, but more intrusive. But I would for sure go to sleep. Guaranteed. Especially because this asshole is always trying to serve me wine with dinner and then put the moves on me.

What else even is there? Seriously, do men have to think this goddamned hard?!

On dildo night Mavis cooked dinner at the lake house in South Haven: salmon, rice, bok choy, and these purple green beans from the farmers' market that turn green after you cook them. Miniature lemon chess pies. Bourbon. *Glasses of wine.* This was going to be an event. We crawled into bed afterward, queueing up that Denzel drunk-pilot movie on the iPad, and I was asleep within thirty seconds, not even kidding. Mavis nudged me awake with a rolled-up *New Yorker*, peering at me disgustedly over her reading glasses, hair tied up in its bedtime topknot. "Seriously? You're just going to sleep?!" And at that moment I turned into every chubby sitcom dad on every show you've ever watched while picking at the peas on your dinner plate.

"Nope!" I rolled out of the bed and into the bathroom to change into my night caftan, this gauzy black thing that your aunt Susan lent me and that I think is pretty sexy but am probably totally wrong about. I tore open the nondescript plastic pouch the harness came in, slipped my penis through the rubber O-ring attached to the back plate, and secured it at the base. Once I was satisfied that it was firmly in place, I stepped awkwardly through the nylon leg loops, then pulled the loose ends through the backpack strap fasteners to tighten them under my butt meat. Mavis looked on, unimpressed. This is worse than waiting for some flaccid dude to get his dick hard. I connected and tightened the top strap and immediately started giggling because my nipples fucking got caught in that shit and I had to, like, free them. I don't know what the fuck I was picturing. I mean, I guess I thought it would be like a horn sticking out of my stomach or something? But the fabric backing molded to my mons pubis and the dick dangled between my legs like, well, like an actual dick. Except purple and silicone and unlikely to require Plan B. "IT FEELS WEIRD," I said, frozen, standing next to the bed like an idiot.

I lay on my back and she straddled me, grunting as she struggled to jam my huge member into a vagina that had clearly dried up while watching me fool around with all of those stupid levers and pulleys. I circled my hips and laughed while she humped me, feeling nothing below my waist other than a leg cramp that, with my luck, was probably a blood clot. She dismounted moments later, her smoking inner thighs smelling like a Barbie doll someone had set on fire. "That was dumb," I whined. "Let's just eat some more pie."

She e-mailed me her feelings about the whole thing afterward, because that is what some ladies do.

> If you really wanna know the truth (and this gets all mushy but it's real) the longer we're together, the more emotionally intimate and committed we get, the more I want that intimacy

and connection during sex. Not all the time, it doesn't always have to be fingers laced intense eye contact weeping afterward sex, but I love that we can and do have that. And the strap-on isn't that, at least not yet, and it's also not yet just fun taboo banging—we're not skilled enough at it for that. so we've gotta practice if we want to get there. And we have such limited time it's hard to see strap-on expertise becoming our sexual priority. Not saying I want to stop playing around with it (or try one myself), just giving you a little glimpse into my heart.

Oh brother, all these feelings. This is the part I've found I'm less good at, all the *processing* we have to do. All the *thinking* and the *feeling* and the *talking* that is required. Licking her asshole? Not a problem, bro. I just held my breath and did it until I thought she was going to shit in my mouth and then I backed off. Talking about my emotions for an hour after I just put in thirty-seven minutes of really taxing physical labor?! PROBLEM. I'm not one of these Neanderthals who pretends I was hatched before having fully developed the feelings part of my brain, but talking about them all the time is exhausting. I can't just pat her on the back and say, "Good job, sister," I have to stare into her eyes and tell her how much these experiences move me. And I have tried, but I can't stop laughing. And that shit is rude.

Couldn't she have just said, "Meh, your sex game is whack," while rolling over to fetch her nighttime-specific hand cream and reading materials from the library? Why we gotta be all heart glimpsing about it?! Man, having a penis has turned me into such a dick.

fuck it, bitch. stay fat.

I mean, isn't this what we really want to do anyway? Because we already know how one loses weight: eat less and exercise more. Or get surgery. Why are we still playing around with the Oreo diet or the whole-milk-and-unpasteurized-cheese diet or the diet where you still get to eat a pound of pasta?! Either you're ready to eat vegetables and get on a treadmill, or you are not. And I'm ready. I just lost five pounds and here's how: for two weeks I quit drinking booze and soda and I stopped eating dessert. I didn't exercise—someone please tell me how you fit heart-rate-raising exercise into a schedule that includes working a real job and trying to get a good night's sleep?—but I tried to set reasonable goals like "Don't order one meat on top of another meat at lunch."

Dieting is crazy and turns most of us jerks into insufferable babies. Either (1) you're a crabby asshole on the verge of tears all day long because you're desperate for a handful of Cheetos, or (2) you're perched atop a high horse made of fewer than twelve hundred daily calories, glaring down your nose at me and pointing out how much saturated fat is in my unsweetened iced tea. Man, don't you *hate* a fat-skinny bitch more than anything else on the planet? You know who I mean— your friend who used to eat mayonnaise straight from the jar but who recently lost twenty pounds doing Whole30 because she was going through a midlife crisis and is now suddenly an expert on health and nutrition, totally qualified to rip the corn dog out of your greasy little clutches. HOLY SHIT, SHUT UP, GIRL. Can't we all just decide that if you're over the age of twenty-eight you don't have to worry about being skinny anymore? Thin is a young woman's game, and I'm perfectly happy to chill on the bench this quarter with a chili dog. And if I happen to burn a few calories while texting, then great.

Now, let's not be crazy. Should you work out? Of course you should. But you don't need some magazine intern clucking at you from behind the computer screen about taking a jog around the block every once in a while. It doesn't even have to be hard—just go to Curves a few times a week and trade a couple of meals a day for some Special K or a salad (but not the meat-and-cheese kind). And drink water. To make your belly feel full and distract you from how much you would die for a Dove bar. Also running to the bathroom all the time has to qualify as minimal cardiovascular exercise.

The hard part isn't the knowing what to do, it's the doing. I just had a yogurt. It had 150 calories in it and 2 grams of fat. I wrote it down in a little notebook full of lies that I keep in my backpack to motivate myself to try to eat better. In theory, that notebook is supposed to hold me accountable for all my food choices so that I can get on a path to better eating. In reality, I willfully ignore its existence every time someone brings a pizza to the office or the nights my friends coax me out to the bar or the entire week I spent in LA pretending I didn't just vow to end my love affair with cheese. I know *what* I'm supposed to do; I just need someone to tell me *how*. Every single day until I die.

Seriously, though, every woman in America is probably an expert on health and exercise based solely upon her subscription to *SELF* magazine. Do you really need another article about how important it is to eat a big breakfast full of healthy fats and whole grains to curb afternoon snacking? NO, YOU DO NOT. You need bitches to write about how comfortable maternity jeans are for women who aren't really pregnant. And sexy ways to remove a bra that has four hooks. I'm always amused when they encourage you to eat "instead" foods, like eating an apple when you really want to rub a bacon cheese-burger all over your boobs is a fair substitute. Why not instead list which ice creams have the least calories, by the pint? Oh, sure, you can tell a woman just to run five miles and take up crafting after she gets dumped by some asshole and her friends won't call her back because they're tired of listening to her dissect every single aspect of their relationship ("Do you think we'd still be together if I hadn't hated on that *Flight of the Conchords* show in 2009?"), but she'd much prefer knowing whether an entire pint of Talenti has fewer calories than one of Häagen-Dazs. That's an "instead" a girl could really go for.

"¡Dale!"

I became legitimately obsessed with Zumba before the grinding of bone on bone in my knees made it impossible to enjoy. *Obsessed*, even though I am wary of most forms of physical activity, including sex. It all started when I had taken some files to the kennel area of the hospital and found all of the techs and assistants gathered openmouthed around the giant flat-screen computer monitor that hangs in the treatment area.

They were watching a YouTube video where an upbeat Latinx woman in sherbet-colored workout gear stood in front of a dance studio full of gorgeous, scantily clad thirtysomethings in clingy dancewear, leading them in choreographed Salsa-lite dance moves. "What are they doing?" I asked Betty. She rolled her eyes and was like, "This is *Zumba*, Sam," like I was the asshole for not knowing.

"I thought Zumba was a region in Mexico." I shrugged, starting to walk away so I wouldn't inadvertently step in dog puke or get sprayed by anal glands, then did a double take. "Wait a minute, are they dancing to Pitbull?!" I shoved Betty out of the way, tossed the files on the floor (sorry, animals!), and started to cha-cha and shake my jelly along with the sexy young things in the video. Pitbull makes me want to take my pants off. We painfully mimicked that video three times, and by the end I was sweaty and hoarse from screaming "*¡Dámelo!*" at the top of my lungs for twenty minutes. I signed up for a class the very next day.

Working out is a bummer. Walking on a treadmill for forty-five minutes while listening to the same Metallica playlist over and over and trying to read the closed captioning of a television show you don't even care about is a total drag. The elliptical machine makes uncoordinated people like me look stupid. The stair machine reduces mere mortals to tears within four minutes. The stationary bike feels like uncomfortable butt sex. Who wants to put the Twinkies down and get out of bed for any of that? I'm not sure that I have even once experienced the shot of endorphins surging through your body that is supposed to occur when you're exercising, unless I didn't recognize it because it feels the same as a heart attack or vomiting up your breakfast onto the sparkling white gym shoes you bought because flip-flops are frowned upon at the gym.

A couple of months ago my vegan Russian trainer moved to Hawaii so she could run ultramarathons in a temperate climate and mack on girls in grass skirts. At first I was sad, but then I thought, "Now there will be no one to scowl disapprovingly at my attempted push-ups! Hooray!" During our last training session, right after I'd completed seven of the fifty sit-ups she'd asked me to do, she said, "You are my most disappointing client." And I interpreted that as "This tiny human says it's okay for me to keep eating red meat and cupcakes in bed. Good talk." We did some partner stretches, and after she adjusted my knee for the fourth time, she said, "I worry about you. We are going to text after I move." I nodded in agreement while my brain said, "Fine! Joke's on you! Texts don't have eyes!"

A week after she left I got a text from THE RUSSIAN.

THE RUSSIAN: What's for lunch?

ME: Lean Cuisine!!!

THE RUSSIAN: and what?

ME: Water . . . ?

THE RUSSIAN: AND WHAT?

ME, breaking into a liar's sweat: Um, oxygen?

THE RUSSIAN: WHAT ELSE?! [I could hear her shouting in my brain.]

ME, still trying to be on that bullshit: Granola bar.

THE RUSSIAN: You're lying.

ME: Okay, okay, you caught me. A granola bar and an apple.

THE RUSSIAN: . . .

ME: And a Diet Coke.

THE RUSSIAN: . . .

ME: Oh, and I had half a doughnut this morning.

THE RUSSIAN: . . .

ME: Okay, fine, a WHOLE doughnut.

THE RUSSIAN: . . .

ME, sighing at my screen: *Two* doughnuts.

THE RUSSIAN: . . .

ME: And I might have also had a beer before work.

THE RUSSIAN: I hate you.

I'm not going to lie and say that I started caring about myself, because for real I mostly don't. But at some point I was just like, "Yo, I do not move," and I'm not old enough to get away with that yet. I'm lazy and research is boring, but I got on the Internet anyway to try to find out whatever I could about this Zumba torture I was about to subject myself to.

"Ditch the workout and join the party!" the official website shouted at my eyeballs. Zumba "is the only Latin-inspired dance-fitness program that blends red-hot international music and contagious steps to form a 'fitness-party' that is downright addictive!" I am suspicious of words like "addictive" and "contagious," and I immediately blanched while clicking through all the pictures of lean and toned soccer moms gyrating in crop tops and neon bicycle shorts, their perfect bodies beaded with sweat, their toothy, openmouthed grins screaming, "I AM HAVING THE TIME OF MY YOUNG AND CONVENTIONALLY ATTRACTIVE LIFE."

I am a negative person by nature, and I typically shy away from anything that requires me to be having visible fun. I like to do stuff that I can sit quietly in the back and enjoy, and I have spent my entire adult life perfecting a bored-yet-slightly-amused-and-entertained facade. And I just don't understand being excited about exercise. It's like doing a cartwheel on your way to have a root canal; my face just doesn't light up at the prospect of abdominal isolations. Also? The pictures. Look at that instructor guy with his *shirt off.* I'm not trying to embarrass myself tripping over my feet doing watered-down salsa steps while some red-hot international instructor rolls his eyes at me in disgust and bounces quarters off his ridiculously chiseled backside.

The Sunday morning of my first class, I got up and put on socks and my old New Balances while remaining in my pajamas. I can't compete with these jerks doing a revolutionary new fitness concept while wearing bikini tops, so I decided it was in the best interest of my self-esteem to go to the opposite end of the clothing spectrum and just look like absolute trash. Because even if I busted my melon open while trying to cumbia to the beat, at least my jibs would be appropriately covered. I took thirty-seven Aleve and a Norco and tried to inconspicuously stretch my Achilles on the train platform so it wouldn't snap in the middle of a routine. When I got to the gym I paid the fifteen-dollar drop-in fee and found my way up to the dance studio. I hovered nervously near the back of the gym, anxious for all the JLo look-alikes to start pouring in and making me feel bad about that container of Greek yogurt I'd eaten in the locker room.

And then your mom came in wearing booty shorts and the shirt she wears to wash the dishes, flanked on either side by your aunt Judy and your recently retired fifth-grade teacher. Her sewing circle showed up next, as did her crochet buddies, and all the ladies from book club, with the exception of Kathy, whose son had strep so she decided to stay home with him. There's the woman who cuts your mom's hair, and Diane, who works part-time at Eileen Fisher in the mall. The school-board ladies, the PTA, and the hockey moms came running in, too, clad in biker shorts and racerback tanks with their hair pulled up in banana clips and scrunchies. I don't know what I had been so worried about.

"I thought this was for attractive young people?" I wondered aloud to no one in particular.

A lady down the way looked me up and down. "Yeah," she said, eyeing my flabby triceps and pulling a protein bar from her fanny pack. "ME, TOO."

The music started, and our teacher, a boisterous woman who was wearing a sports bra and a noisy coin skirt whose constant jangling set my molars on fire, started shouting and dancing and pointing out people who sucked as we tried desperately to follow along. I was winded after the first song, and twenty minutes in I told the woman struggling next to me to call me an ambulance. I was sweating in the grossest possible way, sweat dripping from my hair into my eyelashes before rolling down my nose. Your mom is pretty good at Zumba, but thank goodness she ain't got no rhythm. The only thing that kept me from looking like a complete moron was my blackness, which kicked in right when I needed it most. I might not have gotten every single step, but at least I wasn't clapping on the one and the three.

Despite the fact that I really did almost keel over and die, I was hooked. It is physically impossible for me to smile while skipping and jumping and fist pumping, but I loved it. Thumping, loud music at nine thirty on a Sunday morning in a room full of WASPs who are coming down off a chardonnay bender? More, please! These ladies yelled and whooped and screamed for an hour, then they toweled off and hopped in their Lexus SUVs to congregate over skinny lattes at the Starbucks two streets over. The minute that first class was finished, I vomited my right lung onto the locker room floor, then went downstairs and signed over half my paycheck to become an official member of the gym. It was "fun," my heart rate was high enough to make me feel like an actual sentient human being, and, for your information, Ricky Martin made a lot of good dance music, so bite your hateful tongue. And it's lame knowing that I need the withering gaze of your hot-flashed, perimenopausal mother to get me to samba my way to maybe living past the age of thirty-nine, but admitting defeat is the first step, right? I live in fear of the day I go flying off a moving treadmill, but pretending I can bachata to Gloria Estefan for an hour is something I can do. Plus your mom said she would bake me gluten-free cookies and give me the number to her masseuse next week. And that girl has a tight ass. I've been noticing.

I texted THE RUSSIAN a couple of weeks ago to rub my newfound dedication to working out in her skinny face.

ME: I'm into Zumba now. It's super fun.
THE RUSSIAN: What is that? Some new thing you eat?
ME: . . .
THE RUSSIAN: Sounds fattening, whatever it is.
ME: I hate you.

"Maybe I Can Just Eat Plants?"

I am a sucker for a headline screaming "How I lost the weight and kept it off!" or "200 pounds down and counting!" from the cover of a magazine in the checkout line at Walgreens. But then I buy the magazine, only to find out the big secret was SlimFast or bypass surgery and that is totally fine, for real, but who ever got full off a "shake," and United HealthCare is like

YEAH RIGHT, TUBBY, so I guess I'm stuck throwing these deck chairs off the *Titanic* one at a goddamn time. Right now I am sporadically trying to be vegan, because I love animals and being a good steward of the environment. LOL JK. I have inflammatory bowel disease and nothing is more inflammatory than meat and milk, but wow oh wow, I've never tried anything so difficult in my life and I was *homeless* before.

Eating with any sort of intention is terrible, especially when you (1) work hard all week, and (2) have trouble with plebeian tasks like grocery shopping and basic caring for yourself. Mavis is a health person, but she lives two-plus hours away. And that's good for, say, not wanting her to know how much *Family Feud* I actually cry tears of joy while watching? But bad for wanting to holler "Let me get one of them wheatgrass spirulina drinks you're making!" from the comfort of my bed while burning one calorie distractedly scratching at a patch of dandruff.

Fail to plan, plan to fail: I know, I know. And I am the queen of excuses, so let's just run through a few of them so I can prove to those of you who doubt me that there's really no possible way for me to be good at this:

1. I get up too early in the morning.
My alarm goes off at 5:50 a.m. First thing I do is check to make sure I'm not dead. If I am, in fact, still alive, I usually sob uncontrollably until there's nothing left in my tear ducts but salt dust, then grope blindly through my apartment to the bathroom, where I say a little prayer for a hole to open beneath my building and swallow us all. I can hardly muster the strength to take a bird bath and pull on my yoga pants that have never seen the inside of a gym, let alone cook steel-cut oats and make a kale smoothie.

2. I work with people who eat their feelings, too.

This sisterhood understands that the solution to a dreary morning/a shitty interaction with a petulant dog mom/gloopy, crampy menstruation/a disappointing season finale you stayed up late to watch is a delicious, overpriced lunch delivered by a young bicycle messenger with a hot beard and muscular calves. I never *want* to spend fifteen dollars on a meal I will eat on the toilet because there's no place else to get some peace and quiet, but I always *do*, because I am a stunted adolescent who was never taught constructive ways to deal with her emotions. I wish, more than a person has ever wished for anything, that a piece of rye melba toast with a smear of almond butter provided the temporary happiness found at the bottom of a carton of massaman curry, but, alas, it simply does not.

3. My joints still hurt.

After much half-hearted consumption of every legume, sprouted grain, cheese made from nuts, and root vegetable snatched from the loving clutches of the earth, I know that the degenerative disease currently snacking on my sacroiliac joint will maybe hold off for an hour so I could stand in front of the stage and get sweated on by Drake, but I'M SO SAD and THIS IS AMERICA so I WANT MY BONES TO STOP HURTING while I EAT CHEESE. I have an $800 tiny robot computer that can tell me the weather in Tokyo and knows to suggest "hoe" when I finish typing the phrase "yeah right," but science can't figure out a way for me to have a little yogurt without my having to rely on a walker the next day?! Pffft.

4. Staying committed to things is hard.

I have seven different body washes lining the edge of my bathtub right now.

5. The list of trash foods you can apparently still eat while trying to be vegan:

- spicy sweet chili Doritos
- Nutter Butters
- Swedish Fish
- Fritos
- Goya flan
- unfrosted Pop-Tarts
- Snyder's of Hanover jalapeño pretzels
- Pringles
- Oreos

I'm not sure if these are all really real, but that kind of seems beside the point considering that I'm attempting to whittle a third-grader off my backside. If I have to try to wipe the memory of the sharp, sweet sting of Italian salami from the taste buds in my mind, then I'm not going to ruin whatever progress I make by shoveling fistfuls of Pop-Tarts in my mouth every day.

This is what I'm like: I don't ever buy juice, because I've got so many fitness articles and printouts from the nutritionist burned into my brain about empty calories and mindless sugar consumption that I don't even go near it. My eyes don't even wander over to the juice section. And that sounds so good and so health-conscious but the real gag is that I don't want to waste a thousand calories on apple juice, a cheap and unsatisfying provisional solution to my despair, when I could invest those same calories in something that will really dull the sharp edge of life's blade, like a slice of the birthday cake that was half-price because little Timmy's parents never picked it up. So yeah, there's never going to be a twelve-pack of beer in my fridge (empty calories) but you might find a chocolate gift basket I sent to myself and signed someone else's name for (empty calories that stave off sadness for approximately twenty minutes).

I don't know that I'm always happy in this big body. Or what there is that I can actually do about it. I was not born to delicate people; my mom was six feet tall and my dad was short and broad with oversize hands that he gifted me along with my life. This rotting meat corpse they created is riddled with inexplicable disease and is as wide as it is tall. I was never destined to be a waif, or to have a less-than-terrible relationship with food. I grew up poor, anxious, and unhappy, with cheap carbohydrates the only affordable substitute for joy. If I had a depressed kid right now, I'd drag him to a doctor and ask for some Wellbutrin, but that was never an option for tiny me. Even as a kid, when I did all the fantasizing that little kids do, I never pictured a tall, strapping man hoisting me into his tuxedo-clad arms, the itchy netting of my veil rustling against his beard as we descend the steps of a church of his choosing as a crowd of our loved ones throws confetti over our heads. I had an incredibly realistic imagination, and I knew that no husband of mine would ever be *picking me up*. After exchanging legal vows and a chaste kiss in front of the judge, my future husband and I would walk with grim determination from the courthouse, hand in hand and Velcroed into our most sensible shoes, get into our roomy midsize sedan, then eat the Tuesday afternoon lunch special at IHOP. We'd toast with overcooked sausage links because IHOP doesn't serve booze, then drive to our unpretentious ranch-style house to make love one time and never again until we died.

So I bought a bunch of vegan cookbooks. I soaked the overnight oats; I made the fake cheese out of cashews and an onion and a carrot and a potato; I resisted the temptation of milk chocolate even though dark chocolate tastes like ants. And it felt fine. *I* felt fine. I made this amazing chickpea masala in my own kitchen that tasted almost as good as takeout.

Pretty sure the first time I faltered was at the movie theater. I love, love, love going to the movies, and when I do I like, like, like to have popcorn. And a fountain Coke, because I live for the burning snap of a freshly carbonated beverage. I went to see *The Hateful Eight* alone on a Saturday afternoon after work. I bought my ticket and willed myself to go straight to the theater, to not even glance at the concession stand, but I could not resist the siren call of the self-serve soda machine. I changed my inner mantra from "you don't need anything" to "fine, just get a drink," but as soon as I rounded the corner and heard the kernels popping their glorious staccato I jumped into the popcorn line and promised to make Cuban black beans and rice for the next three days. I was able to control myself enough to get both a small popcorn and a root beer (curveball! this girl is full of surprises!), but the minute the first buttered bite hit my tongue I was like, "Lord, I've made a dire mistake." (The vegan thing, not the popcorn, just so we're clear.)

The next day, as I was chopping tomatoes and red peppers for gazpacho, I decided that although I would continue to try my best to steer clear of meat and cheese, going forward I would never again publicly refer to myself as vegan. Then, if I decided to eat some carnitas or have an eggnog at Christmas, no one I know from the Internet could look down his judgmental nose at my choices. Carnivore in the streets, person-who-has-eaten-a-carrot-masquerading-as-a-hot-dog in the sheets.

Million-Dollar Mermaid

A solid 75 percent of the time I am awake, I am in pain akin to that of childbirth. Sometimes you can read the excruciating discomfort on my face, but I've gotten really good at masking it so that it just looks like I'm stifling an unpleasant bit of gas. People are always asking me what Crohn's feels like, and my answer is this: it's like a compact car is trying to drive through my small intestines, all the time. Seriously, and it doesn't matter if I eat or don't eat or whatever. Oh, here's something fun—I don't care what diet you're on or what herbal supplements you take. If they work for you, I'm happy. I don't know if it's something about me, or if people walk around just dispensing unfounded medical advice to everyone they've ever met with a health issue, but more often than I'm comfortable with, some asshole with a high school diploma wants to sit me down and talk at me about how they can cure my wretched-gut disease. There's always some bag of dicks with a beer in his hand, a triple cheeseburger on his plate, and a cigarette in his mouth trying to talk to *me* about healthy eating. And with zero trace of irony! I appreciate the effort, I really do, but this shit is auto-immune and I have a gastroenterologist. If all I had to do was put down this taco and take those herbs your grandma swears by, I'd already be cured. Thanks, though.

This arthritis and I decided that feeling like garbage all the time is for the birds and that we were going to have to do something about it, and that something probably needed to be swimming. EXCEPT. Aside from the fact that I seriously do not possess the kind of body I am comfortable displaying in a bathing suit, and how I adore and admire those girls who do, scrolling through their gorgeous round tummies and dimpled bottoms proudly sticking out of their fatkinis on Tumblr. But I'm not there yet, and I really am not trying get my bikini area waxed. Or shave my armpits. Or risk being in a pool full of sexy, young hairless aliens looking like my real self. In my imagination the local YMCA is a shining beacon full of healthy, tan, chlorine-scented muscles gleaming beneath the fluorescent lights overhead, a happy place full of health-conscious singles mingling over protein shakes and energy bars, goggles and towels draped gently around their necks as they flirt and laugh about the number of calories they've burned on that complicated-looking stair machine. And those mental images are precisely why I decided to take senior aqua aerobics. I need to be around some pancake arms and spider veins and *National Geographic* titties, for real.

But first: a bathing suit. Typically, I'd wear a thong and a couple of small halved coconuts for this sort of endeavor, but I thought it would serve me best to be modest—for the first class, at least. After I'd barricaded myself in a corner at Lane Bryant, shivering and cowering like a child in a horror movie, handfuls of jewel-toned polyester clutched to my chest, a saleswoman approached me and hesitantly asked if I required some assistance.

"I'd like to see your most opaque turtleneckini," I declared, "and your finest ankle-length swim bloomers." Her eyes widened with concern as she tried to determine whether I was insane. Were you guys aware that those things don't exist?! I was shocked, too! Anyway, a friend told me I should get a two-piece in case I needed to go to the bathroom and didn't want to do so while completely naked (why didn't I think of something as practical as that?), so I pointed to the wall of mix-and-matchables and snatched a black tank top with a built-in full coverage underwire bra and some sort of panty-skort-culotte type of contraption for my bottom half. Literally the closest I could come to being fully clothed yet appropriately dressed for water calisthenics.

I got up early on the following Monday and put on my bathing suit under my clothes, because while I don't care about your grandma comparing my stretch marks to hers, I didn't want to make my introductions while trying to secure my breasts in those stupid cups. Helen Keller was rolling her eyes, muttering, "Not even going to trim the sides, eh?" under her fishy breath while I was figuring out how to step into that silly bottom piece. I threw a shoe at her head, just barely missing her horns.

After I paid—it costs eight dollars to participate in the aerobics—I staked out the quietest row of the locker room where I could sit and listen in relative peace to Shirley and Elaine squawking about Medicare and using double coupons to shop at Kohl's, until it was time to get into the heated baby pool.

I was immediately transported back to my days as the poor kid at summer camp whose mom sent along the previous night's meat loaf and an off-brand thermos full of milk for lunch instead of peanut butter and jelly with a Hi-C like everyone else. Every day, I would plead with her: "No one else brings Tuna Helper or liver and onions. Please stop ruining my young life." I was that kid with the stinky home lunch that had to be *heated up*, while everyone else brought delicious shelf-stable potato chips and pudding cups. No wonder I got pushed to the ground so often. Quit playing like you don't know what I mean—everybody knows that one kid who brought the metal fork from home. AND THAT POOR, SAD BASTARD WAS ME. Anyway, all of these milkshakes had brightly colored beach towels with them, and I flushed with shame as I pulled my house towel out of my bag. Stop laughing. I have pretty decent towels, but they are plain white and boring beige and don't wrap all the way around my body. These ladies brought towels in swirling purples and pinks and blues and greens made specifically for fun times at the local pool. They obviously have mothers who actually love them.

I took a cue from the other ladies and wore my cover-up out of the locker room (what is that thing called, a beach robe? pooljamas?), grabbed my goggles and tube and hand buoys, then tried not to slip and crack my skull open on the deck. One glance at my feet and I thought, "A pedicure should have happened yesterday," then slipped into the pool before anyone noticed my bruised-looking toes. When I was a baby, poor people sent their kids to the YWCA for day care, and as a result I learned to swim before I could even speak full sentences. They for real just throw you in the swimming pool the minute you get there, pull you out twice a day to poop and eat a couple of graham crackers, then toss you right back in. You go home on the bus and sleep straight through dinner until breakfast the next morning. It's a dream. Being in the water doesn't scare me, but explaining my horrifying scarlet birthmark to strangers does, so I avoided the crowd in the center of the pool and hung back near the ladder.

As we were doing K-treads to the lively medley of Patti LaBelle's greatest up-tempo hits, a lady waddled in, and I caught some weird looks being exchanged among the other women. She had a house towel, too, so I just assumed these elitist snobs were giving her a hard time for it; I made a mental note to later ask someone in better shape than I am where to procure appropriate beach accessories. The new lady didn't say anything, just slid on her floaties and asked one of the too-hot-to-be-working-this-shift lifeguards to help lower her

into the pool next to where I was sweating with the other old-
ies. One of the Bitter Bettys in front of me (I think they were
all named Martha or Lucille or Janice) turned to sneer before
rejoining the group in their uniform leg kicking. I couldn't
stop looking back and forth between them; it was the real-life
sequel to *Mean Girls.*

During the otter roll (please kill me) there was more vicious
whispering aimed in our general direction, which I almost
didn't notice because I was having a bitch of a time struggling
to keep my breasts secured inside my top. All of that "gentle, low-impact movement" was doing a really efficient job of
gently removing my tits from where I'd strapped them down,
and shoving one back in once it has escaped is the worst. That
class was hard as hell. Next time you're at the pool, no more
snickering behind your hands when you see lumps of curdled
cottage cheese bicep-curling water weights and bunny-kicking
in the shallow end. I have a newfound respect for active seniors.
After that brutality all I wanted was to go to the day care room
and find my sleeping cot and take a nap.

In the locker room after class, a bottle of amlodipine I'd
dropped rolled over to where the outcast was changing back
into her pleated pants. She picked it up, and when she returned
it to me, I couldn't help but ask why the other women hated
her so much. Turns out they all live in the same assisted-living
facility, and Outcast had recently taken up with one of the few
eligible bachelors who could still eat solid foods and drive a
car at dusk. The other women didn't like her, and they liked
her even less when they found out that old Levitra was sticking
his mothballs in her. I sat on the bench wrapped in my house
towel, mouth agape, through the entire story. When she finished I was like, "You are the coolest," and started pulling my
hoodie on over my bathing suit. Outcast smiled at the compli-

ment and told me she looked forward to getting splashed in the face by my uncoordinated arm movements next time. "And you're going to get a yeast infection if you wear that bathing suit home. You young girls think you know everything." I never went back.

Whole Wheat Ricotta Crepes

So I tried Nutrisystem. I'm not even sure where I got the idea, but I went online, gave them all my money, checked off a bunch of delicious-sounding food items, and waited for them to be delivered to my job. Because that's where I am between the hours of 7:30 a.m. and 6:00 p.m. Every day. As soon as the first boxes arrived, I knew I'd made a huge mistake. I try not to be a conspicuous person, because I don't like talking to people about anything I'm doing, But especially not about something as ridiculous as needing to pay hundreds of dollars for portion-controlled meals. I know there are people who can spend hours talking about diets, and maybe if I were one of them I could actually find one that sticks, but I am too easily embarrassed to get into the minutiae of what I eat, and when and how often, to ever have a conversation about it. That's why I won't go into debt trying to see a therapist—I'm so humiliated all the time that it forces me to be dishonest, and what is the point of therapy if you can't come clean about what your problems are without wanting to pull a hat down over your eyes or jab yourself with a pair of scissors?

I burned with shame as I filled the communal freezer with a month's worth of tiny meat loaf sandwiches and single-serving desserts, hoping no one would catch me and demand a detailed explanation of my path toward health and wellness. Online, the white cheddar mac and cheese had looked plump and inviting, the tortilla soup spicy and delicious. In real life, the tiny cans and dehydrated cups look like something you'd make for a baby. They were kind of delicious, though? But in a hot-lunch-program kind of way. Like, if you are the kind of person who would never lower yourself to eat a McNugget, you are most certainly not going to be able to handle Nutrisystem. That vacuum-sealed goodness is not for people who insist on doing shit like soaking their own beans and making bread from scratch. Thank God I grew up living that peel-and-eat life.

The drawback was that everything I ate made me have the kind of farts that make you check your underpants for burn holes afterward, the kind of farts that sear your asshole as they exit, the kind of farts that have teeth. Even with the IBD, I've managed to jury-rig a pretty predictable poop schedule, but those coconut almond bars and arroz con pollo and bean Bolognese had me cutting people off midsentence to run to the bathroom. I would have to meticulously plan what trains to take to avoid being stuck on one with a meal-replacement bar racing through my lower intestine at max speed. I would fart without even realizing it was happening; I couldn't walk down the street to get a coffee without people crossing to the other side to avoid the gassy cloud following me around. And when I wasn't burning calories from breaking a continuous stream of putrid wind, I was sweating on the toilet as three ounces of food karate-chopped its way through my intestinal tract.

After two months I went to see Dr. Jackson for a skin problem and she was like, "Your face looks so slim! Wanna hop on the scale just for fun?"

First of all, no. The words "scale" and "fun" do not go together in my mind, especially since she insists on using the old-timey triple-beam scale where you have to stand, trembling, for the 229 interminable seconds it takes for her to slide the rider back and forth (a little to the left, no back to the right, wait a little bit more left, oh no waaaaaay over to the right) while you pretend you can actually hold your thighs together for as long as it takes for her to come up with "STILL TOO FAT." But that day I'd lost some weight, and she clapped her hands excitedly while I wondered if maybe my right foot hadn't been all the way on. She asked what I'd been doing, and I told her I was trying Nutrisystem, but truth be told I didn't know whether I'd actually lost weight, or if the colonic effect of those protein shakes had just flushed out the seven pounds of undigested food hanging out in my colon. My stomach churned and gurgled, then she listened to it with a stethoscope, her eyebrows raised in alarm. "You might not be the best candidate for a program like this." She sighed, pointing at my midsection. "It sounds like a soccer match is going on in there."

"But I still have three weeks' worth of meals!" I protested, delicately fingering my newly svelte jawline.

"Fine, eat them." Dr. Jackson tucked her notes in her armpit and shook my hand, as she does after every session, and started for the door. "I'll e-mail the pharmacy your prescriptions. And maybe you should buy some diapers."

Cow Pose.

I recently started yoga. And by "started" I mean "I've gone to two classes in the last few weeks." Between my real job and my freelance jobs and the hours I've set aside to watch television, I don't have any time. So finding activities that fit into the narrow window I have not dedicated to making money for someone else is rare. I hated the physical therapy I was doing for my broken foot that never healed, so my podiatrist suggested yoga. Gross, right? The only class I could find that's (1) cheap, (2) near the train, (3) at a time I could actually make, and (4) not taught by a person I know in real life was for pregnant women. And I signed right up. The flyer at Metropolis coffee shop advertised the class as "incredibly easy, laid-back, no pressure." I guzzled my scalding coffee—I hadn't put enough sugar in because a handsome stranger had been standing next to me and I didn't want him to know I'm a child—and studied the faded pink sheet of paper. I figured it would be my kind of party because the word "easy" was underlined five times with a thick black Sharpie. Who the fuck wrote that? I mean, nothing says "easy" more than "a pregnant lady could do this," I guess? If I saw a pregnant woman skydiving or bungee jumping or performing open-heart surgery, I would think smugly, "Hey, I probably could do that."

I didn't hesitate or think twice until I walked into the room in my comfiest outside pajamas and found myself surrounded on all sides by gestating bellies and nervous preclass chatter about back pain and morning sickness. Oh, right, these women are actually pregnant. I was so busy thinking about how no one would ask me to touch my toes that I kind of ignored the whole carrying-another-human-being aspect of this physical and spiritual practice. In general, I've got enough stomach jibs to pass for early second trimester if anyone decided to really get up close and inspect me, but I decided to keep a low profile and chill in the back, not saying a word. If there's any place where staying mute with your eyes on the floor is appropriate, a yoga studio has got to be it.

I loved that first class. It was air-conditioned and the yogini used the word "gentle" about eighty times, which is music to my joints. My foot felt good, my self-esteem wasn't shattered into a million pieces, and everyone appeared to be having as hard a time as I was getting up off the floor. I went back a couple of times, but nobody likes an outsider. Seriously, skinny people want your fat ass out of their clothing stores. Straight people want your gay ass out of their bars. And white people want your black ass out of their presidency. So my empty womb and I were scared to admit that we weren't packing no embryo. I really liked the teacher and I hope Diana's baby isn't breach and I would love to know what names Maureen decides on for the twins, but I don't want to look like a weirdo with a pregnancy fetish or some other *Dateline*-type shit. Nor do I want to be the douchebag who couldn't cut it in regular yoga. (Because, yeah, I couldn't, and let's not even talk about that two-hundred-degree sauna yoga, are you kidding me?) But I'm not savvy enough to keep a good lie going. I can't keep rolling into class and not talking. OR GROWING. Plus, I don't trust myself. One of these days I'm going to forget where I am and ask one of these girls for an emergency tampon and the whole lot of them will realize what I've done and line up to beat the crap out of me.

Living Is a Mistake.

Mavis wanted to host a brunch for me to meet all of her close momfriends. I wasn't nervous about it, because I'm charming and do well with moms. I couldn't decide what to wear, because I'm at a time in my life when nothing I put on feels good and even fewer things look good, and the T-shirt and jeans I would like to spend my days wearing aren't always appropriate. Nor is the hoodie. And, if we're being honest, the jeans don't always fit right. Jeans and bras, man: ARE THEY EVER 100 PERCENT COOL? So while homegirl was downstairs baking the quiche and cutting fruit into appetizing shapes, I was trying on and taking off the three hideous shirts I leave in the half a drawer designated as mine. I knew before I even got my clothes on that the day was going to be a toilet. Sometimes you just know.

It's hard not to feel like an animal on display when someone throws a party for people to meet you, even though I am always 100 percent flattered when someone wants me to stammer awkwardly through an introduction and try to come up with a sincere response to "I've heard a lot about you!" that isn't "Oh my god, am I not satisfying her sexually?!" Women started to arrive, wearing their nicest smiles and loaded down with church doughnuts and breakfast casseroles, and I felt better than I'd expected. My clammy nerves had settled down, I was picking at my breakfast in a convincing way (I hate eating in front of strangers), and I had just begun to relax when I felt a weird hitch in my wobbly chair. Three seconds later, I went CRASHING TO THE FUCKING GROUND, taking a platter of French toast bites with me.

The five stages of Holy Shit I Just Broke a Chair in Front of People:

1. **Denial.** "I'm not on the floor, you're on the floor!!"
2. **Anger.** THIS IS WHAT HAPPENS WHEN YOU BUY CHAIRS AT A RESALE SHOP, BITCH.
3. **Bargaining.** "Please, God, if you kill everyone in this dining room right now, I promise I will try to recycle all of the SlimFast cans I swear I'm going to start buying."

4. **Depression.** "I am fat enough to kill chairs. I don't deserve oxygen."

5. **Acceptance.** "Welp, since I'm already fat, fuck these toast points; let's get a pizza."

Turns out Mavis hadn't put the chair together correctly, but tell that to the bruises spreading like wildfire across my tender ego. I spent the rest of the brunch standing awkwardly in various places in the dining room until enough time had passed to usher everyone out without it seeming chair-related. I took a handful of aspirin and started cleaning up the leftovers, picking at what was left on the trays and serving dishes we'd eventually have to drive around delivering to their rightful owners. The doughnuts tormented me, nestled so sweetly in their box, but, bitch, I just had a chair collapse underneath me so please pass the fucking watermelon balls. We bought new chairs the next goddamned day. METAL ONES.

My friend Anna once got up in this kid's face during gym class because he kept asking how much I weighed. The truth was that I didn't actually know, because my mom was too broke and too much of a wreck to take me to the doctor. But what I did know was that it was the very first time I had to change clothes in front of people, and as humiliating as it might have been to try to hide my bulging, discolored body from girls who were at the ideal height and weight for their ages, I also had to ride the shame wave of having a mother who couldn't pay for both the school-issued shorts *and* the T-shirt, so the dingy white shirt with a red lion on the front that didn't get washed enough was paired with Women's shorts (capital W, to distinguish them from the slender Misses and the dainty Petites) found in the two-dollar bin at ESCCA, the place where your well-off classmates' parents donated the family's old clothes. So yes, Rebecca, I actually *am* wearing your dad's old sweatshirt today. Anyway, these ESCCA shorts were more of a tomato red (let's say a Pantone 032) than the official deep red (Pantone 1807) of the Nichols Middle School Lions, and they stood out in stark contrast to the ones my peers were dressed in, whose names were written in permanent marker on the white strip of material on the right thigh that my home shorts noticeably did not have. I don't know enough about sociopolitical stuff to write intelligently about classism in this country, but purchasing and maintaining a $50 short set required for twenty minutes of halfhearted daily physical activity is a big deal to people who can't keep a phone on, and it's thoroughly humiliating for the person singled out at the start of every period for not being "dressed correctly for class." Would it have killed that leather-faced monster to cut me a break, just once?

I learned how to operate under both the physical and emotional weight of unrelenting shame very early. Fat babies are adorable, while fat children are a little less so. Fat teenagers are chided into either end of the eating-disorder spectrum, and fat adults are either admonished for not figuring out how to get new bodies during adolescence or straight up dismissed altogether. I wish that I was an emotionally healthy human without years of accumulated trauma, one who just *decided* to be a fat caricature of a person perched gleefully atop a mountain of doughnuts, shoving candy bar after candy bar between my teeth while cackling demonically over how much money my eventual care will cost taxpayers or whatever it is comments-section trolls always accuse fat people of doing. And I don't need sympathy or special consideration because, ultimately, who even cares? You hate me, and I hate me, too. We are on the same team. I guess what I'm saying is that maybe we could all just mind our own fucking business for once, and that when you can actually see a person's scars, maybe be a pal and don't pick at them.

Do you think that fat people don't know? Because we definitely do! We're repulsive to look at, and undeserving of both love and easily accessible, relatively inexpensive yet well-made clothing. We get it! We have seen the messages in movies and magazines, on the Internet and TV, and we understand. If we wear something formfitting, we're delusional pigs who have the audacity to think we look attractive, but if we wear shapeless sacks that hide all our offensive, stretched-out flesh, we're sloppy dirtbags who need to get our shit together. It's a lose-lose, unless you lose weight, but good luck keeping it off without reconstructing your entire brain and DNA. I'm sure people get skinny and stay that way, and if they want to invite me over for little cups of green tea and a handful of unsalted pretzels to split between us so they can tell me how they did it, man, I'm down with that. Especially if they know the secret to making a radish feel as good on your tongue as a salty-sweet piece of smoked pork belly that's all caramelized on the outside but soft and fatty on the— Wait, what was I even talking about?

A couple of years ago, some woman thought I was someone else she'd been beefing with online and tweeted a slew of things that I assume were intended to be hurtful at me, including such darling missives as "You're a shitty writer and you should die" and "You look like you're one hot dog away from a heart attack." I don't know how you say something like that to a person you've never met, a person who has never done anything wrong to you, with the entire Internet watching, but yeah, okay. I probably am. My heart is enlarged and in the early to middle stages of failure because for a long time I couldn't afford this medicine I was supposed to take. Now that I can, the damage is irreversible so I'm just gonna do what I can until it suddenly stops beating and hope that when it quits on me I am wearing something flattering and not behind the wheel of a car. And when it does happen, despite all these years of trying, despite all these fits and starts, I will still be dead, and maybe you and that faceless Twitter person will think I deserve it. And that's okay. I am fat and I am mentally ill, and those two things have been intertwined since before I even knew what those words mean. If this is how I'm going to die, then why not just let me. Maybe there is a way to solve those problems, but maybe I'm tired of trying. Maybe I stopped going to swimming because I was afraid of what would happen if, after months of treading water, it still didn't work. Maybe I quit yoga because I was afraid of what would happen if I lost a ton of weight and that still didn't fix my insides. I can't afford therapy, but I can buy a sandwich.

nashville hot chicken

By this point in our nascent relationship, Mavis and I had figured out how to mash our moist and sweaty sex parts together
with marginally enjoyable results, suffered through awkward
introductory meals with each other's closest friends/families
(including a surprise birthday party I totally almost ruined by
being a pouty asshole), and gone in on a family cell phone
plan: IT WAS TIME FOR US TO PLAN OUR FIRST
JOINT VACATION.

Thoughtful romantic that I am, I texted, "Hey, instead of
flying first-class to Jamaica to drink rum out of coconuts and
risk skin cancer roasting under the sun, how would you feel
about instead spending nine hours wedged into a rented car
with my dead dad's ashes to go to Nashville and eat biscuits
and gravy and listen to terrible country music for a week?" In
hindsight I realize that that is a heavy fucking thing to ask a
normal person with actual human feelings to accompany you
to do. In my mind it was like *Weekend at Bernie's*, but in real life
she has a mom she talks to on the phone once or twice a week

and isn't used to my whole LOL I KILLED MY MOM shtick. This could be an emotional minefield.

I'm not sure that I can articulate this exactly the way I want to without alienating anybody cool, but my parents have been dead for so long that it almost isn't even sad to me anymore. I can't remember their voices or what they liked to put on their pizza; I couldn't tell you what teams my dad rooted for or what shade of lipstick my mom liked to wear. They had no part in my adult life, so it's not like I miss our Sunday dinners or their career guidance. And, if I'm being straight up, I know that if the trajectories of their lives had continued down the paths they were on, I'd be sharing a one-bedroom apartment with my mom and giving her a daily lottery ticket allowance while my dad spent every day passed out in a racetrack bathroom. My life would be the kind of sitcom that's more situation than comedy, full of scenes in which my adorably confused mother called me in my sad beige cubicle five times to remind hapless me to pick up her cigarettes at the gas station where my potential love interest works on the way home from the office as my Stereotypical Angry Employer stands huffing over me, the audience collectively worried that this is the episode that my likable yet annoying and overbearing mother will get me fired. My dad would make a cameo during sweeps week, all dressed up in a Salvation Army suit, smelling like Old Spice, and make a lot of promises he had no intention of keeping, then disappear at the end of the episode not to be seen again until the season finale.

There would be lots of walking-home-late-in-the-rain montages in which I'd adjust my unwieldy purse and clumsily drop the bag of Doritos I am going to eat for my dinner on the floor. The gas station attendant—who is secretly handsome under his oil-stained cap and thick, out-of-style glasses—works up the nerve to do something about his long-standing crush. He won't, though, at least not this season; he'll just watch me with longing as I tuck the pack of Virginia Slims next to the sensible office heels in my workbag. "Ma'am?" he'll call out as I reach the door, and everyone at home on the couch will totally lose their shit because maybe he really is going to put down his wrench and sweep me into his strong, alternator-fixing arms. I'll turn around hopefully, because I have a secret crush on him, too, and, duh, I've never been kissed and an Aretha Franklin song is swelling to a crescendo in the background, and holy fuck I might *finally* get to have sex, but that hope shatters into a million pieces as I realize he's just holding out a pack of matches to take home to my mom. Roll credits, sad trombone.

That is for real what my life would be, shame-spiraling into spinsterhood as my mom made an ever-evolving list of reasons I could never move out and abandon her. We would definitely have too many of whatever pet we could both agree on, and she would sit smoking in her armchair and nodding along with Oprah while calling me constantly throughout the day to either (1) remind me of things she needed me to bring home, or (2) recount to me, in explicit detail, the happenings on her various beloved television programs. We'd be the type of people who had both of our names on household accounts. You know what I mean? Like when you get a new MasterCard and there's that "Do you want to add an authorized user?" box, the one I currently check FUCK NO on while doing the untethered single-person running man. I would answer a begrudging yes and get a second card with Grace Irby on it. We would undoubtedly be sharing a bed, one that I definitely made the quilt for, and I would never post anything on Facebook other than videos of frolicking baby goats and inspirational infographics while wishing real hard every night that someone at the church would force her nonverbal son who is "too sensitive to get a job" to take me on a date to Baker's Square and ask to touch my privates after. So I guess what I'm saying is that it's okay they're dead.

Our family tree is so goddamn sparse that if you shake it you'd probably start a fire. My dad was born in Mississippi but spent his formative years in Memphis, where he fathered my brothers before ditching them to move to Chicago and eventually meet my mother, who already had three young girl children of her own.

I have neither seen nor spoken to either of my brothers since they attended my mom's funeral in June 1998. That's part of the reason I've never done anything with our dad, because it's just my luck that the minute I decided to dump that asshole in a barbecue grill or sprinkle him outside the shady SRO he lived in for a while, one of them would turn up and be upset that I hadn't included him in the decision. Our father was terrible—he tried three times and still couldn't get the kind and loving parenting thing down—but it still nagged at me that they might want to say good-bye or something. (My sisters don't give a shit—he was the kind of jerk stepfather who yelled a lot about nothing and nailed the windows shut after they'd snuck out of them at night to go meet their boyfriends.) My brothers are not men who Facebook. They are not gentlemen who tweet. Once every couple of years, I will do some lightweight Google sleuthing and call the first handful of phone numbers I run across, but they have all led to dead ends. The last time I was in Memphis I was fifteen and spent the entire time taking pictures of heartbroken women earnestly sobbing over Elvis's grave with a disposable drugstore camera, not risking getting my head blown off going door to door asking "Are you my brother?" in unfamiliar neighborhoods.

So I ended up with SB on a technicality. The thought of physically handling his ashes in order to transfer them from the box they came in to a nicer container horrified me, plus I ain't got no fireplace. Where the fuck was he supposed to go? Should I have, like, displayed him? Not doing that ever. But isn't it wildly disrespectful to just, um, throw him away? Is there no discreet disposal service I could use? WHY DID THEY MAKE ME HIS GUARDIAN? I HATE BEING IN CHARGE OF THINGS. It would've been an easier decision if I had a house. Because then I could just dump him in a hole and plant a rose bush in it or something, and when houseguests admired my garden I could explain to them how I'd ingeniously repurposed my father's cremains and look like a thoughtful and sentimental person. But I'm broke and can barely keep the tiny succulents in my studio alive, so instead of doing anything with him, I hid the giant can of rocks and dust that used to be Samuel Irby in that Gap bag on the top shelf of my hall closet and decided to ignore him. It would be a fitting metaphor for the bulk of my childhood. Plus I didn't think my dad would give a shit, really; I was more haunted by the ghost of the old boyfriend I'd purchased those fucking Gap sweaters for.

I'm not sentimental; I don't save birthday cards or baby pictures or newspaper clippings, I have no real traditions, and I throw everything away the minute it stops being shiny and new. Still, one day I realized that dusty box full of my dad's ground-up bones and brains had been sitting between the cat carrier and a bag of mittens for seven years, and I was determined not to move it to another apartment ever again. My dad died eighteen years ago: it was time for my dude to get free and stop grossing me the fuck out every time I needed a goddamn jacket.

I decided to take him to Nashville, to dump the ashes of my dead father in one of Tennessee's thirty-plus rivers or tributaries so he could float on and become one again with the earth or whatever, but also to kind of try to have a vacation. Like I said, he was technically from Memphis, but I've been there. A lot. There are only so many times you can trudge through the excruciatingly depressing mausoleum that is Graceland without wanting to scoop your fucking eyes out with a grapefruit spoon, so I wasn't doing that again. I needed to get rid of him, and it needed to be in a place that felt like it had at least a little bit of sentimental value in case any of my future children (read: cats) ever ask about their grandfather. It also needed to be someplace close enough that I could drive there without dislocating my fucking knee, yet far enough that my boss couldn't get cute and try to call me in to work. My hipster friends with good taste like Nashville, there are a lot of Kinfolk-looking blogs espousing Nashville's many hidden gems, and Nashville has a shitload of good restaurants. If my daddy had really wanted to split hairs about his final resting place, he should've left a goddamned will instead of overdrawn checking accounts and a bunch of gambling debts and worthless old scratch-off tickets. That motherfucker was getting scattered in Nashville.

I am for sure about to be called a nigger with the hard R. That is what I was thinking while Mavis and I sat in my rented Toyota Camry outside a Hucks gas station in Madisonville, Kentucky.

According to the faded signs in the window, you could get a pack of cigarettes here for less than three dollars. You can't even get a newspaper in Chicago for three motherfucking dollars. Should I move? I mean, I don't smoke and the South is terrifying to me, but last week I spent thirteen dollars on some trash called "young raw coconut juice" and that is really not the kind of life I want to be living anymore.

Anyway, we had been in the car for seven hours, me behind the wheel as we darted between terrifying big rigs and 1976 Toyota pickup trucks driven by mulleted, shirtless teenagers. Mavis thought it would be more romantic to take the small and beautiful back roads due south rather than the ugly congested highway with its bright lights, densely populated McDonald's, and the kinds of white people who care about driving fuel-efficient hybrid cars, so we had been singing along with a two-hundred-song Spotify playlist I packed with BONA FIDE JAMS like "Return of the Mack" and the Human Nature remix of SWV's "Right Here" (if you weren't a teenager in the early nineties then I am terribly sorry for you) to keep me awake on the road while driving through hundreds of miles of desolate farmland.

A man wearing thick white athletic socks shoved into Adidas shower shoes shuffled past the car, studying my stylish urban Mohawk with an intense curiosity. "My barber fades it by hand," I almost called out, my polite northern way of asking exactly what the fuck he was motherfucking staring at, but decided against it. Mavis is a healthy person, reason number 137 why I am convinced she will quickly grow tired of me and my bullshit, right after "votes in local elections" and "has never eaten a Hot Pocket purely for enjoyment of the taste." Healthy people keep themselves properly hydrated, and this was the third time we'd had to stop and find her a bathroom in the kinds of towns where Confederate money is still accepted as legal tender. I'm the opposite of whatever she is, the kind of person whose extra-large drive-thru Diet Coke had lasted from Broadway and Thorndale to the middle of Kentucky, and I hadn't once had the urge to pee. Or shit, for that matter, since I had eaten only a handful of saltines and Imodium for breakfast. I don't need that kind of stress, man. I would rather fight Moby Dick on a raft with a hole in it than be stuck in a car in the middle of nowhere groundhogging a giant poop. Or squatting on the side of the interstate with nothing but Mavis's skinny legs for cover.

Mavis emerged from the sliding glass doors, loaded down with water bottles and whatever healthy snacks are to be found in a country-ass gas station. A blazing neon sign in the window blinked an advertisement for hot fried chicken and gizzards and, maybe I'm disgusting, but there really was an internal struggle between the part of my brain that is averse to eating food left out in the open under a heat lamp and the part that knows that chicken was probably *delicious*. I spent the entire rest of the drive dreaming about those room-temperature giz-zards as my stomach growled loudly in protest.

I really dig a fancy fucking hotel and we picked the Fucking Fanciest. Nothing like rolling up to the tastefully appointed valet and handing him the grocery bag you packed your one outfit in as you hold out your arm and painfully unfold your plastic travel slippers and stained yoga pants and cramping limbs from where they've been molded around a steering wheel for half a day. I'm not going to continue to put too fine a point on this, but getting with someone the total opposite of you is the goddamn move. This is how I pack for a five-day trip:

many underpants, maybe an extra bra, multiple socks, maybe two T-shirts, a hoodie, and a bag of dehydrated sriracha bacon and a fountain drink for the car. This is how Mavis packs: many separate top and bottom options, including but not limited to multiple shorts and shirts, dresses short and long, skirts, running/exercise tanks and shorts, a special moisture-wicking-type bra, athletic socks, several sandals, a pair of gym shoes, at least one romper, an extra carburetor, a full silver service, a twin-size bed, several different types of Tylenol, and a cooler full of dry snacks and drinks and coffee. It never even occurred to me that I might do anything other than survive off of whatever I could find in a vending machine or from room service. She is a real-life adult. It's impressive.

The morning after we arrived, I awoke in a bed larger than my entire apartment and suddenly remembered why I rarely ever take vacations: trips cost a lot of money and I don't ever really feel like doing anything I couldn't already be doing in my own bed. I never wake up excited at the promise of a new day; instead, I grudgingly tear my eyelids apart while dreading whatever soul-crushing obligation is on the other side of my door. A job, a phone call, a lunch: I would rather be dead than do any of it. Mavis was already out in the world—the note she'd left next to the bed let me know that she had gone out for a run and LOL WHAT DO THOSE WORDS EVEN MEAN. I toddled around the room in a sleep haze, wiping crust out of my eyes and debating whether I could accept a room service order without a bra on. Like, what if it's more than an exchange of plates or whatever and I have to awkwardly tuck my tits into my armpit to sign a receipt? I like traveling to other places to do the exact same thing I do at home: read books in bed, occasionally get overpriced takeout, and groan exasperatedly at tourists chattering excitedly out-side my door over whatever thrilling activity they are about to go do.

Shit we did in Nashville, in no particular order:

- Saw Dave Chapelle's return to standup.
- Ate doughnuts in the parking lot of the Donut Den during a tornado.
- Learned what a "meat and three" is.
- Cried while eating Hattie B's hot chicken.
- Listened to a terrible version of that "Black Velvet" song sung by your drunk stepmom at this overcrowded bar with delicious okra.
- Drove around all damn day Easter Sunday looking for an inconspicuous place that wasn't a golf course or chil-dren's playground to dump a giant can of ashes without alerting anyone to our possibly illegal (?) agenda.
- Xanax.

Shit we did not do in Nashville:

- Go to the Country Music Hall of Fame.
- See the Parthenon.
- Hit the Grand Ole Opry.
- Venture outside a whole lot.
- Eat anything we probably couldn't find in Chicago.
- Talk to anyone other than my friend Lena, who was living in Nashville for work.
- Much of anything, really.

Even when I had stopped believing in God as a teenager, I would still drag myself to church once a year to contemplate my mortality while celebrating the risen Christ and surveying all the elaborate headpieces worn by the women of the congregation for Easter service. When I was little and forced week after week to attend our death-boring Methodist services, Easter was always a welcome change: better songs, a well-rehearsed play, a fierier sermon. Plus, Easter has the best candy, so of course it was my favorite. To this day, I weep like a child when those purple bags of Cadbury Mini Eggs show up in the Walgreens seasonal aisle at the first dawn of spring.

I didn't have very much of an attachment to that dusty can of gravel; I don't know if I'm a robot or dead inside or what, or if the passing of time leeches the sentimentality out of loss, but guilt was the only emotion keeping me from just dropping it in a garbage can outside of a 7-Eleven. I'm not much for ceremony, either. If ever there is a wedding in my future, you can bet your sweet ass that it will take place in some nondescript room in a courthouse, followed immediately by appetizers and margaritas at the closest Chili's. I don't like to make a big to-do, although it did seem fitting to sprinkle his ashes on Easter, if for no other reason than to see if I'd find him randomly hanging out in my kitchen three days later.

I wasn't sure how to appropriately eulogize a dude who had once punched me in the face for washing the dishes wrong, and it really never even occurred to me that I might write something down for the occasion. People always assume that because I'm a writer, I just show up to special events with some super poignant shit written on a scroll in my purse. I write butt jokes on the Internet, you guys. Please stop asking me to "say a few words" at your kid's baptism. Also, the only semiprivate spot on the river we found after driving around in the nice clothes I remembered at the very last second to pack was a very public boat launch down a sharp incline. Even though it was three in the afternoon, I was terrified that some kids out to enjoy the shit-smelling river on a warm day in a kayak would happen upon us and call the fucking police. (I read *To Kill a Mockingbird*—I'm not trying to be caught with a pretty white woman doing *anything*.) So even if I had written a speech, I would've been too fucking jittery to read it.

I could tell that Mavis was dismayed by my bored lack of liturgy, so I made a big show of slowly prying the lid off the can while I tried to come up with something moving to say. "Is it tacky to Instagram this?" I asked her, but before she could answer, a car full of hooting and laughing teenagers crunched through the gravel at the top of the hill and parked next to the idling Toyota, and I for real was not trying to explain just what the fuck we were doing to a bunch of children who were about to go skinny-dipping in my father's cremains. "It's bad manners just to dump him in the water! Shouldn't you at least say *something* nice?!" Mavis asked, a borderline hysterical edge creeping into her voice. I waited for the wind to die down while keeping an anxious eye on the cutoff shorts and tank tops untying the boat from their SUV above us. "Thanks for always cutting my meat into tiny pieces," I said finally, tipping the can toward the gently rippling waves. The sun sparkled on the surface of the water . . . which remained blissfully undisturbed, as nothing was coming out of that fucking can.

"If I have to touch these ashes with my bare hands I am going to kill myself," I barked at Mavis, who stood downriver, wringing her hands nervously and keeping her eyes trained on the whooping and hollering kids stripping down to their bikinis up by the car. I shook the can a little harder. Still nothing. What a fucking asshole, undoubtedly mocking me from the other side of the rainbow bridge. "Stop embarrassing me!" I hissed, banging the side of the container to loosen him up (gross) before violently shaking it out over the water. As the better part of the cremains shook loose from where they had settled, a huge gust of wind came from the east. OF FUCK-ING COURSE.

Mavis's face was like Munch's *Scream* painting, all horrified wide eyes and open mouth, as I turned toward her with my dead father's charred bones and fingernails splattered across my face and crackling between my teeth. It was like coming home from a day at the beach, except replace "sand" with "gritty Sam Irby penis and entrails" lining my nostrils and in between my toes.

"FUCK!!!" I shouted, tasting burned human flesh on my tongue as I shook eyeballs and elbows off my dress. What hadn't ended up in my face hole was floating like a large clump of dust slowly down the Cumberland River. Is that really all there is? I've had more pomp and circumstance while taking out the fucking recycling. Horrified, I stood frozen at the edge of the water.

As we climbed back up the hill, past those children whose lives I would be living if happiness weren't a goddamned lie, I could feel bits and particles squelching between my toes; I made a mental note that this would be the last day of my life that I was going to ever wear motherfucking flip-flops. Mavis drove to Bolton's Spicy Chicken & Fish so we could get a couple of pieces to take back to the hotel, and I stood outside the car in the parking lot bent over a trash can shaking out my hair and digging little black specks out of my ears while she flirted with the old dude frying up her catfish inside the restaurant. I tossed the gold funeral-home can in a dumpster and said one last thank-you to my father for blessing me with short, fat fingers that couldn't get as deep into my ear canals as I needed them to go. When we got back to the hotel, I contemplated plucking out each of my eyelashes one by one, shaving my entire body (eyebrows included), then hosing it down with bleach, but *SVU* was on, plus we had just gotten some ribs, so instead I took a Klonopin and brushed my teeth in the hot shower, wondering which of my dad's parts I was watching ride a frothy cloud of extra-strength dandruff shampoo down the drain. Roll credits, sad trombone.

i'm in love and it's boring

I found the apartment in the rental listings of the *Chicago Reader*. The ad was for a "spacious, airy, unbelievably huge!" one-bedroom not far from the one my roommate and I were currently arguing about dirty dishes in. "$600 a month! No credit check! No deposit! Move in today!!!" I called the number and was bounced between receptionists before finally getting one who could help. We scheduled a viewing for later that day, and I was pleasantly surprised to find an apartment that really was massive, not the shoe box I'd been expecting, with large windows that flooded the space with light and gleaming hardwood floors. I knew I wanted it the minute I crossed the threshold, but I went through the motions of peeking into the closet and checking the water pressure in the shower so the landlord could rest assured that I was a Serious Person. I offered him the first two months' rent in cash on the spot, and he handed me a basic lease to sign and said I could move in whenever I wanted. After I closed the door behind him, I sat on the closed toilet and texted my boyfriend: "Dude, I found us the perfect place."

When I was in love with Zachary Jones, I knew it, because my stomach used to hurt whenever I thought about his face, and I would drag myself barefoot around that apartment we were *supposed* to be sharing, drinking cold vodka in my pajamas while listening to "Wake Up Alone" by Amy Winehouse and waiting for him to text me. I knew it was love, because I was twenty-six and had crashed my 1987 Honda Accord in the parking lot outside of Pizzeria Aroma when, over the cell phone I shouldn't have been talking on while driving, he said "I love you" and sounded like he meant it. I knew it was love, because he gave me a mix CD three weeks after he ghosted on my birthday party. The party was also supposed to be a "this is my actual boyfriend, not just some imaginary guy I've been talking your ear off about" party, so I sat there pink-cheeked and burning with shame while everyone asked where he was, again.

It was always my young dream to fall in love with a DJ. I was a very earnest clubgoer, and when I wasn't shuffling around the dance floors at Slick's and Sinibar and Betty's Blue Star, I was studying records at Gramaphone. I fantasized about hauling bags of house records to my car from the Darkroom at 2:00 a.m., my clothes damp with sweat, sticky with spilled drinks and reeking of cigarette smoke. I daydreamed about late nights fighting through crowds to fetch bottles of water from the bar for the faceless imaginary boyfriend hunched over the tables, oversize headphones bobbing as he nodded to the beat. I barely slept, toiling all day at my various jobs before racing home to slam a quick dinner and draw on some eyeliner before leaving right back out to go to the club.

I met Zac at an MF Doom show at Sonotheque, a place

I loved so much I cried when it closed. I was actually there with another dude, this younger kid, Jason, who I was trying to figure out whether or not I had feelings for, and Zac stood watching us huddled together shouting unintelligibly into each other's ears. When I realized this giant human nursing the same beer for forty-five minutes was staring at me, I figured it was because I was wearing gym shoes in a disco and tried to hide my feet behind my bag. For two hours, he watched me over the heads of tiny backpackers furiously composing battle raps in their heads until the show ended and the lights went up and everyone scattered like roaches to the darkest corners of the room. Zac had disappeared (had I dreamed him?), so I hovered awkwardly near the bar waiting for my friends to pee and close their tabs and tried to shake off that shy, embarrassed feeling you get when you think someone likes you but you figure out they were really interested in your friend or some shit.

I smelled him before I saw him, clean like soap yet spicy and masculine. All of a sudden, a stubbled cheek pressed against mine as he bent close to speak. His lips smelled like Carmex. "Is that dude you were sitting with your boyfriend?" His voice pierced my heart like a knife, and my voice caught in my throat. I shook my head, deciding right then and there that my feelings for Jason were most definitely of the friendly variety. He asked for my number, and I mentally had to calculate whether there was enough money in my bank account to get my cell phone reactivated by the time he was going to call me. I could probably hustle up a freelance copyediting job right quick and get Sprint their money, so if he was one of these cool guys and waited a few days, I'd be all good. But what if he, you know, *liked me* liked me and tried to call later that day? Then I'd either look like a broke bitch or a lying asshole, and, yeah, I'm probably both, but he ain't gotta know that yet. I snatched a pen off the bar and wrote down the number to the house phone I had initially sneered at when my roommate insisted (thank goodness for sensible people). He smiled, revealing a row of perfect teeth that stood in stark contrast to his deep chocolate skin even in the almost-dark, and enveloped my hand in his big bear paw. My insides turned to jelly, and I fought the desire to get on my tiptoes and kiss him.

The courtship was amazing. Until I met him, I had been an unwitting victim of a lot of Netflix and Chilling, except that wasn't a thing then. Let's just say I spent a lot of nights on various boyfriendly futons watching HBO for whatever amount of time is long enough to feel like a not-prostitute before having unenthusiastic sex. I was twenty-five, man. No one was asking me to dinner! It was like, "Oh, hey, cool, you gave me your number at that De La show! Wanna come over and watch me and my roommates play *Resident Evil* for three hours?" So I would say yeah, and shave my legs, and get all my shit on, and go to some kid's house to watch him smoke weed and play Xbox, and then when he lost, we'd go to his room and have loser sex atop the pizza boxes and Jordans and DVDs scattered across his bed. And by "have sex" I mean "lie stiff as a board with all my muscles taut so his roommates wouldn't hear the bed squeaking." Lather, rinse, repeat for the entirety of my early twenties until this adult human male picked a time and a restaurant that served food on real plates. In the cab on the way home, I whispered to myself, "This is it."

I knew it was love because he was busy with school, and I was not busy—at least, not busy in big and important ways—and it's cute when you're not busy to mail care packages to your boyfriend who literally lives thirty minutes away but hasn't called in a week because *he is so fucking busy*. That inner cringe when a friend asks "Have you ever even been in his house?" is obviously what love feels like. I was in a pretty hopeless place: working too much, sick all the time, *desperate* to be loved in a real way. I needed an anchor, and into my lap one fell. He talked about helping me finish school and taking me on tropical vacations and didn't care that I can't have babies. How did I get so lucky?! And all I would have to do in return was wait, while trying not to drown.

I became pretty good at pretending to be a super-chill girlfriend, but sometimes I felt like I was really going to lose my shit pacing around that apartment waiting for updates: would he get out of class early enough to hang out tonight? Could he take Saturday night off from work to meet me out for a drink? What about if I drove to the hospital during his lunch break and just made googly eyes at him in the harshly lit cafeteria for a few minutes? Hours stretched to days, and days stretched to weeks, and there I was trying to be cool while pining for someone too unavailable to be my boyfriend, secretly delighting in the agony because it was proof that I was actually—no, fucking *finally*—in an adult romantic relationship. I would bore my increasingly irritated friends with melodramatic whining about how my one true love didn't have time to hang out because of his chemistry final, then sit alone in this new apartment I'd rented so I could give him a key without being disrespectful to my now ex-roommate. A key he used maybe three times over the course of our entire relationship. Because he never found the time to come over.

I knew I was in love, because even though I spent my weekends locked in my crib organizing my ketchups and moping around to heartbreak music, it was worth it because I could finally relate to what the hell those bitches were singing about. I had mastered the unrequited crush early in life; every boy who leaned over to help me solve a geometry problem or who smacked a volleyball back over the net before it smashed into my face became the object of my never-ending devotion. Until he asked someone else to homecoming and I learned, again, that just because a dude runs across the whole school with the clarinet you left behind in the band room tucked under his arm to bring it to your Latin American history class doesn't mean he's in love with you. Sometimes people can be decent. So I gathered all the songs about loneliness and longing and made bleak mixtapes to listen to while ripping pictures of Christian Slater out of back issues of *YM* and *Seventeen*. And that was fine, but what I really wanted was a reason to sing all the tortured, love-gone-wrong songs. What I really wanted was to sing "Tear in Your Hand" at the top of my lungs and mean it.

I had sex one time in high school, but that was a joke. As soon as he squirted that thick ribbon of cum all over my pubes and inner thigh before I'd even begun to enjoy myself, I decided that I wouldn't be doing that with a person I might have to do a group project on NAFTA with ever fucking again. In my later teens, I'd learn the hard way that sex doesn't equal undying romantic feelings. But boy, those first few lessons were brutal. They resulted in many "Yo, I thought we were just homies who kicked it sometimes" conversations. So when I finally happened upon this handsome stranger, one who had all the hobbies and interests of the prototypical lovers I breathlessly detailed in my journals, one who took me on dates that he paid for, one who made actual love instead of trying to fuck me in the face, I thought it was kismet. It had to be. So what if he didn't ever have time to have long philosophical talks with me or fit a quick lunch into his grad school schedule? He told me he loved me and wanted to spend his life with me, and he proved it by never ever calling or using the extra toothbrush

I'd carefully arranged in the medicine cabinet in what should have been our bathroom. All I had when I moved was some pots and pans and the shit in my bedroom, so the dining room and living room and guest room sat cold and empty for the entire time I lived there letting the words to "Carrion" by Fiona Apple echo through the empty spaces, waiting for him to give me a reason to fill them up.

The torture of loving someone through difficult circumstances seemed so glamorous in music and on television. I knew I was in love, because opposite work schedules and organic chemistry were conspiring to keep the two of us apart. What cruel irony to meet the seven-foot-tall record-collecting beefcake of my dreams only to be prioritized somewhere between "get a root canal" and "study for the MCAT" on his to-do list! I spent years of my life romanticizing something that amounted to little more than the kind of relationship a person has with her high school boyfriend once they've gone away to separate colleges and he forgets there's someone pining for him halfway across the country. The gut-wrenching pain of casual rejection was my oxygen as I waited for him to put his stethoscope down long enough to help me pick out a couch. At least I got a lot of shit done while waiting for him to finish school. I circled a lot of particleboard furniture in the IKEA catalog, fucked a couple of muscular jerks with fat fetishes I brought home from the gym, and read the entire Harry Potter series during the summer I unknowingly was waiting for him to dump me. God, I was dumb and cautiously optimistic for way longer than I should've been. I mean, "in love."

How do I know I'm in love if I don't want to kill myself all the time? Mavis is the nicest person I've ever met, and it was hard to recognize I was in love with her because she never let so much time elapse between "hey wats up winky-face emoji" texts that I had deleted her number and had to respond, "NEW PHONE WHO DIS." She has never replied ". . . uh okay sure" when I tell her I love her. She's never patted me on the back while telling me that she thinks of me as a *really good friend* despite our regular carnal relations; never said, "Nah, I don't read your shit because you really aren't that funny to me"; never disappeared for a month and then popped back up all nonchalant. She has never, not even once, made me miserable. How is it possible that what we have is even real?

You know how when you're in your mid- to late thirties, and you're dreaming about where you are going to live hopefully by age forty-two, and you're picturing your reasonably affordable one-bedroom apartment in a moderately safe and attractive neighborhood: who is living there with you? Is it the withholder? The serial cheater? What about the commitment-phobe, or perhaps the grifter? Yeah, no. It's none of those. It's some mythical being you haven't met yet, one who doesn't have any suspicious Facebook activity that can trigger hours of pointless scrolling down strangers' profiles, looking for infidelity clues.

I have developed a very special set of skills as a coping mechanism for falling in love with shitty people. I can go days at a time without so much as a smoke signal. I have no problem eating in a restaurant alone or living without physical contact for weeks or believing that a person who definitely was sleeping with several other women was also somehow devoted to me. That's the deal, right, that it's not real unless it feels like someone reached into your chest to pull your heart out while you stand by helplessly? I can work with that. I have not, however, figured out what to do when a person I am romantically involved with keeps her word and looks after my feelings. If Mavis showed up at a reading, drunk and inexplicably wet, and heckled me onstage, I would know how to handle that kind of love. I understand a love that argues with you in public and occasionally puts down your body and knocks on your door only at midnight.

I've never been loved like this before, and I resist it, every day, because I do not deserve it. Real love feels less like a throbbing, pulsing animal begging for its freedom and beating against the inside of my chest and more like, "Hey, that place you like had fish tacos today and I got you some while I was out," as it sets a bag spotted with grease on the dining room table. It's not a game you don't understand the rules of, or a test you never got the materials to study for. It never leaves you wondering who could possibly be texting at 3:00 a.m. or what you could possibly do to make it come home and stay there. It's fucking boring, dude. I don't walk around mired in uneasiness, waiting for the other shoe to drop. No parsing through spun tales about why it took her so long to come back from the store; no checking her e-mails or calling her job to make sure she's actually there; no sitting in my car outside her house at dawn to make sure she's alone when she leaves. This feels safe and steadfast and predictable and secure. It's boring as shit. And it's easily the best thing I've ever felt.

Today is Zac's forty-third birthday. We met on the eve of his thirty-second. That totally blows my mind. Like how can I be this old? How could this have all gone down a decade ago? And how are the scars lurking under the surface of my skin still so easy to find? I remember the first time I ran into him in public after we'd broken up: my friend Julia and I were at the Silver Room block party, withering under the blistering July sun, when I heard a familiar laugh behind me and my stomach fell right out of my butt. I turned around and made eye contact, then immediately started to cry, but all cool-like behind giant sunglasses. It felt like all the wind had been sucked out of my lungs, an acute pain that I could feel radiating through my whole body. I clutched Julia's arm, tears streaming down my cheeks, and was like, "Yo, I gotta go. Right now." And then we pushed our way through the crowd of sweaty, gyrating bodies to get a cab home. It had been, I don't know, six or seven months? And I thought I was fine after we broke up. I didn't fall apart like I thought I would.

But when I saw him again something cracked open inside me, and I went home to my new apartment (this time just one room, big enough for a full-size bed, a bookcase, a kitchen big enough to wedge a little writing desk under the window, and a bathroom the size of a closet, perfect for the three boxes I'd moved in with) and called a friend to say that I thought I might be dying for real and played Portishead records in the dark for the rest of the night. Reminded, again, that love feels like a fucking dumpster fire in the pit of your stomach.

I saw the little gift icon on my iPhone calendar this morning and immediately texted him, which I have not done in literal years. But this is a sign, right, randomly digging up all these fucking feelings on the anniversary of his birth without even having realized it? I have never written about him, and I never planned to. I like to make fun of people, especially myself, but I've always felt so protective of that twenty-five-year-old idiot moping around those barren rooms with her barren womb feeling so grateful for the hope that came attached to this person. I had no idea whether he had the same number, but I wrote "happy happy day, champ!" and pressed send. He wrote back within minutes, which never happened when we were together. How you doing blah blah what are you up to blah blah how is your family blah blah blah are you seeing anyone and then he said:

I regret how we ended our relationship, because I really thought something permanent would have come about with you, but I see now that it was bad timing. We had a lot of laughs together. Your soul is always with me and I always keep you close to me, and yes, I know it was hard as hell but one thing you should know is that I really loved you and I never stopped.

Eight years ago reading that would have melted the stalactites hanging from his space in my heart, formed by ice that thickened every time I changed my outgoing voice mail message so it would sound like it belonged to a carefree person who obviously had missed his call because she was too busy out having fun; the ice that had grown thicker still with every evening spent cleaning the top of the refrigerator and polishing the faucets and all the other pointless shit you do when you think your boyfriend is coming over and you want him to know how clean and put together you are. Eight years ago, I would have poured myself a drink and put on some red lipstick and rented a hotel room in the hopes of seeing whether our bodies still fit together the way they used to. I sat with that text for a minute before responding with this: "I really loved you, my man. We could've been a good thing." Which is probably lies? But it doesn't even matter, because this is now, and I'm totally fucking bored.

a bomb, probably

Everyone I know is having a goddamned baby and what that means is you can't just stop by your homegirl's house unannounced with a bottle of Carménère and a couple of tubes of Pringles to watch hours of makeup tutorial videos on YouTube anymore. Because that baby might be sleeping or eating or doing its taxes, and you are going to mess it all up with your loud, single-person bullshit. That baby does not have time to listen to an in-depth analysis of the string of unanswered text messages you recently sent to your latest unrequited crush. Nor does it have time to deconstruct the most recent episode of *The Bachelorette*. Unless you're coming over armed with a bowl of creamed peas and a cardboard book for that kid to chew on, just stay in your tragic one-person dwelling and hope like hell that the next person they hire at work will be someone not stupid to whom you can relate.

I am in a relationship now with a woman who has children, and let me just say that most certainly was *not* how I was expecting my destiny to knit itself together. I thought for sure I would be spending my stress-incontinence years picking moist dog food crumbs out of my aging shih tzu's slobbery beard while earnestly considering circuit court judicial endorsements in my local newspaper, but now it looks like I really do have to learn what molly is and how to know if your kid is on it. Being in a relationship has turned me into a total asshole. Hold up, not that kind; I still don't vote regularly or eat rutabaga or use words like "plethora" in regular conversation. But I *do* do lame stuff like "thinking about my future" and putting money away "just in case."

Right now I'm "babysitting" and here's what that looks like: the girl child is in the sunroom gobbling high-fructose corn syrup by the handful, watching irritatingly loud cartoons, and building a bomb, probably, and I'm in the dining room paralyzed with fear that she might ask me to tell her a story or cook her something nutritious or—God forbid—help her with her homework. These kids are going to find out real quick that my perceived intelligence is a web of lies built on a crumbling foundation of charm and quick wit. The other night, the boy child was working on his algebra homework at the dinner table, and when he asked me to look over a problem, I was like LOL and pretended to be choking on a brussels sprout. I was doing some long division by hand yesterday and dude blurted, "Is that even *math*?!" while squinting at the numbers and turning the paper upside down and shit. "I think it's hieroglyphics," murmured the girl. Bitch, I don't know new math! I don't even know how to figure out a 20 percent tip on an odd-numbered check!

Want to know the hardest thing I've ever had to do? Not yell a string of offensive curse words when I banged my finger in a kitchen drawer with an impressionable child in the room.

I've had colonoscopies that were easier than holding my pulsating hand in a dish towel and looking into those wide, blue child eyes and simply saying, "Ouch!" In my mind I was kicking every stupid pot and pan in that motherfucker while howling "SHIT FUCK YOU SON OF A BITCHING DICK!!!" and foaming at the mouth, but kids don't need to hear that, so I just took a handful of aspirin and ground my molars into stumps as pain radiated up my arm.

Five years ago, at a cozy, sunlit corner table at our favorite breakfast spot, my friend Anna looked up at me from her bowl of chia porridge with tears shining in her eyes and said, "Samantha, I'm pregnant!" And I started crying, because she's been my friend since we were ten years old and I love her more than anything. Then she said, "It's two babies! They're the size of lentils!!!" and by that point we were both sobbing and hugging and curious onlookers shot us scathing death-looks because the brunch line at that place is always bananas. I made a concerted effort not to reach out and put my hands on her belly because I read somewhere that that's rude, and please somebody give me a medal for that restraint. I couldn't believe that this jerk who wore hemp necklaces and put Ben Harper on every single mixtape she made in high school was about to be somebody's mother. Technically two somebodies. Horrifying.

I became an aunt to my sister's kid when I was six, but that was way different. My niece was never going to look across the backseat of Mom's Chevy at where I was buckled into the booster seat and wonder why I hadn't put a down payment on any property yet. She never questioned why her Adult Aunt was sneaking her lunch of neon-orange mac and cheese directly from the pot it had dried in because she didn't have any food at home and her direct deposit hadn't cleared the bank yet. I'm sure that Anna and her fine-ass Canadian husband had already started setting aside money for those lentils to go to college, but shouldn't they have asked *me* if *I* was ready for kids? If I had enough Fun-Aunt money set aside for regular trips to the American Girl store? If I had the energy to pack up my apartment and move into a place someone had already childproofed? If I was ready to stop shouting swear words all the time?!

I am hCG-challenged and at an age when all my late nights and drunken partying is dangerously toeing the line between "fabulous and exciting" and "sad as a motherfucker." The age at which the sluts I used to drink too much and cry with are all dressed like Kohl's ads, driving sport utility vehicles with roof racks affixed to them, and having stable relationships with men who wear sensible shoes and make wise investments with their beer money. Goddamn it, is there anyone left who wants to be drunk at three in the afternoon and go get manicures?! I see you, potential new friend: banging terrible dudes, drinking backwashed beers some stranger just left on the bar, and basically whiling away your early thirties pretending that your life is an extended episode of *Sex and the City* when all of a sudden, BOOM. Every vagina within a ten-mile radius is pushing out an eight-pound screaming red ball of human who will eventually need braces and many winter coats. And you and I are still eating cheese fries and jelly beans for dinner.

I swear, now that I am finally beginning to come to terms with being that special kind of pigperson who is barely treading water while being neck-deep in a frothy sea of embossed wedding invitations heaved at me by my so-called friends, it seems others have come up with a whole new way to make me feel like an emotionally stunted teenage boy: THEY ARE CREATING NEW PEOPLE. No big deal, right? Yes, everybody knows somebody who was pushing a stroller to class in the ninth grade. But back then it was like, "Too bad you have to take your baby to gym class, I'll just be over here wearing my velvet choker and sobbing to Liz Phair." Now it's like, "Girl, you are making me feel like a lesser human being." My dead parents aren't around to harp on me about my slow grandchild production, and while I am grateful for that little bit of orphan silver lining, no one told me that, having already survived a series of teenage years during which bodysuits were the rage, my thirties would be another unimaginable assault on my very low self-esteem.

The twins started kindergarten last fall, and every year, I am still one day early or two days late for their birthday. I forget when they're within earshot and say mean things about dead people or recount in excruciating detail the highlights of my most recent gynecological exam. My friends and frenemies all have little ones now, and I'm not any smarter or feeling any more put together, plus when I visit them I can't set my bag down anywhere for fear of dropping a metal flask onto some tiny soft skull. If "it gets better," I'ma need to know when. I suppose I could just wait for all their children to drop out of dental school and stab a convenience-store employee while trying to steal a box of real Sudafed before I feel haughty and superior about my choice to let everyone else do the breeding, but with my luck these little dudes are going to grow up to be, like, funny and charming Instagram models who automatically take my arm when we're walking in the snow. I hate them already.

You can't tell by looking, but I was a nanny for a while in high school and through my early twenties. It was just like *The Help* except swap in liberal white guilt and Land Rovers for Jim Crow and cotton gins. The most important thing I learned was the difference between the boxed-macaroni-and-cheese parents and the holistic-kale-anti-vaccination parents. Macaroni moms are the easiest to be around, obviously. Because, duh, you can totally let their kids zombie out in front of the TV and order a sausage pizza. I am not good enough to be around my no-screens-in-the-house flaxseed friends. For real, I can't be having your kid in our adult conversation because you don't want him to get high on *Sesame Street* and fruit snacks. GO AWAY, BABY. And I have neither the intelligence nor the patience to navigate the kid aisle at Whole Foods while trying to find the gluten-free, carob-sweetened, agave soy organic vegan oxygenated wheatgrass bites or whatever so that my newest nephew has something to snack on while trying to stay alive for two hours in my apartment. I might put my knives away and hide the porn, but educational toys and petroleum-free jellies are not within my purview.

You need to know all this stuff, of course, because some of these new moms will lose their impacted shit on you if they catch you pouring anything other than Hawaiian volcanic water into their child's bath. Yes, that same person you watched pull a disgusting dollar bill from between a stripper's ass cheeks with her *teeth* will now try to break your jaw for serving her kid some cheese with hormones in it. And she's not wrong, she just needs to understand that *I don't know what the fuck a heart of palm even is, Katy*. That's why I took the boy to McDonald's. THEY SERVE APPLES NOW, SHIT. And I've changed plenty of cloth diapers in my day, but it is not humanly possible for me to stay on top of all the ways I might be destroying your young offspring. There's only so much reading and interacting I can do, parents!

I have come to find out that the only leverage you can get on a kid is doing something that he's too young to do, and since ten-year-olds these days are already refinancing their second mortgages and maintaining better 401(k)s than I do, the best way to stay ahead of the game is to do things that they legally can't, like going under the needle and drinking a High Life with your breakfast. You have to find a way in with kids, and if they're old enough to figure out what a total loser you are, you have to do it immediately. Danger and contraband are the currency of youth, and the less similar to their responsible, bill-paying parents you seem, the better you'll get along with your surrogate children. That's why when Auntie Sam comes over to babysit she brings dirty needles and a ComEdison disconnect notice in her purse; they're putty in my hands after I tell them what it's like to run out of toilet paper and how to disguise your voice when you accidentally answer a collections call. The fact that I live somewhere else and am not fussing at them to clean up their Legos is usually enough to hit the cool-points jackpot, but when I need a boost, I tell them about the one time I got into a bar brawl. Or that time I got shot. (I never got shot.)

If your idiot friends start procreating while you're still trying to get on the VIP list at the club every week, you definitely have to learn baby talk. Not "goo goo, gah gah," you asshole, you need to learn what "Montessori" means. Seriously, you better verse yourself in home births and butt paste, because gone are the days when your girl has time to listen to you whine about that one dude with the nice car who never called you after he teabagged you in the parking lot behind a bowling alley. You are going to be talking about baby poop. All the time. Its smell, its consistency, its color, its length, its taste, whatever. Prepare to let your life be taken over by infant diarrhea. And while we're at it, you better get accustomed to looking at some giant, lactating boobs, because your breastfeeding friends will have zero qualms about unhooking their flesh-colored front-loading bras right in the middle of your dinner. And don't worry about being a pervert for staring, because it might be the least sexual event you will ever see in your life. All that rooting around and the squishing noises. When Anna was in town when the girls were six weeks old, she was partially naked half the time and like 80 percent disoriented, and I had to learn quick how to conduct a conversation without trying to gauge the size and shape of my best friend's exposed areolas. But even if public boobs freak you out, you won't even care, because every time that tiny alien screams its little head off demanding food or a diaper or a change of scenery, all you'll want is for her to get those jugs out and shut that noise up.

OH MY GOD THE MONEY. You thought what you had to spend when the parents got married was bad? Well, hold on to your prepaid Visa card, friend, because that was only the beginning. At least weddings happen only one time. Babies have birthdays every year. Three times a month I'm standing in Target squinting to read the instructions on some inappropriate toy or another, trying to figure out whether it makes too much noise or requires too much skill or comes equipped with too many parts a little kid could choke on and die from. Only to then fuck up the wrapping paper and spill vodka on the card the kid can't even read yet when I get home. You will need to take out a monster loan. Or if your credit is messed up, you better start waiting tables during all your single-person free time.

You won't mind, though, because your exhausted BFF will smile so hard and be so grateful that you picked up a pack of onesies on your way over to regale her with stories from your super-exciting, STD-dodging single-girl life. By the end of the first month, you will be seriously considering signing up for the Babies "R" Us e-mail list. Because baby stuff is cute, and seeing a little diarrhea-soaked human being dressed in a perfectly matched outfit that you bought for him is an incredible feeling, especially if he is too young to tell you how much he hates it and how all the other kids at school get their bibs from Gucci. You won't be able to walk by a pastel display at Walmart without dumping half of it into your cart. You'll coo at little monkeys and bears and marvel at the tininess of little frilly socks, spending your way to eviction because the asshole you sat next to in US history junior year couldn't figure out how to properly use a condom, and you will love it.

Try not to feel too salty when going through your bank statements. (Or just be like me and never even open them.) Just keep in mind that eventually those kids will be old enough to drive you around and send you cards and look after your cats while you're in Florida for the winter. And couplefriends with babyfriends are the best, because they always have extra stuff just lying around for your pitiful single ass to mooch off them. No way in hell I'm going to Sam's Club; that's why I keep smug marrieds around! I haven't bought my own toilet paper in three years. I just wait until one of them is like, "Come eat dinner with us, you lonely piece of shit!" and while the fish sticks are heating up, Mom and Dad pack me suitcases full of two-ply extra-strong kid-proof toilet paper and economy-size bags of animal crackers. The friends with deep freezers and large pantries are even better, because you can walk out of there with nineteen individually wrapped chicken breasts, four bottles of toilet bowl cleaner, one-thousand-count boxes of

Swiffer cloths, a ten-pound bag of frozen shrimp, and six pints of strawberries. Who needs Peapod? People with kids are so exhausted they don't have time to notice that one of the forty-six boxes of Kleenex they just purchased is missing. They literally have no idea what is in their houses at any given moment. If something is gone or broken they'll just assume one of the kids did it. You think I'm kidding, but the last time I bought Ziploc bags, Gladware containers, Handi Wipes, sponges, dish towels, and Q-tips was, ummm, never. That's what (baby) friends are for.

This year, on my days off, I'm trying stay up super late (it's 10:37 at night right now—who am I, a rapper?!) and sleep as late as I possibly can. Now that a lot of my friends are having babies, the only recourse I have against feeling like a huge dork for still trying to maneuver my way through my first real romance is doing all the things those mother hens can't do anymore: I curse at the top of my lungs in the solitude of my apartment! Eat pizza for breakfast! Take several long, uninterrupted showers every day! Turn my phone off! Watch R-rated movies! Poop in blissed-out peace! Buy unpasteurized cheese! And pointy furniture! Leave my vibrator in the dish drain after I wash it! Never ever watch public television! But also never turn the television OFF! Get some mercury-laden sushi! Spend an entire day reading under the covers! Go out for drinks! Throw away all of my bite-size foods! Make sand castles in the cat litter box! Never buy any fresh fruit! Use my outside voice inside! Take a bunch of Tylenol! And a bunch of Advil! And don't forget: DRINK A SHITLOAD OF COLD MEDICINE!!!

the real housewife of kalamazoo

The only time I fantasize about jettisoning my fast-paced, action-packed, exciting city for the Purell-ed, easy-to-park-your-oversized-vehicle embrace of the suburbs is when I think about how nice it would be to never have to race the motherfucking Zipcar from Target to the Whole Foods hot bar to the Laundromat in under three hours ever fucking again. Strip malls are boring and CHILDREN ARE SO FUCKING LOUD, but there is something to be said for the ability to deposit your car right in front of the window that you will be hawkishly staring out of for half the night to make sure no one so much as breathes on your windshield. I've owned four cars. All pieces of absolute garbage, and all purchased with whatever loose change I could scavenge from couch cushions and broken pay phones. They were all junked after a year or two of having been driven into the ground and destroyed by life on a crowded city neighborhood street. It's totally the worst, and I want to finally own a car with power windows that doesn't have a fucking tape deck.

Every once in a while I get really tired of the city. It typically

coincides with getting really tired of absorbing the projected
rage of entitled assholes with purebred dogs, but occasionally
I'll see a horse or a flower through the grease-spotted window
of a crawling Amtrak train and daydream longingly about a car
I can park right up next to my front door and a pair of elastic-
waisted jeans I can pull right up next to my tits as I crush potato
chips to go on top of the tuna casserole I am making for dinner.
This is not to suggest that I am cosmopolitan, by any means,
but I do live in a bustling metropolis where dudes stand over
you on a crowded bus with precariously gripped open containers of hot coffee and having cool hair is of primary importance.
I am always on the lookout for signs that I am aging disgrace-
fully, and my constant agitation at all of the congestion and
noise and close proximity to other actively sweating humans is
proof positive that I don't have long for the Second City. BUT
COULD I REALLY MAKE IT IN A SMALL TOWN?

Pro: I would be rich.

When I was hanging out in unincorporated Missouri with my
friend Lara, I saw a house for rent for $500 a month. An entire
house. For rent. For less than I paid for the glasses I'm wearing
right now. Is this real life?! I pay almost twice that every month
for a couple of rooms and a kitchen whose sum square footage
is probably less than that of your garage. What I'm trying to say
is that I could have a house, with a driveway and an upstairs,
for the price of half an ounce of La Prairie neck cream. I weep
thinking of how little I'd have to work to maintain my basic
quality of life in a town like that. Fifty out of the 168 hours of
my week are spent mad because work is interfering with all the
Internet articles I'm trying to read, forty-nine are spent trying
to get some sleep if I'm lucky, ten are spent suffering through

some sort of commuting nightmare, eight are pure panicking, eleven are brooding, and the last forty are eating shitting writing reading watching wishing hoping and hating. What is it all worth?! Sure I have money to buy an iPhone, but no time to figure out how the hell to use the Passbook. If my rent was less, I could work less, and working less means I could shave a couple of hours off the time I have set aside for moping and sort out how to set a recurring alarm.

Con: I don't know how to fix small engines or any other worthwhile small-town shit.

Where would I work out in the middle of the heartland?! I whine and complain about my job a lot, but let's be real: I graduated high school almost twenty years ago and since then, I have had a lot of jobs and not a lot of higher education. And I can't go to any more school. That ship has sailed, and I am thrilled to be left standing in its wake. I didn't like school when it wasn't weird that I was there, so the thought of sitting next to your daughter in Intro to Psychology makes me want to die for real. I can do fractions, but not when your son, that smug little bastard, is smirking at my gray hairs. Maybe I could go $100,000 into insurmountable debt at one of those quick colleges they advertise on television during *Days of Our Lives* (I could be a medical assistant, I guess? If I tried real hard?) but I would rather mop a hundred fast-food floors than ever awkwardly try to make friends in another goddamned cafeteria.

Pro: Everyone seems so dang nice.

The first time a Michigan person gave me an enthusiastic "Hello there!" at the co-op, I spent the next five real minutes hiding in the natural-soap aisle checking to make sure I didn't have watercress in my teeth or a bloody nose or something else to incur such sarcasm from this otherwise pleasant-seeming human on a random Thursday afternoon. Chicago is in the Midwest, and yes, we're probably way nicer than New Yorkers, but don't get it twisted—we are still not making eye contact and saying hi to you while you measure out your buckwheat groats in the bulk section of the health food store. Lots of people are theoretically nice, but when you need them to jump your car's dead battery they act like the text didn't go through. And that's fine. We big-city folk understand that "Call me if you need help moving next week" loosely translates to "BITCH, I DARE YOU." But I might need a hand getting my firewood into the house, and it would be amazing to shout over the fence for Bill and his unironic cargo shorts to come over and give me one.

Con: I can't be 100 percent sure these people won't call me a nigger to my face.

Hey, remember that time I stopped in West Virginia in the borrowed Subaru my homegirl and I were driving across the country and a little white child no older than eight amusing himself with a length of wire and an old flat tire wiped the mayonnaise from the corners of his mouth just long enough to call me and my friend "dirty nigger lesbians" as we minded our own business filling up our gas tank? That tiny guy lived in a small town! I was pretty shocked, since the last time I'd let her finger me had been in DC and I'm pretty sure she'd washed her hands after, so how could he possibly know what we'd been up to three states ago?! Also I had showered in Baltimore, so "dirty" might have been overstating it a bit; disheveled I can handle, but dirty?! GIVE ME A BREAK, CALEB. I've never had a fistfight with a baby before, but I briefly considered it before reminding myself that (1) jail is real, and (2) in ten years the coal mine would introduce him to karmic retribution better than I ever could.

Pro: Frito casseroles.

I didn't eat for two days so that I could spend all my Weight Watchers points for the week last night on a nineteen-dollar octopus salad from Longman & Eagle. WOULD DO AGAIN. I grew up eating the kind of boxed trash you heat up and pour milk in for dinner: macaroni and cheese, Hamburger Helper, imitation Trix. Poor people food is my food; banging a couple of cans together over a shallow Pyrex dish before sprinkling some noodles and cheese on it then baking it for twenty minutes at 350 degrees is like tugging a threadbare thrift-store sweater onto my stomach, a warm comestible hug. I love all that homestyle shit: casseroles and bundts and cobblers and sheet cakes and rolls; recipes that require Crisco and food coloring and have oxymoronic names like "cheeseburger pie" and "lasagna soup," recipes that cost eight dollars to make and last for a week.

Con: What if I forget what ramps and garlic scapes and morels are?!

If I had to pick a favorite food to eat while sobbing over the kitchen sink, it would probably most definitely be beanie weenies. There is no greater sad joy than cutting up a dollar-store hot dog and putting it in a simmering saucepan of Bush's honey baked beans. To further illustrate the direness of my current situation, I should disclose that I am writing this while eating a frozen bean burrito that might not really be cooked all the way through. I can count the number of fancy meals I have in a month on one hand, but that doesn't mean I don't want the option of rejecting your invitation to go to them. Living in Chicago spoils you, because there are hundreds of places fifteen minutes from wherever you happen to be at any given moment where you can find locally sourced farm-to-table organic meals made by a chef who's probably been on TV. I might not take advantage of them as often as I do, say, Pizza Hut's two mediums for $6.99 deal, but the point is that if I wanted to I could stick up a bank, steal an outfit from a person who doesn't wear pajamas as regular clothes, and order the lily bulb/rambutan/distillation of caviar lime at Alinea any time I want. (Yeah right, I could never get in there.)

Pro: Life would be so simple.

I could wake up to the sound of crowing roosters or methheads at sunrise, consume a platter of buttered carbohydrates, hitch up my overalls, and grab my watering can from the shed. That would be a dream. I'm sick of news, and buying stuff, and trying so desperately to have fun all the time. I just want to watch old *Catfish* episodes on the couch and record videos of Helen's cat snores.

Con: BUT WHAT IF I GET BORED?

Please ignore that I have shunned all available social and physical activity on this lovely Friday evening in order to sit in my darkened apartment, bathed in the blue light of this computer screen while I gaze dolefully at a YouTube video of Justin Bieber singing karaoke in a car. Boredom is a fallacy in my tiny life. I have a fancy phone with lots of apps on it and relatively decent LTE coverage, I haven't been truly "bored" since 2007. And even back then, there were televisions and books and Myspace and pets. But if I wanted to go out and get into something fun, I theoretically could put a jacket on and go do it.

Pro: It's just so goddamn beautiful.

I'm tired of looking at stomped-out cigarettes floating in puddles and rotting old food stinking up the sidewalk. I am getting So Fucking Touchy lately, and I know the problem is me, that Americans have the unalienable right to fill their potholes with dirty diapers and the slimy celery they forgot was in the produce drawer; I would never deign to take that away from anyone. I'm sure nothing feels better than dropping a used Kleenex three feet to the right of a public trash can. But I'm growing tired of grimy cabs and the E. coli factory that is our stretch of Lake Michigan; I could stand to have some trees and weather in my life. I mean, I don't really want to *touch* nature, but I do sometimes like looking at it.

Con: Nature is terrifying.

Last summer Mavis and I spent a weekend in a remote hippie cabin in the woods. It is the plot of every horror movie you've ever seen: white person convinces black person to pack up his/her hair grease, wave cap, and reparations money in the hopes of spending a long relaxing weekend in [vaguely authentic-sounding pseudo–Native American word] [Lake/Falls/Island/Coast] doing white-people things like lying in hammocks and eating fresh apricots. Black person dies before you've even made a dent in your popcorn.

I had my sunglasses, my car snacks, and my road-trip music; I was ready to meet Mavis in the woods. I plugged the address into the GPS on my phone and waited for the pixels and giga-bytes or whatever to plot my route. Finally, Siri heaved a long, weary sigh. "Bitch, are you sure?"

WHAT? I restarted my phone and reentered the address.

Another pregnant pause. "Sa-man-tha, there are no black people within a hundred miles of this destination," bleeped the computerized voice. "Would you instead like directions to the Essence Fest? I think Mary J. Blige is performing."

"THAT WAS LAST WEEK!" I shrieked, pounding the address into the phone again. "JUST TELL ME HOW TO GET TO THIS COUNTRY SHIT." Another long pause as she calculated directions. I watched a map slowly appear on the screen, my course charted in blue. "Anything in the whole town comes up missing over the next three days and your black ass is going to jail," Siri warned nastily, and I threw the phone into the backseat. I spent three hours on tranquil highways and hilly back roads littered with raccoon and deer carcasses, vainly attempting to eat a sandwich like a civilized person while also dodging families of ducks as they toddled across the unmarked road. I passed dozens of tiny houses set back from the high-way with ancient cars and boats rusting under the sun on their front lawns. I could smell the methamphetamines cooking in the air. "IN A QUARTER MILE, TURN LEFT AT THE COW," Siri cackled viciously. "IN TWO HUNDRED FEET MAKE A SLIGHT RIGHT AT THE HORSE ONTO A DIRT ROAD, AND TRY NOT TO GET MAULED BY A BEAR FOR THOSE FIG NEWTONS HIDDEN IN

YOUR BACKPACK, STUPID." I could've died out there for real.

I am on the precipice of abandoning my whirlwind single-person existence for what is essentially a trust fall into my new relationship, but I cannot envision my life in a crib that has stairs. Or a crib with more than three rooms. Or a crib that has well-meaning neighbors who drop by without giving you a heads-up to take out the trash and hide your prescriptions prior to their arrival. I currently live across the hall from a person who, seemingly unprovoked, screams bloody murder. And upstairs from a person who sings arias in a lovely tenor at hours and decibels that regularly make me want to kill myself. Those people are referred to as Screaming Woman and Opera Dude, respectively. I am literally never going to talk to them. I will never know their real names. See also: Smooth-Jazz Guy and Bedhead Lady with Obvious Cats. If I walk into the building and see someone headed toward the elevator, I idle near the mailbox until I hear the gate slam shut, then hustle over to it before some equally awkward stranger comes home and ruins my meticulously executed plan for riding the elevator up to my floor in peace. I do my laundry at five on Monday mornings because I am generally very polite and four years ago I was forced into twenty minutes of witty banter with a decently hot gentleman while trying to hide behind my back a pair of underwear that needed pretreating. One night, Smooth-Jazz Guy and I exited our apartments at the same time, and I froze at my end of the hall, pretending I couldn't possibly figure out which of the four keys on my key ring was the one that locked my door. I could just *feel* him waiting to say something about Peabo Bryson to me, and once I could finally stall no longer

I walked toward him as he exclaimed, "Hey, [fellow black]! I never knew you lived here! Come by for a drink sometime!"

What's worse than being stung to death by thousands of bees? Sitting in an apartment adjacent to yours balanced precariously on a stranger's bed while sipping a glass of Chivas Regal and listening to Najee, or sitting in an apartment adjacent to yours balanced precariously on a stranger's bed sipping a glass of Chivas Regal and listening to Najee?! I AM NEVER EVER DOING THAT. And it has nothing to do with him— I'm sure he's charming and hospitable and has an incredible selection of Take 6 records. But yo, I would rather be mauled by that *Revenant* bear than strike up a friendship with someone who would inevitably do horrible things like "knock on my door" or "sign for my FedEx packages." I have been alone for so long that the idea of community is legit terrifying to me. I'm anxious and easily flummoxed, and I don't want anyone seeing the maxi pads in my trash or how many books I leave next to the toilet. I don't want people to know that there's only bologna and Crystal Light in my fridge. Seriously, I don't want to have to explain why I have so many bottles of hand soap on each sink (I like variety, okay) and half-melted Diptyque candles scattered everywhere (I SAID I LIKE SOME GOD-DAMNED VARIETY).

The idea of being part of a community is daunting. Despite how open I am on the Internet, I am fiercely private IRL. Which is to say that I am often a hermit because I never want anyone to see my actual pores or clothes. I have grown increasingly uncomfortable with large groups of people, but this isn't really that. This is more like "Why would you ever want to come inside where I live?" or "I just don't get why we have to talk in your living room when there are dozens of perfectly good restaurants five minutes from here." But this summer I am moving. To a neighborhood like one on TV. Where I have to keep a bra on all the time because kids are always just letting themselves in for impromptu playdates and you never know who might be dropping by with a bag of extra grapefruits from their CSA box or some vegan Korean food fresh from the farmers' market. (That very specific example happened once, thank you, Sarah Hill!) In Chicago I have this tiny little universe that has a dead bolt and a door buzzer, but you'd never come over anyway because there's nowhere to park and Opera Dude really does get in the way of meaningful conversation a lot of the time. However, in Michigan, we have giant windows with no blinds (WHITE PEOPLE), a skateboard ramp in the driveway, and a tire swing hanging from the big oak tree in the yard, and do I even need to finish this sentence? I will never be able to just let my tits hang ever again.

I tell anyone who is ever interested that my ideal long-term romantic relationship is one in which my partner and I have separate apartments in the same building. Or in buildings across the street from each other. Or in buildings on opposite sides of town. Or in buildings on opposite sides of the state. Or in buildings in different states altogether. I have very little interest in joint cohabitation. Seriously, almost none, save for the fact that if a person had a big television and was willing to pay for premium cable and give me 70/30 ownership of the remote, then I would maybe *consider* it. I mean, come on. Hers and hers houses?! Such a jam. Up until now, Mavis and I have spent two years in different states and that has been a dream—95 percent of the time I can watch *Love & Hip Hop* without pausing every five seconds to explain the difference between Yung Joc and Lil Scrappy, I can use a spoon to cut pizza, I can sleep like a fucking starfish spread across the bed: it's glorious. I can keep my shit together for 5 percent. I can keep the laundry folded, the dishes put away, the lumps fluffed out of the duvet, and the bathtub spotless for 5 percent of the time. 5 percent Sam buys fresh-cut tulips and displays them in stone vases; 5 percent Sam throws out the expired yogurts and keeps chilled rosé in the fridge; 5 percent Sam is the kind of person you want to live with.

But 95 percent Sam is gonna be a problem. I'm not sure what I'm gonna do about all my gross habits. My cans of Mexi-corn, my seventeen Q-tips after every shower, my irregular mopping, my dresser covered with pill bottles, my cat food everywhere, my cat hair everywhere, my pile of indiscernible black laundry, my dirty Birkenstocks scattered in corners far and wide, my dinner in bed (these people sit down to break-fast, lunch, and dinner at the table and I will literally die if they expect me to do that, by the way, who the fuck eats actual *lunch*). How can I really hide who I am from these people who only know a sanitized version of me if they are everywhere I am, all the time? I'm gonna have to start a swear jar at work in the few months before I pack my valuable belongings into one and a half trash bags and move them to a house with children running around it. No bullshit, I gotta figure out a way to stop saying "bitch" so much before one of these shorties rolls up on me while I'm cussing Helen out for being such a vile little piece of garbage and runs away screaming to tattle on me. Every morning when that naughty, uh, *scamp* bites me awake at five o'clock I'm really going to have to grit my teeth and say, "Good morning, cat!" instead of "I'M EUTHANIZING YOUR BITCH-ASS TODAY, YOU FUCKING BITCH" like I normally would.

I don't know, man. I'm just dubious of spending the major-ity of my awake minutes with someone I show my privates to who also needs to know how much money I am making and is keeping a mental checklist of all the times I forget to drag the recycling to the curb. And also being in a town without real bagels. People are boring and terrible. I am boring and terrible. My funny runs out, my cute runs out, my smart sometimes hiccups, my sexy wakes up with uncontrollable diarrhea. I have an attitude. And a sharp edge! I'm impatient. I like the whole bed. I hate anyone touching and moving my haphazardly arranged possessions all the time. Plus, I'm a downright horrible sharer, and I can't guarantee that I won't write my name on something in the refrigerator I don't want her to eat. These quirks, if I'm being generous, have had thirty-six years to consolidate into one giant mass of "mine." How do you get over that? Am I going to need hypnosis?!

There's so much single-person stuff I still need time to do! And, I know, you're all "Fuck other people?" but I'm over here like "Nah, my dude. I mean eat lunch meats rolled up in a tortilla because I don't have any real bread while watching *Jackie Brown* on my laptop" or "Try on all of the lipsticks in my apartment while taking a series of poorly lit selfies I'm never going to show anyone . . . again." I do so much shit I don't want anyone else to see, or know about, that I never want to have to explain to another human being. And I want to keep doing them. I enjoy listening to the Young Turks really loud in the bathroom while I take a long shower, then spending a considerable amount of time moisturizing my various parts. This is not a bad thing, it's not even a particularly creepy thing, but it is the kind of thing that might be weird when other people are living in your house. Waiting for that bathtub. Wondering what's taking you so long and who your imaginary talking friends are.

I want to still have time to sit staring at the wall for hours with both my headphones and the television on, daydreaming about what I would wear to the Golden Globes, as if I'd ever have a reason to go to the Golden fucking Globes. I want to watch porn by myself, and movies by myself, and *Black-ish* by myself. Basically anything I ever want to see is best enjoyed alone, under a blanket, with a hot-water bottle propped against my back and no other noise whatsoever. I like to dance to MIA while I cook, if you understand "cook" to mean "make food that I sample so frequently during its preparation that the end result is already leftovers." I can't do that horrifying shit if I live with some foxy lady and her kids! I mean really, do you think she's going to be supine across my freshly changed bed linens looking hot and awesome and still want to rip me out of my chonies after watching me cry for hours at videos of people surprising each other? The answer is no. No, she will not.

But I still want to do it. So does that mean this next phase is doomed? Because I can keep my apartment clean and safe and inviting for a night, for a weekend, for maybe even a week, but that day-to-day shit ain't happening. I am obviously destined to die alone, in giant panties that come up to my chin, with half a gallon of pasta sauce I haven't even added oregano to par-tially digested in my stomach, mouth frozen in a silent "Fuck."

thirteen questions to ask before getting married

Mavis and I are getting married next month and she just sent me this article from the *New York Times* like "LOL ISN'T THIS HILARIOUS?" but joke's on that hoe, I'ma answer this shit without telling her and put it in the fucking book. I see you, bitch.

1. Did your family throw plates, calmly discuss issues, or silently shut down when disagreements arose?
The man whose ashes I ate punched me in the face once for incorrectly washing a cast iron pan, so I guess that qualifies as "throwing plates"? But here is the thing—in my haphazard and inconsistent childhood, I was never living with any person long enough to ever establish any sort of real patterns. In the Cooper-Irby household there was no such thing as, say, Meat Loaf Mondays. Or Christmas Eve at Grandma's. (And thank God for that because my skinny, mean grandma would've set a plate of sardines and grits out for Santa and embarrassed my ass because homeboy was looking for cookies.) I come from a

fractured group of individuals who don't even all have the same last name, let alone any traditions, but, once, my dad hit my mother in the head with a frying pan during an argument, so I guess that's how we get down. Maybe you should pick fights in a room with a lot of soft stuff in it. HOLD UP, I THINK I FINALLY RECOGNIZE A PATTERN.

2. Will we have children, and if we do, will you change diapers?

HELLO, PATRIARCHY. I'm not having any babies. I want to give a smug answer about how much money and free time I have because I still don't got kids (so much, so so much, and if you don't get that reference go do your googles), but let's talk about my real fears when it comes to my parenting a child.

2a. I pretty much stopped learning things after high school.

Now, don't get me wrong, I read shit all the time. Even smart shit like *Vanity Fair* and *The New Yorker*, even though it seems like it takes me four months to get through a single issue. I watch Rachel Maddow and listen to a couple of podcasts when I remember they exist, but I don't know how to do trigonometry. And I cannot remember anything from a single history class I've ever taken, so unless tenth graders are being tested on *BuzzFeed* listicles and how to keep track of all the bogus e-mail addresses you've created to sign up for multiple thirty-day Tidal trials and ModCloth discount codes, I do not know anything of use to a modern-day child. I can show a kid how to make a satisfying meal out of stale saltines and leftover aloo gobi, but that is basically it. I wasn't parented past the age of thirteen, and it shows. I once blew a car engine because I had no idea what an oil change was. I didn't even have a coat last winter, I just doubled up hoodies and wrapped a scarf the size of a tablecloth around my shaved head. IN CHICAGO. I have a lot of what polite people call "life experience," which is a nice way of saying I possess skills like "can find a café with free Wi-Fi blindfolded" and "able to spot an overdue bill from a glance at the back of the envelope."

2b. I hate going outside, and talking to people can be excruciating.

I'm depressed, man. Lexapro gave me night terrors, so I stopped taking it and haven't yet tried an alternative because I value my newfound ability to sleep through the night. I didn't have out-door parents, and I'm not all that mad about it. You say "walk in the park," I hear "runny nose, itchy eyes." You say "picnic in the grass," I hear "bugs stinging and birds pooping on me."

And exactly what am I supposed to do during soccer prac-tice every week? Or during Girl Scouts? Have you ever lis-tened to people with kids talk to other people with kids? It is a strange and confusing language that I don't ever want to understand. I don't ever want to listen to two people debat-ing over whether school lunches should be non-GMO. I have absolutely zero opinions on things like that. Also, I would buy my kid a hundred TVs just to get him right on up out of my goddamned face. So many things that people have to do to make good, well-rounded people out of their children are such a hassle for the parent. If she has to learn to play the cello, I have to: buy the cello, find the instructor, and drive her to the lessons. Not to mention the half hour every afternoon I have to subject myself to living in a house WITH A CHILD TER-RIBLY PLAYING THE CELLO. And sure, I would probably get a lot of reading done squashed behind the wheel of my sensible midsize crossover vehicle in the parking lot behind the ice-skating rink to avoid gossiping with the other moms about which of our standout left wings will be arrested first for assault, but then I'd be the type of person who was forced to purchase something called a midsize crossover vehicle.

We're talking a minimum of sixteen years that I would be responsible for taking a young, defenseless creature out into the wild and protecting her from people who say damaging shit like, "Aren't you a pretty princess!" Years of talking on the phone to women named Caitlin who want to make sure I know that my snack for the slumber party has to be gluten- and sugar- and peanut-free. Years of neighbor children being forbidden from crossing the threshold of my home because I let my son eat microwave snacks while talking on his personal cell phone and playing murder games on the computer in front of the television while I lie on the floor under the dining room table with an ice pack on my head with strict orders for him not to interrupt me unless the house catches fire. And even then, what the fuck am I going to do? Call 911, you stupid kid.

I could go on. I could add another 296 things to this list and still not even scratch the surface of why my having a child is a bad idea, the first of which is that you already have some, and if your white kids were to gang up on my black kid, I would have no problem starting a race war in our home. I can see it now: I come home from the bar where I spend my afternoons crying and wishing I had made different choices in my life to find White 1 and White 2 playing slave auction or some other horrible game with my baby. I burn the house down with all of us in it, screaming whatever lines I can remember from *Django Unchained* at the top of my lungs. So yeah, we're not going to adopt.

3. Will our experiences with our exes help or hinder us?
Well, I can't be hindered by dead people, so I'm all good.
JUST PLAYING, WISHING SOMEONE WERE DEAD
DOESN'T MAKE IT REAL, SAM.

**4. How important is religion? How will we celebrate
religious holidays, if at all?**
I was raised in church. And you tried to hold my hand in
the middle of that one service I took you to, the one during
which my sister led the choir in a rousing rendition of a song
I'm pretty sure was called "Jesus Does Not Like Lesbians," so
I'm confident in saying that you've never been to church a
day in your life. If I had to declare a religion for a census, I'd
probably choose "agnostic," because the parts of the Bible I've
read are just, like, a really boring soap opera that's dragged on
for too many seasons, but I *refuse* to believe it's a coincidence
that when R and I broke up in the front seat of his Pontiac
"Breakdown" by Mariah Carey came on the radio at the exact
moment he was avoiding eye contact and mumbling, "I don't
think this is gonna work out, dawg." To which I very earnestly
responded, in song, "I be feelin' like you bringing me down,
taking me around, stressin' me out; I think I better go and
get out and let me release some stress (stress)," in time with
the music. If that isn't the universe intervening to keep me
from beating a motherfucker to death with a broken window
scraper, I don't know what is. I sat there for the last 1:47 of the
song with the door cracked and sang my lungs out while R
provided backing vocals before I got out. And then we never
spoke again. LOOK AT GOD.
   Even though I don't care about organized religion, I still

feel some type of way when people who weren't forced to sit in stiff ruffles and too-tight patent leather mary janes for four hours every Sunday morning get to just, you know, buy an Easter basket without having done any of the work. Those jelly beans and Cadbury eggs were my annual reward for memorizing the Twenty-third Psalm and not falling asleep during Sunday school, and yet somehow there are kids who get to sleep in every weekend and have never had to identify Bible passages from memory who get the same number of jelly beans I do?! It doesn't even matter, but I resented it. How did you earn those Christmas presents if you've never had to spend hours after school making a life-size diorama of the manger that will be displayed in the church's vestibule three weeks past the time it should've been carted down to the basement?

Here's how we're going to celebrate holidays: Sunday mornings I'm going to walk around yanking curtains open at the crack of dawn, singing "Victory Is Mine" and cooking eggs and bacon while bumping the gospel station at top volume, then I'll rush you to get dressed because we need to get to service in time to get my favorite seat behind Sister Augustine. We're going to leave our phones at home, get to church at ten thirty on the dot, tithe our combined 20 percent, kneel before the pastor during altar call, "mm-hmm" during the good word, then go home at four to eat dinner and watch some wholesome TV. *Touched by an Angel* or some shit. After many months of this, then, and only then, will you have earned the right to call that dried-up spruce the cats keep launching themselves into a "Christmas tree."

5. Is my debt your debt? Would you be willing to bail me out?

Bail you out of what, jail? Yes, of course, especially since I like to keep a bail bondsman on the payroll at all times just in case.

The smartest decision I have ever made in my entire dumb life was dropping out of college. Other than a few early mistakes that are being excised from my virtually nonexistent credit file every year—why did I ever agree to have a home phone with a roommate who ran up $700 in international calls?—I don't have a single crushing financial obligation. No student loans, no tax liens, no baby mamas snatching up half my check. And see, the way my money is set up? Your debt is gonna have to be yours, champ. Unless I get to claim that master's degree, too.

This is not to say that I won't lavish you with gifts and pay for exotic vacations to places in America that have large black populations, but I'm not filing my taxes jointly ever. First of all, I like to do that work on the Internet and keep it moving. I saw you sitting at the dining room table with your old-timey visor and graphing calculator adding up expenses and sorting through receipts, and, yeah, I'm never going to do that. It relaxes me to think that by paying the most possible taxes, I'm keeping my karma right, so just let me live with that delusion. Second, I want to have a secret bank account for emergencies like Miu Miu sunglasses and last-minute reservations at Maude's, and I'm pretty sure you don't live like that. You pay off your credit card balance every month and none of your bills are behind, so shouldn't I really be asking this of you? I will give you whatever you need, provided that you catch me after my direct deposit clears but before the Old Navy coupon codes hit my in-box. If you need money the same day Lane Bryant does their semiannual bra sale you better wake up early in the morning to ask me for it, because as soon as I wipe the sleep out of my eyes I'ma be clickety-click clacking. Do you know how expensive keeping my nipples off my kneecaps is?! So do what you can to plan your emergencies around sale season.

6. What's the most you would be willing to spend on a car, a couch, shoes?

I wear one pair of shoes. One pair only, every day, unless it's snowing. And even then I change out of my boots and back into my one pair of shoes as soon as I'm safely out of the elements. I have one pair of Finn Comfort Augustas, they cost $375 a pop, and I replace that pair annually. Who knows if I'll remain faithful to you, but I will never cheat on these perfect shoes ever. They come from a place in the suburbs called Waxberg's, where a gentleman named Irving measures my feet and watches me walk and forbids me from ever having another pair of flip-flops cross the threshold of my home. I'm not trying to put too fine a point on it, but these jams changed my life. If they went up to $500, I'd still buy them. I might have to cancel my Spotify to work them into the budget, but it can be done.

I've already bought a couch for you and that couch was $900. So . . . $900.

I'm gonna buy a car this year and it's gonna be great. I have never before purchased a car from a reputable dealership, the kind of place where the salesmen wear ties and offer you water while they roll their eyes at your credit score before offering up some loan-shark contract that involves putting up your firstborn child or the deed to your house as collateral. All of my rusted-out matchbox cars were purchased from somebody's dying grandma or from tiny lots where you can pay for your new Chevy with a combination of expired food stamps and lottery tickets. So now that I am an adult who is going to be living in a house with a driveway, I am going to buy a big black truck with a booming system and shock absorbers so I can silently weep as I float over the potholes without disrupting so much as an eyelash. I'm going to glide into the drive-thru, effortlessly lowering my childproof window to whisper my fried chicken order directly into the mic instead of dislocating my shoulder trying to roll the window down before shouting unintelligibly at the helpless person inside who can't understand why a person whose car is barely three inches off the ground wouldn't just bring her lazy ass inside.

I will take every road trip and helm every carpool on brandnew fully inflated tires, an iced coffee in every cup holder, while getting free oil changes every three months because that's the kind of thing written into the fine print of a multipage lease agreement rather than a bill of sale hastily scribbled on the back of an unpaid FedEx invoice (you know this is too specific not to be true). I don't care what it costs. I am a grown-up lady who doesn't have any cartilage in her arthritic knees and I deserve to have a car whose seat slides back electronically. No auxiliary cord? No problem! Because the Bluetooth already connected to your iPod and Beyoncé's dulcet tones are soothing your weary eardrums before you've even fastened your seat belt. In my old Escort, I used to have this little device that would play a Walkman through one of the staticky radio stations at either of the far ends of the dial. I would make a mixtape, put batteries in a portable cassette player, connect it to the adapter, set the dial to 88.2 or 107.8 or whatever, then cruise around to the barely audible strains of "Essaywhuman?!!!??!" et al. for approximately forty-seven minutes before the batteries tapped out or the connection died. *That* is the story I need to tell when people ask me "How could you *possibly* be sad?!" in earnest.

7. Can you deal with my doing things without you?

In fact, I would prefer it. I like a lot of alone time, you know, for things like scrolling through the Jibri website for four hours, trying on clothes in my mind. Or plucking my chin whiskers while sobbing over that movie where Winona Ryder is dying from a heart tumor and Richard Gere is in love with her but somehow just can't stop fucking other people, so yeah, maybe I need to be alone as I process all that imaginary grief for the ninety-seventh time.

I don't understand couples who do everything together. If I'm going to see you at home, I don't *also* need to see you while agonizing over which flavor of Hot Pockets to get. I would like to have my own relationship with the dry cleaner, thank you very much, not smile off to the side while you guys have your familiar little "light starch on the gray slacks!" morning banter. I'm going to the coffee shop you hate, so it can be *my* coffee shop. You're getting groceries from the white chick with dreadlocks over at the organic co-op? Well, fine, I'ma get my provisions for the week at Target, along with a car battery, six lightbulbs, a desk calendar, and a handful of Revlon lipsticks. I like having my own shit.

The thing is, I have no idea how to exist within a family unit. Despite my efforts, I have never lived with a romantic partner before; the last time I shared a house with someone, we divided the light bill in half and wrote our names on our respective milks. I don't know how to coexist in a place where people don't scribble names on their food or hide their pharmaceuticals on the top shelf of the closet. I still live like I'm in a foster home, hiding my trash at the bottom of the can because I don't want anyone to know how many Little Debbie oatmeal pies I ate under the covers after dark. And I am still like "Will she notice how much of this body wash I used . . . ?" while tucking the bottle behind a bigger one for fear that you're going to yell at me about how I always use up the expensive shit. Forget being hit or kicked—the real terror of my childhood was tiptoeing around trying to disguise all the precious resources I was using up. Sometimes a person's damage is obvious: yelling, violence, defensiveness. But in some cases it looks like walking around with a plastic bag full of trash in your backpack when you didn't spend last night at home because of a baseless worry that someone will look through it and hold its contents against you.

I am still learning that no one is going to mark the level of the shampoo before I take a shower so they'll know whether I use a squeeze. And that I don't have to hide my dirty clothes. However, I *will* put a password on my computers and shit, I know how you feel about unauthorized screen time. And also those naked pictures of you on my desktop.

8. Do we like each other's parents?

Is this a trick question? My parents, as I can't stop reminding people, ARE DEAD. Which means you are one of the lucky people on this planet who never has to suffer through any of my mom's silent scrutiny of your potato salad (she would eat it, but she would not approve) or humor my father as he not-so-secretly drinks every drop of cognac you have in that high cabinet where we keep the plates yet gently berates you about how children in his house weren't allowed to whistle, let alone speak to him while looking him in the eye. He would fall asleep in the rocking chair while my mom washed all the dinner dishes and excused herself multiple times to anxiously smoke cigarettes in the driveway, and then she'd serve her contribution to the meal: a cake from a box mix baked in her finest cat-shaped mold. At some point in the evening I would have to take you aside to explain that I was going to sell the children's piano to fund the latest of my father's harebrained schemes, but that he'd assured me that *this one* was going to be the one that finally paid back a return on my investment. There'd inevitably be a fight of some kind, resulting in your having to drive my sobbing mother home and my body-slamming an old-ass man in the middle of the TV room while your kids cower in fear in the kitchen. So I guess what I'm saying is that death can sometimes be pretty great.

I will have to keep your parents at arm's length because yours is the kind of family that goes on extended vacations in the wilderness together, and I'm afraid that if they like me too much, they will expect me to go with, and I am doing no such thing. You get only one chance to drag me to the woods, and I already let you take me to that isolated cabin in the middle of nowhere for three days with no phone and no Wi-Fi, so see you when you get back. I can't remember the last time one of my sisters and I went to the grocery store together, and I can't think of anything less relaxing than revisiting a fight that began in 1993 while slowly developing a bacterial infection from a wet bathing suit. I imagine there are two types of orphans: people who can't wait to jump into a ready-made family or build their own from scratch, and the kind I am: get your heartwarming holiday cards away from me ASAP. You know what I can do, since I don't have a mom anymore? Write "I love big dicks in my pussyhole" on the Internet without worrying about getting a disappointed phone call immediately after.

I haven't had to justify anything I have or haven't done to anyone in my whole adult life (PS: it feels amazing). I also haven't had to suffer through a forced Thanksgiving dinner or Aunt Barbara's retirement party or cousin Julie's baby shower, and, sure, I have an iPad, but unless you let me stay in the car, your padre is totally going to be all "FOR REAL, SAMANTHA" and hit me with the "I didn't raise you like this" eyes. And the thing is? No, he did not. And I respect that moms gotta mom no matter whose kid they're talking to, so I'm definitely not inviting your girl over for a bottle of—I don't know, what do moms drink? Sauvignon blanc? Costco wine?—so she can knit her eyebrows together in concern while waiting for me to offer up an explanation for why I wrote "LinkedIn is emailing people that today is my 14th anniversary at my job, but damn, I wanted to write my suicide note myself" on Twitter this morning.

9. How important is sex to you?

Is there such a thing as the opposite of important? Because that's what I would choose. Maybe this is the depression talking, or maybe years of masturbating with the most powerful vibrators on the market have broken my vagina, but at the end of a long day, the last thing I want to do is stand up more. Or put on clothes that someone else might find visually arousing. Hopefully lesbian bed death is real and not another unattainable fantasy the Internet has lied to me about, like poreless skin.

10. How far should we take flirting with other people? Is watching pornography okay?

I used to bang this dude who was really into female body-builder porn. And while that's not necessarily my bag, because I like to watch soft naked bodies jiggling like chocolate pudding on a spoon, I was totally down with it. I didn't do a single triceps curl for the entirety of that relationship, either. I walked in on him jerking off to an ass like a library book bouncing up and down on some shriveled steroid dick, then walked right out and down the block to Dragon Gate. Because, listen—if he is getting what he needs from watching two leviathans bang into each other like bumper cars while oozing streaky orange self-tanner, then I am just going to get these eggrolls and post up in the other room with a pile of magazines.

I am partial to mature lesbian porn, because I'm old, and while I would never call it "lovemaking," that is *exactly* what I wanna watch. I like watching two ladies (or men) with a few miles on 'em kissing passionately on the mouth and having real orgasms. I am forever here for gratuitous cumshots and clenched ass cheeks thrusting away for twenty real minutes (how do they do that?), but I have never been excited to watch two straight girls kiss like it's icky while plucking at each other's clitoris like a banjo string. I don't need soft music or a backstory, but I would very much like to believe that these people are both at least marginally attracted to each other and experiencing legitimate pleasure. Porn is a quick and easy way for me to release some tension through a vaginal sneeze without having to undo my bra or take my shoes off, and I will never stop watching it, especially now that it is free, and I ain't gotta hide my sex DVDs at the bottom of my sock drawer when company comes. Sex is messy and exhausting, and if you'd like to masturbate alone while I am sleeping or watching sports, have at it.

Flirting is one of my main forms of social currency. I don't mean actual gross hitting on people, but if your mom comes up to me at a reading, then I'm going to look deep into her eyes and say, "You look amazing in magenta, Margaret," without breaking my gaze, and she is going to swoon and buy six copies of my book and, duh, love me forever. I'm not kidding, Margaret is going to shout down the other members of her book club when they try to dismiss this trash as vulgar and disgusting (they might have a point) and storm out of Betsy's house in a cloud of Chanel perfume because I wrote "I would love to toss your salad, girl" inside the front cover of her copy. Listen, I would never lead someone to think that I would actually want to have sex, because yuck, see above. But everyone loves eye contact and eating butts!

It's so weird to me that adults in committed relationships have a problem with something so seemingly innocuous as flirting. I would never expect you to walk around with a paper bag over your head to avoid catching the eye of a stranger, nor would I discourage your making friendly conversation with whomever you might encounter during the day. And look, if you needed to fuck somebody else, we could talk about it. People change, our desires evolve, and it feels foolish to me to expect that what you'll want two, five, or ten years from now will be exactly the same thing that fills you up today. I mean, the way I feel about fidelity has evolved over the last ten years of my life. It's a hard-and-fast rule that we don't apply to any other thing in our lives: YOU MUST LOVE THIS [SHOW/BOOK/FOOD/SHIRT] WITH UNWAVERING FERVOR FOR THE REST OF YOUR NATURAL LIFE. Could you imagine being forced to listen to your favorite record from before your music tastes were refined for the rest of your life? Right now I'm pretty sure I could listen to *Midnight Snack* by HOMESHAKE for the rest of my life, but me ten years ago was really into acoustic Dave Matthews, and I'm not sure how I feel about that today. And yes, I am oversimplifying it, but really, if in seven years you want to have sex with the proverbial milkman, just let me know about it beforehand so I can hide my LaCroix and half-eaten wedge of port salut. ("Milkmen" always eat all the good snacks.)

11. Do you know all the ways I say "I love you"?
I guess so, but the most important one is that time I came home after an Amtrak ride from the pit of hell and my pajamas were already laid out and my night banana and half-full glass of room-temperature water were waiting on the bedside table for me.

12. What do you admire about me, and what are your pet peeves?
Likes:

- You look real good in a pair of tight-ass jeans.
- You can eat more food than anyone I have ever met and I'm pretty old.
- Your laugh.

- That time you dropped your credit card at a tollbooth was pretty hilarious.
- You don't stink even though you wear homemade deodorant.
- You scoop all the cat poops, which is sick.
- I asked you to learn all the dance moves in the P Diddy and Ma$e "Been Around the World" remix video and dance them with me and you did.

Dislikes:

- I do not enjoy being kissed in the middle of the grocery store.

13. How do you see us ten years from now?

Living is a mistake. If good things ever happened to me, I would say that some grief-stricken mutual friend of ours will be sobbing gently while digging up the yard of one of my many enemies to plant trees fed by our biodegradable burial pods so that he forever has to live his life in my shade. But everything is garbage, and the universe never gives me what I want. So, sadly, we'll still be alive, and I will definitely be luxuriating in the recliner you haven't let me buy but I'm scheming to get anyway. That's a good foundation for a healthy marriage, right? Having a plush, comfy rocking recliner that clashes with the house's current midcentury modern design just show up on your doorstep and being like *shrug* when your wife objects? I mean, it's already here, we might as well watch an *SVU* marathon in it . . . ?

yo, i need a job.

Dear Sir or Madam,

   I am writing to you regarding your company's customer service representative opening. I have been working as the client
services director, which is a mostly fictional title, at an animal
hospital for the last fourteen years and have developed substan-
dard phone manners while also somehow managing to maintain a tenuous grasp on my sanity. I am used to an incredibly
busy and fast-paced environment, serving as a personal assistant
to seven doctors, each with drastically different personalities
and demands, as well as being an unpaid servant and chamber-
maid to literally thousands of wealthy suburbanites and their
unruly pets.

My duties included, but were never limited to:

- answering phones without an attitude
- swallowing my pride while people talked down their
  noses to me about cat vaccines

- feeling chagrined as clients made jokes like, "Brought you a present!" while tossing steaming bags of dog feces for parasite screening on the desk next to my iced tea
- getting bitten on the leg more than once without murdering anyone involved
- staying awake for eleven hours at a stretch despite the 50 mg of Benadryl in my system, because believe it or not, I am allergic to stupid cats
- sniff-testing the effectiveness of industrial-strength institutional-grade air fresheners against the smells released from animal mouths, butts, and inner ears
- fielding questions like "Why is there a worm coming out of my dog's penis?" (A: That is his penis.)
- giving meticulously detailed driving directions to the practice over the telephone in 2016
- ordering enough office supplies to both cover the anticipated needs of the clinic and also offset the collateral damage inflicted on the supply closet by the staff. (Who needs thirty-six blue ballpoint pens in their house, I mean, who?)
- making playlists full of dope yet inoffensive midtempo jams as a subtle reminder that they had chosen a hospital with cool-ass motherfuckers working there yet ones who are savvy enough to know that you can't have the word "shit" unbleeped during business hours

I'm very good at covertly grinding my teeth down to stumps as gentlemen who've clearly chased a soiled diaper with bitter espresso wheeze instructions on how to best do a job I have held for the entirety of my adult life directly into my face. And while my brain says, "Go kill yourself," my mask remains a placid lake of serenity, whose surface remains unrippled despite the frothy rage boiling just beneath its surface.

I am also exceptional at keeping a straight face at the same time a person asks, "Ugh, is this table clean?" while pointing in disgust at a sterilized table upon which she has been asked to set a creature who is enthusiastically licking its own asshole. Or when a man primed to spend upward of $100 on pain pills for a dog complains about how much his 100 percent optional companion animal is costing him, despite his having paid twenty-five hundred real American dollars to bring that purebred host to all manner of insect, arachnid, and parasite into his home.

I excel at remaining outwardly calm on the telephone while women yell at me about cat dandruff on speakerphone from within the lush confines of their roomy Land Rovers. I'm totally able to keep a cool head as someone explains to me in a condescending tone how of course she can't come in to get [redacted]'s flaky dry skin checked out at four thirty; she has a job. Don't I know what having a work schedule is like?!

I'm superb at seeming interested in the thirty-seventh conversation of the day about the weather, or feigning surprise at how congested Main Street is on a Tuesday afternoon. I don't give a shit about traffic. Or weather. Or any combination thereof. Want to know what the last thing the hourly wage drone trapped behind a desk in a windowless office for eleven-plus hours wants to hear from a person who clearly has a lot of in-the-middle-of-the-fucking-day free time on her hands? How beautiful it is outside. How gorgeous the clouds are and how wonderful the air feels. Oh, you didn't have to wear a jacket today? WELL GLORY BE, DIANE. I don't care! For me, today is the same temperature-controlled sixty-eight degrees it is every other goddamned day. Storm clouds? Sixty-eight degrees. Blizzard? Still sixty-eight degrees. I mean, sometimes I turn on the ceiling fan if I really want to feel like I'm living my best life, but even then it's still only sixty-eight degrees with a light breeze. Dude, every day I dream of chewing my wrists open and emptying them until I'm dead. I really ought to get out and enjoy that sunshine, I get it. But then who would sell you your dog's outrageously priced limited-protein food?!

I can and will answer to many names that aren't my own, "Hello, Stephanie? Sabrina? Salmonella, is that you?" I have been referred to as the "nice African-American woman" on the phone more times than I can count. Which is interesting because I am decidedly not nice. "Mildly unpleasant" would work just fine, I think. Speaking of my awful voice and face, even though a lot of Dianes have been looking at the same scowl for the past fourteen years, three months, and handful of days, many of them think of me as their friend. Which is surprising, even to me, and so my friend-making-under-duress skills will obviously be an asset in my new position. I totally understand why watching this metamorphosis over the last decade would fool someone into thinking he knows me in real life. I scheduled their rag doll's tooth surgery! I faxed their bichon's Bordetella vaccine to the kennel! And sure, they often don't remember my name, but they've invited me out to lunch (dreading that I might take them up on it), asked me over to their actual houses for dinner (really, really dreading that I might wear my work jeans stinking of Roccal-D into their homes), and on one special instance, paid for my books that one semester I decided I was going to finish my degree (okay, that was actually amazing). The nice ones come in with boxes of chocolate and cases of beer and bottles of wine, grateful that an adult woman who got a thirty-three on the ACT dedicated most of her life to explaining the difference between fleas and ticks to college freshmen who use their meal allotment money to buy corgi puppies from shady Craigslist breeders. One time, when I was in Whole Foods with a cart full of shit pretending to be rich, I ran into this woman who was so thankful that I'd talked her through getting her dog to vomit up the carcass of a squirrel the week before that she bought all of my groceries. I don't know why I'm resistant to say so, but I am actually quite good at serving a customer.

Upon finding out that I work in an animal hospital, people are usually like, "Aww! You must love pets! Are all the puppies and kitties so cute?!" And then they blink real hard and smile with all of their teeth showing, waiting for me to regale them with heartwarming stories of cats rescued from trees and dogs that save little boys who've fallen down the local well. They picture my day to be like Belle's in *Beauty and the Beast*, except instead of skipping through the French countryside, I'm limping through the suburbs, waving hello to the baker and the cobbler as they tip their caps while I struggle past, carrying a backpack full of a halfhearted attempt at lunch I already don't want to eat and anxiety meds in lieu of a basket laden with library books, ruffling the heads of children I pass on their way to school. This imaginary hospital is little more than a modernized gingerbread house, purring kitties and floppy-eared dogs bounding after me with their bushy tails wagging as I flip on the lights and turn on the fans and cast open the shades to let the sunshine stream in. No animals are violent or in critical condition, and all of them are well behaved enough to roam free, maybe alighting on my shoulder as I hand Mr. Martin his parcel of healing tonics and tinctures I've made myself, the price of which he wouldn't dream of haggling over. Cool breezes blow through open windows that no dog is actively trying to commit suicide through, and who needs doctors when the needles and blades just come to life and perform the operations themselves?!

In reality, I stumble through blinding snow from the train at 7:20 in the morning to the darkened door, grope blindly down the pitch-black hallway to find the keypad that shuts off the alarm, then have thirty seconds to enter the four-digit code before those flashing lights and that awful siren start blaring, signaling that the police are on their way and I have to find something in this building other than my secret painkiller drawer to prove I actually work here. I spend twenty-seven real seconds punching in various pass codes until one finally stops the ticking clock, then immediately bend at the waist to dry heave as the computerized voice bleeps "Disarmed, ready to arm." I try to regain composure as I rummage through the communal fridge to find the Coke I swear I left in there, but give up when I hear voices approaching, shoving someone else's soda into my bag, swearing to myself that I will replace it as soon as the liquor store next door opens. When I get to my desk, the fax machine is shooting memos from various referral clinics by the dozen, and the phone's blinking red light indicates that eighteen messages have been left in the twelve hours since we've last been around to answer the phones. Hospitalized patients, realizing that the box-cleaners and food-pourers have arrived to start their shifts, howl and yowl and caterwaul for their breakfasts. The place quickly fills with the brain-rattling noise of the day: the sharp clang of metal bowls in the waist-high tub/sink, the whoosh of water from the hose spraying down the outdoor runs, the slam of a washing machine filled with blankets and towels, treatment orders shouted over the din of bark and meow.

I listen to the voice mails (several hang-ups, a couple "Hello, is this the answering service? Hello . . . ? Hello . . . ?! JEAN, I TOLD YOU THEY WEREN'T OPEN YET!" and at least one "No, I don't have an appointment but I'm bringing my dog right when you open and I want to be seen immediately, I don't care what else the doctor has coming in" just to get the stress adrenaline pumping) while trying to say good morning to coworkers as they answer e-mails and file lab work. By the time we unlock the doors, we've done so many things that it feels like the day should already be over, and then comes the constant deluge of impatient questions I may or may not have the answer to (yes, I know the requirements for filling out an international health certificate for a cat to fly to Romania; no, I don't know whether your dog walker's advice to use cedar oil will get rid of a flea infestation); the hourly pop quiz of every single one of the prescription diets we carry and its indications (because if I sell Hill's a/d to a person who really needs IAMS Low-Residue, I could get in hot water); and the ungraceful mating dance that occurs when someone mindlessly talking on her cell phone has a pissed off, scared, snapping terrier raging at the end of a loosely held flexi-leash as I'm trying to usher her into an exam room.

I can translate the consistency of a dog's stool as relayed to me by its owner into the proper medical terminology:

"Soupy" = diarrhea.
"Watery" = diarrhea.
"Like a melted chocolate bar" = diarrhea.

"Kinda runny this morning but lumpy by lunchtime" =
   diarrhea.
"You know, like, vomit but from her butt" = diarrhea.

There are seven doctors in our practice, which means that in addition to explaining surgery-consent forms and the difference between each of the dangerous vectors that can bite and infect a dog and the products we carry to protect them, I have to be a personal assistant to one dude who likes his messages time-stamped and dated and listed in order of importance and a woman who prefers to be tracked down and delivered her messages by hand. PLUS FIVE OTHER PEOPLE. I just interviewed a young woman who responded to the blunt and very direct ad I posted to find more front desk help, and during the meeting I was like, "Listen, I like you very much, so I'ma be straight with you. Can you: spread a payment across three credit cards without forgetting how much goes on which one, remember which cat in the waiting room is vomiting and which one is here to get subcutaneous fluids, find that list of files the technicians asked you to pull half an hour ago and get them pulled, and send the refills Ms. Bruggeman called in to the pharmacy? All at the same time? Without coffee because no one told Lori we were out and the delivery isn't coming until tomorrow? Because that's what this job is."

To have a child, you have to at the very least find someone to make it with you. I mean, doesn't that constitute some sort of unofficial screening process? Whenever I see someone dragging along a snot-nosed little tax deduction I think, "Someone liked that guy enough to let him pollinate her flower. He must be cool." (No, I don't. I really think, "I bet he only got fourteen minutes of sleep last night, thank the Lord I can't get pregnant.") Or at least you have to get someone to sell you a bag of sperm, and that takes enough money to pay for it, and you probably have to fill out a bunch of paperwork and forms and background checks, too.

But you don't have to do anything to prove you're worth a pet, and that makes our job totally ridiculous 82 percent of the time. Any old asshole can pick up a cat in the street or walk into a pet store and buy a sad puppy-mill puppy. And as soon as they do they call us, asking the kinds of questions that are often baffling to me. Now, I'm not going to get up on a soapbox, because it probably couldn't support my weight, not to mention I am most certainly not the kind of person who does research before making a decision or a purchase. Everything I buy is an impulse purchase, be it a new flavor of sparkling water or a thousand-dollar computer. I get my clothes off the Internet, for fuck's sake: I am not risk-averse. But yo, I wouldn't get a goldfish without at least asking the kid at PetSmart what kind of tank I had to buy for it and how much the food was going to cost and whether I had to find a doctor to take care of it. Not everyone is as lucky as I am to have seen the horrors of pet ownership up close and personal for a decade, but every day there's a situation that makes me drop all pretense of professionalism and hit some client with a "Bro, for real?!"

A couple of years ago we had a cat come in that had been run through a heat cycle in a dryer. Please read that sentence again. Read it again, and imagine the type of person who would allow such a thing to happen. Can you picture it? Are you there yet? Perfecto. Now imagine answering his phone call as he described the practical joke that had gone wrong, and the feeling in my stomach while listening to him try to explain what happened, then multiply that feeling by fourteen years, and maybe you now have some insight into why my outlook is so dreary sometimes. We are exposed to human beings of the lowest common denominator, all day every day, and this is a multimillion-dollar, incredibly busy practice in the suburbs. It costs sixty-plus dollars just to walk in the door.

Once I sat, horrified, as a woman in our waiting room licked a kitten to "clean it" because she "wanted it to feel like it was back with its mother." Another time I watched a woman with long lacquered nails and an expensive-looking boob job eat a dog treat to "see what it tasted like to her dog." You know, because human and canine taste buds are so similar; it's why I have a bowl of Purina One every morning in lieu of traditional oatmeal. And that was shortly after a different birdbrain drank a little bit of her dog's diarrhea medication while Laura ran her credit card "just to see if it worked." Listen, I put a lot of dumb shit in my mouth, but at least I have the decency to do it where no one can see me, like the time I smashed some sour-cream-and-onion potato chips on half an old cheeseburger I found in the backseat of my car and wolfed it down behind a nightclub.

I have seen people pay thousands of dollars for chemotherapy and rehabilitation and get acupuncture for their dogs and psychiatrists for their cats. I would have never understood the logic in that before but now I *get it*. My first week was straight-up shocking. I had no idea that people paid to have their dogs' teeth cleaned! How would you even do that? Coax her into the chair, get her to lie back, strap the goggles on her then hang a Milk-Bone over her face so she holds her mouth open so you can get those molars clean?! (Now I know that you put a dog under general anesthesia and take a digital X-ray of its head and Alyssa scales its good teeth while the surgeon on duty that day pulls out the bad ones, and the first time I ever stood next to the dental sink watching it go down I nearly passed out.) Ultrasounds, neurology, dermatology, ophthalmology, radiation, cardiology, oncology? Man, who knew?! When I was a baby we had two dogs, one of whom remained chained to the garage due to bloodlust and unpredictability, while the other stayed inside with us and guarded my crib. I would fall over dead right now if you told me that either of those goofs had even had shots, let alone that my father had ever put one in his nice car to drive out to Buffalo Grove to get thousands of dollars' worth of chemotherapy. I don't even think the outside dog got dog food, just milk and scraps of raw meat. (Which, with my current level of companion-animal expertise, I would gently discourage my dad from feeding him.)

Things I've learned at my last job that might come in handy in a very specific set of circumstances at a new one:

- Don't give your dog Advil if you suspect he has a fever, and please refrain from giving him Imodium if he has a little diarrhea. Especially if he has diarrhea because you thought he should have some of your burrito. Call your vet.

- And, while we're at it, stop diagnosing your pets at home. Take them to the doctor. Unless you have a DVM license, in which case I'd like to see it.

- Walk your dog on a leash and keep your cat in the house. Every time I saw a dog that got beat up by a possum or a raccoon or a fox or a dingo it made me want to choke-slam somebody.

- Stop leaving chocolate and grapes and shit where your dog can get at them, and please, for the love of Doritos, put your weed away. Because at least once a month a dog just houses its owner's stash, and while it's kind of hilarious, (1) it makes your dog feel like crap, and (2) loud is expensive. I mean, you really can't get a dog if you want to still live like a careless slob. I do, that's why I never got one. Sometimes I leave deliciously stinky underwear on the bathroom floor or fall asleep with sushi next to the bed or forget to tie the trash with the old pork chop bones in it up tight. All careless things that could lead to hundreds of dollars of treatment at my vet and a stern side-eye from the staff at the front desk. I have seen dogs vomit: socks, toys, jewelry, bottles, soap, and underwear. Put your things away already. Are digital pets a real thing yet? I saw *Gone Girl*, go order a robot dog.

- Name your pet something reasonable that people who maybe aren't hip to the zeitgeist can spell and figure out. Yeah, I like *Game of Thrones*, too, but that doesn't mean I'll be able to find your cat Daenerys Targaryen with ease in our computer system. Far be it from a woman with a cat named Helen Keller to criticize, but at least the average third-grader could spell that. When *Lord of the Rings* was poppin', we had a lot of Éowyns and Faramirs and Galadriels coming in for booster shots and heartworm tests, and I never read those books, hoe. And these nerds would take it as a personal affront that I needed a hint at how to spell their dogs' names. Fine, tell me who Kizzy Reynolds is and then we'll talk. JUST NAME IT WRIGLEY LIKE EVERYONE ELSE IN CHICAGO, GOD.

I am calm in a crisis. Like the time that one dog got hit by a car right in front of us on the street or the time that cat had a heart attack as her owner handed me her carrier. Once, after a dog was euthanized, we witnessed a funeral ritual in our office that I found surprisingly moving, even though I'm convinced that whatever spirits there happen to be, they're all in collusion against me. I've held a lot of scared hands, hugged a lot of people who bravely came alone to put their best friends down, and cried a lot of tears with people I don't really know, but I kind of do? Because as they neared the end they were in the office every other week or because I was there when Megan was pregnant with her first baby. He is now ten years old and his sister is eight and they're on their second dog, geez where does the time go!?!

I am also very dependable and incredibly loyal, which some might read as a lack of motivation to better myself or make anything other than a lateral move. But I was twenty-two when I started this job. And you know what? Sometimes it really is okay to just have a fucking job. Not a passion, not a career, but a steadfast source of biweekly income deposited directly into a checking account from which food and medicine and apps one totally forgot about having downloaded will be paid for. A job you are good at, that makes you feel like you're doing something good in the world. I've had a life: I have been a dropout, a deadbeat, *and* a student; I have lived on Damen, on Central, on Hoyne, on Lunt, on Albion, then back to Lunt again; I've purchased ten pairs of glasses, added at least a dozen trash tattoos, read hundreds of books, watched countless hours of television, lost old friends, made new ones, and had my heart broken approximately 289 times. I'm moving away and it terrifies me to leave the one constant I've had in my entire life, but it's time to start a new chapter. So I need a new job, and I'm available to start immediately.

feelings are a mistake

I am trying to adjust to living in a house where there is such a thing as a limit on "screen time." This is a new concept for me. My original plan for once I'd made the move east on I-94 had been to get an office space or—in line with my misguided, unrealistic fantasy of myself as an artist—a studio space. The kind of place in which I would hang tapestries and burn sage sticks and surround myself with real artwork and plants. This is not the kind of person I have been so far in my life, one who "clears energy"; I just push the towers of books and trash on my desk aside to make room for my battered, gravy-splattered laptop and mine the cloud of negative energy above my head for material. My new fictional office involved an artful desk, the kind you'd find in a hip design magazine, and one of those computer monitors that's as big as a garage door and wholly unnecessary for someone who writes about scowling at nature on the Internet. But in my pretend world I also dabble in, oh, I don't know, Web design? Espionage?! Something that requires a big, fancy monitor.

In reality, I've scrolled through the listings for tiny office spaces in abandoned-looking buildings with the sole intention of escaping there to watch R-rated movies uninterrupted, ones with fucking and curse words. Then I wouldn't have to sit with my finger hovering over the pause button as I listen for tween-age footfalls banging down the hall to ruin the fun I've earned for staying alive this long. I want to eat room-temperature soup while watching entire seasons of *The Real Housewives of New York*, free of questions like "Who is that?" or "Why is this show interesting to you?"

I mean, I'm 137 years old—I can have screen time whenever I want! I bought twelve handheld computer devices, and, yes, I absolutely must have them on my person at all times; I pay the Internet providers so I can connect to all of the GIFs and memes I need; I stood by awkwardly as the gentleman from DirecTV connected these 2,469 channels. And sure, I'll probably be so busy watching a video on the laptop and listening to the new James Blake record on my phone that I'll forget about that *CSI: Miami* marathon I wanted to watch on the True Crime channel, but it's worth a hundred dollars a month just to know that if I wanted to watch it, I could.

Maybe I could put my headphones on and enjoy last week's episode of *Black-ish* on the iPad despite the screen detox imposed on this house's smaller people, but can I really enjoy it when a floppy-haired ball of angst with preteen emotions is glaring at me over the top of the book his mother is forcing him to read?! No, I cannot. This must be what it's like to grow up with siblings your own age; you did all your spelling homework and got moist, delicious cake after dinner, but your brother didn't, so his was followed by a side of jealousy and rage that he projects onto you and your delicious cake.

And it stops tasting good, because homeboy has leeched the sweetness from it with his beady, resentful eyes. This is my life on "Turn Off Those Cartoons and Read a Book" Tuesday or "You Didn't Clean Your Room, So the iPod is Going on Top of the Refrigerator" Sunday.

Last Tuesday there were friends over. I didn't even stop to ask who the little blond heads belonged to as they whizzed past me (into our house, out of our house, pounding up the staircase to the second floor, thundering down another into the basement). There are too many of them, and everyone under the age of twenty-seven looks alike to me, so why embarrass myself or them by confusing an Adeline with a Madeline when they don't give a shit about talking to me anyway? Whenever I hear the screen door slam shut, I cock my head for the indistinguishable cacophony of high-pitched squealing, then barricade myself and the cat in the nearest room full of boring adult shit (bank statements, topical analgesics) until they all run away to terrorize some unsuspecting neighbor's tranquil home.

Beelzebub and I were sitting on the bed, debating whether to apply for a reverse mortgage, when I heard the unmistakable feedback of the karaoke machine followed by a Taylor Swift song crackling through its tinny speakers. Moments later, three high-pitched voices warbled through the air-conditioning vent. I nudged Helen awake. "Should we waste a bunch of energy dragging all our shit downstairs or do you wanna just murder-suicide right here?" She considered it for a few seconds, glancing warily around the room, her eyes coming to rest on a pair of recently laundered compression stockings hung out to dry on the back of a chair.

She sighed. "Is our enemy list up-to-date?"

I pulled a faded sheet of crumpled graph paper from where

I'd hidden it deep within a dresser drawer and quickly added 543 names to it. "Now it is. Help me find something sharp."

Helen nodded toward the at-home blood pressure cuff propped up on the desk. "Is that thing sharp?" She smirked.

"Get out!" I screamed, and she heaved herself off the bed and slowly lumbered down the stairs in search of the sharp knives we kept out of reach of tiny pink hands.

Helen made her (half-)white-flight pilgrimage first. I was out of town for a few days and returned to find my dining room covered in shattered drywall after a radiator pipe had burst and partially collapsed the ceiling. I knew something was off as soon as I opened the door and was greeted by a surge of moist heat. My first thought was that I'd left a Lean Cuisine smoldering in the oven and that no one had noticed because I never replaced the battery in the carbon monoxide detector after it died six years ago. But then I rounded the corner to find Helen, coated in a fine layer of asbestos dust and glaring at me from next to the empty bag of food I had left for her to eat while I was away. I immediately threw her in a box and surveyed the ruined landscape. Eighty percent of my considerable trash library was a warped, pulpy mess; there was condensation beaded on practically every surface; the clothes hanging in my walk-in closet were damp to the touch; and my lipsticks oozed wetly from their shiny cases. It was too overwhelming to even think about, so I didn't. After cutting some air holes in Helen's box, I hauled her down three flights of stairs, then stood on the curb googling "how many months can I skip paying rent over some straight-up bullshit" while we waited for an Uber.

After depositing the Antichrist in a dog-size kennel at work,

I went back to sort through the wreckage of my life. I'm pretty much a scorch-the-earth kind of dude, so I spent the night dragging bags of waterlogged pillows and damp clothes down to the dumpster. As I was attempting to dry my mattress with a neighbor's borrowed hair dryer, my landlord let himself in to tell me he'd *shrug emoji* "have some guys take a look" in the coming week. Like there wasn't a giant hole in my fucking wall. Like the goddamned ceiling beams weren't goddamn exposed. Honestly, I'm not smart enough and this thing about my dead cat probably isn't the place to get into it, but what is life when you work a hundred hours a week in order to live in a dump with a toilet that leaks shitwater every time you flush, and the guy who cashes your uncomfortably large checks (which still don't feel quite right, considering the neighborhood you live in) looks at the child-size hole in your wall and is like, "WOW, THIS SUCKS"?

Helen lived at the hospital for a few weeks while our decaying apartment was torn apart and put back together again. She loved it, man. The techs would just leave the cage door open and let her walk around like a queen, one who occasionally let her subjects pet her lustrous fur. Helen didn't give a fuck about dogs and would just sit there, daring them, as they were brought back for shots or treatment. She got really good at laying on stuff and rolling her eyes every time I walked past her perch to grab a box of Heartgard or drop a urine sample in the lab. She was having as much of a blast as I imagine the King of Babylon can when forced to mingle with the mentally inferior inhabitants of earth, while I was spending every night alone in my empty apartment sitting in front of a television that had shorted out because it wasn't equipped to deal with junglelike conditions and still feeling kind of guilty about my miserable cat all alone in a cold, sterile cage. So I asked if Mavis wanted her in Michigan.

"What is 'Michigan' again?" Helen asked, eyeing the atlas I'd handed her warily.

"It's beautiful! They have trees there! And squirrels for you to watch!" I grasped for some enthusiasm.

She turned her nose up at the idea that she could be bothered to pay attention to anything, let alone a "squirrel."

I tried again. "Um . . . apples? Deer?!"

Helen sighed grudgingly, then wrapped some catnip and a handful of salmon treats in a hobo bindle before demanding I carry her out to the car. She cheered up as soon as we hit Lake Shore Drive, emerging from her travel box to sniff cautiously at the lake breeze wafting in through the car windows. She sat on the armrest between us for the entire trip, alternately napping and shaking herself awake solely to express her displeasure at the outfit I'd chosen for the drive. We pulled up to the house in the early evening, the sidewalk dotted with children playing as they waited for dinner.

"I hate it here," Helen announced, peeking out the window at a girl jumping rope next door. "Take me back to the place where I know I can get good ribs."

But she adjusted. The morning after we got there, she'd already peed on the welcome mat by the door, eaten 90 percent of the other cat's food, and was basking in the sunroom, chattering angrily at the birds who dared graze at the feeder hung outside the window. I sat on the couch, watching her perched on the chair she had sneezed on to mark as her own.

I was thinking that Mavis and I could maybe pioneer a new type of marriage situation, one that some relationship expert would eventually dissect in *The New Yorker*. Mavis could continue to hang laundry on a line and churn her own butter in rural Michigan, and I would spend the days counting down to my early death in my dark, refrigerated Chicago apartment, scowling out my peephole at neighbors who made too much noise getting their groceries off the elevator. Mavis could keep picking her own blueberries to make jam under the blazing sun and knitting socks to sell at the Christmas bazaar in the church basement, while I could bankrupt myself ordering $17 cocktails at rooftop bars and waiting four hours for a brunch table downtown. We'd meet up occasionally to talk about married stuff (uh, property taxes? which big-box retailer has the best deal on economy-size containers of soup?!) and pretend we were still interested in having sex. Sounds like a dream, right? But oh no, fam—apparently marriage involves a little thing called compromise, a concept of which I'd been previously unaware. For Mavis, this means having to wake up to a framed photo of Ice Cube on her bedroom wall, but for me, it apparently means GIVING UP EVERYTHING I EVER LOVED.

Everything here is dangerous and/or irritating: mosquitos the size of a fist bite through my winter-weight hoodie (I will never change) and leave itchy, egg-size welts in their wake; loud-ass frogs in our backyard pond croak all goddamned night; bats flap their leathery wings hysterically while trapped in the woodstove; squirrels in the branches over the deck hurl walnuts at our heads maniacally as we grill farm-stand corn for lunch. Sick raccoons fall out of trees, fat groundhogs chew through the fence to snack on the okra and tomatoes I refuse to help harvest, and young cats disembowel field mice and leave them in the middle of the dining room at dawn. Gas is thirty-seven cents a gallon. You can buy shoes at the grocery store. The farmers' market is full of actual farmers instead of bearded hipsters in distressed flannel pontificating about peak asparagus season. This week on *Americana Horror Story*.

But the Serpent of Old was learning to love her new life, or at least pretend to love it just to spite me whenever Mavis hovered nearby to get a picture of her to post on Instagram. By the time I packed my good cassoulet pan and a bag of assorted sensible cotton briefs and joined them in the Wolverine State, it seemed that Helen had adjusted quite nicely, mastering the art of intimidating the other cats with a punishing look and learning to use stairs for the first time in eight years relatively quickly. After a couple of weeks of giving me the cold shoulder, she busted open the door to my bedroom and sat at my feet demanding to be picked up and placed on my pillow. "Are you happy that I'm here?" I asked tentatively after she placed her moist butthole *right* on the spot where my eye had recently been.

"LOL NO."

"Of course you're not." I shoved her off the bed and started counting the twenty-nine assorted vitamins and medicines I have to take every morning. "Why did you even bother coming in here?"

"I enjoy watching you suffer. Hey, did you know that these people eat *three* different vegetables with every meal? Also they don't consider milkshakes a food group. You could learn a lot by following their example." And she sashayed out of the room with her tail swishing lazily behind her and an unidentified human finger between her teeth.

I have followed their example, okay? Under Helen's mockingly watchful eye, I started doing healthy things like "eating roasted cauliflower" and "deciding to read a book even though there is a television in the room." Which brings us back to my newest adversary: days with a limit on screen time. Helen doesn't care. I mean, she's a goddamn cat, so why should it matter if I'm two weeks behind on *Queen Sugar*? I've learned that every child in the neighborhood can feel a television's electromagnetic waves from three blocks away and will wander into the room on some "Hey, whatcha watching?" shit just as it reaches a crucial point in the episode.

But then she bit a kid. I didn't even see it coming until it was too late. One minute we were settled on the pointless couch in the room with no TV, watching as tan legs in postage-stamp-size shorts whizzed past us to grab precut vegetables and other snacks at the bottom of the food pyramid from the kitchen, and the next, Helen was pressed into the couch's corner with her ears flattened against her head. I tossed the book I was pretending was an episode of *Survivor* on the floor, hooked my hands under two scentless armpits, and lifted Addison? Madison? out of harm's way, only to be caught off guard when Helen latched on to my arm instead. After I wrestled my arm away, we sat looking at each other for a second, her eyes angry and mine surprised, my blood smeared across the tiny patch of white on her chin. "What has gotten into you?" I asked as what sounded like an entire third grade trampled up the stairs to get away from her. Helen responded by bear-hugging the smooth, slender ankle of a mom who'd just arrived to collect her Caitlin and plunging her teeth into the softest part.

Later that night, at midnight, Helen and I were sitting alone in an exam room at the emergency vet. The harsh yellow lights overhead made the cat hair stand out in sharp relief against my faded black hoodie and pajama pants. Helen, in her carrier on the table across from me, was seething. It had taken snow boots, two pairs of fireplace gloves, three old towels, and a folding chair to trap her in the hard plastic case. The doctor entered shaking an X-ray, disconcertingly cheerful considering the time of night and the severity of my situation. Maybe he was nervous. He told me that Helen's chest cavity was small (I know) and her lungs were constricted (mm-hmm) and her heart was abnormally small (FOR SURE), and while none of that explained why she'd lost her shit, fainted, then rose up to launch herself in my general direction again, it definitely was the reason for her labored breathing and a possible cause of her "emotional breakdown." Helen snorted at that.

The doctor droned on about her poor quality of life, how she had suffered from a URI and a compromised immune system since she was born, how I might have to chase her down and put her in a headlock every day to force Prozac into her, how he couldn't guarantee that her behavior would ever go back to normal. I started adding up all my credit card balances in my head, trying to calculate how much I was willing to pay for this cat. "Well, why don't we start with—?"

"I'm ready to die," Helen interrupted, tapping the bars of the cage. "Get the paperwork ready, I want the shot." The doctor excused himself and left us alone.

"Well, that was abrupt."

She rolled her perpetually leaky eyes. "It's embarrassing seeing you wash kale and floss your teeth every day. I don't want to go back to that. If I don't die now, I definitely will after another week of your natural deodorant and wholesome family entertainment."

"I was watching porn this morning on my phone!" I scoffed.

She started making slashing motions across her throat.

"Fine. Do you want a hug or something before I go?"

Almost imperceptibly, Helen moved her head to the left. Not a nod, but not *not* a nod. I unlocked the carrier. She stepped dubiously onto the table, then climbed down into my lap. I hadn't held her since she was a little baby. Every time I've moved to lay a hand on her in anything even resembling an affectionate way, I have been met with everything from mild resistance to misdemeanor assault. I felt her relax in my arms, her body warm and liquid, and I patted her head with the tip of my index finger. She closed her eyes and rested her head gently against my mangled and oozing arm. I tried to remember whether I had brought with me to Michigan the old bottle of amoxicillin from when I'd gotten my tooth pulled. I stroked Helen's back and heard the faint rumble of a purr coming from her throat.

Our fever dream was broken by a knock at the door. The enthusiastic grim reaper popped his head in, asking, "We all good here?" Helen dug her rear claws into my thigh, and I would've body-slammed her to the ground if homeboy hadn't been watching. Instead, I shoved her as nicely as possible onto the chair next to me and smiled while cursing that asshole back to hell, all the while reaching for the clipboard so I could give him permission to send her there. A technician came in with a portable credit card machine, and we all stood around as the chip reader took approximately forty-seven awkward minutes to process my payment. The tech left, and Helen Keller gave me a sour look. "Thank you for being my Annie Sullivan, I guess," she said as I put my wallet back in my bag and shrugged into my coat.

I helped her back into her carrier and lingered near the door. She had sneezed a huge glob of mucus onto my pants.

"You want me to, uh, read a few stanzas of 'The Rainbow

Bridge' off my phone or something?" I asked, one hand on the doorknob.

Again with the eye rolling. "Well, you're the lesbian . . ."

I snatched the door open. "LOL BYE."

I cried all the way to the twenty-four-hour grocery store and ate half a rotisserie chicken in the parking lot. It was the tribute she would have wanted.

we are never meeting in real life.

It's a sweaty, balmy night circa 2002, probably definitely around 1:00 a.m. It's the witching hour, with fifty-nine minutes until the lights come on and you can realize that you're just not into the person you've spent the whole night shout-talking to. I'm in the basement at Sinibar, lurking next to the bar, trying to order myself another Jameson, because that's what I like. Or maybe that's what I want people to think I like. I'm not even sure I had a personality back then; I just tried to haphazardly arrange other people's projections and shit I thought was cool into something captivating. Meeting people in public with the idea that they might want to get my underpants off has always been difficult, because I'm fat and bars are too loud and crowded and dark for me to just pull out 250 out-of-context-pages of the YA novel I've been working on for years to try to impress some dude I wanna fuck. I've spent a lifetime glaring at dance floors full of people who didn't splash on cologne and pay twenty dollars to get into the club to meet someone "interesting."

Jameson in hand, I tip the bartender and am about to drink the whole thing on the spot (I HATE GETTING BUMPED

INTO AT THE CLUB) when I feel someone sidle up next to me and put a hand on my drinking arm. "Oh, hey, it's you," I say to this stranger, which is one of many reasons that I would rather die than make a person's actual acquaintance, this need to fuck every human interaction up with a jolt of disconcerting awkwardness. It catches him off guard, I can tell. He recovers quickly and asks what I am drinking. He chokes back a laugh when I tell him, because no one wants to make a nine-dollar investment in a weird idiot who oozes discomfort and wore her dad's New Balances to a nightclub. My dude is already in too deep to turn back now, however, so he orders one for me and another for himself and I reconsider my decision to pass on the bread basket at dinner. I have approximately six sips until I become relatively incoherent, but the music is loud, so I can blame it on the DJ. Homeboy ushers me to a secluded corner of the room and toasts the drink in my left hand while I drink from the one in my right before launching into a soliloquy about all the cool shit he does that makes him sexy. I am right there with him, I am almost ready to take home a copy of his mixtape and listen to it for real, when he says, "You came in with the girl in the purple, right?" Right. "Yo, that girl is beautiful. Do you know if she's into slam poetry?" And since the tiny lime-slicing knives behind the bar are too dull to effectively cut my wrists open along the vein, I choose to attempt suicide the old-fashioned way: listening to a hot dude who doesn't want to fuck me ask a bunch of questions about the friend I came here with. I chug my whiskey in the hopes that my death from alcohol poisoning will be immediate and painless.

This exchange typifies 98 percent of my former social life, and you know what I've realized? I spent too much time trying to mold myself to fit the romantic ideals of humans who proved themselves unworthy of that effort, and I regret it. Never again will I be with someone who is unwilling to accept me as I am, or who has any desire to mold me into something that makes me uncomfortable. Mostly this is because I'm too anxious and overwhelmed to meet new people and try to make my interests sound more fun. I have unsuccessfully tried to be a girl who is into obscure collage. I have unsuccessfully tried to be a girl who is into the electronic music that just sounds like a bunch of *bleeps* and *bloops*. I have unsuccessfully tried to be a girl who reads graphic novels. And experimental fiction. And David Foster Wallace. I have stayed up late watching bootleg kung fu movies on shitty laptops; I have grimaced through expensive meals that were little more than adorable art projects on a plate; I have shivered in an icy stadium seat cheering for a team I have no stake in, and I have cooked lobsters (which I don't like) for someone who wouldn't dare eat a burger from McDonald's (which I do).

Before I gave up on life and meeting people in public, I used to let my friends set me up on blind dates, mostly because I hate myself. I don't really feel alive unless I'm actively wishing I was dead. This is how your friend, who loves you, sets you up on a blind date: first, she browbeats her boyfriend into exhaustively scrolling through the mental Rolodex of every man he's ever worked for, talked to, or shared an elevator with until he can come up with one who has a job, isn't married, and might be convinced to eat dinner across from a woman she's only willing to describe as "very smart" and "super funny" with "an amazing personality." Then, she forces you to cannonball into the middle of the dating ocean holding an inner tube with no flippers or oxygen tank. And I appreciated the consideration, I really did. It warmed my cold, dead heart every single time I got blindsided by people who had no idea what they were in for and had a difficult time masking

I really did want to tug on a Spanx and s.

from that dude your husband met in the gr

ing lot after he backed into your guy's Volvo \

off his engagement and blather on about televisi

pretends to never have heard of over a plate of midpi ιasta.

Yes, please. Sign me right up. Oh how I love to fatfish the unsuspecting!

This is why the Internet is a miracle. I mean, I don't care about watching real-life murders on the dark Web or angrily tweeting at CNN anchors, but it is a magical thing that I can just open up my computer and cultivate superficial relationships with people who may or may not have stolen their profile picture from an Instagram model without having to pluck my mustache hairs first.

You can just take your tiny robot out of your pocket and see that, no, I don't really have an interest in modern architecture. Or, if I'm pretending to, I can take twenty seconds to figure out which buildings I like best from the googles and impress you with my ability to deftly copy and paste. Don't get me wrong, I am horrified by most of the Internet, but I am happy it's there. Because having a beer with some kid you met on the Internet isn't really a blind date. I mean, you've seen some blurry, faraway, dimly lit pictures, haven't you?! And you know she likes foreign films and quiet evenings cooking together at home, don't you?! Well, then that asshole who won't text you back next week is not a stranger. Or is maybe less of one. At least you know that when you jump out of the Uber they're not going to be like, "OH, HAI. Are you the person the girl I'm supposed to be meeting brought along as her bodyguard?"

I know my blog is hilarious, but I'm not that smart in real life! If you run up on me in the grocery store, YOU ARE

...NG TO BE DISAPPOINTED because (1) there is probably diet peanut butter in my cart, and (2) it sometimes takes a lot of staring at the wall in contemplative silence to come up with these jokes and my off-the-cuff stand-up could use some work. And I'm pretty funny on Facebook, but you can erase and edit shit on the computer, then read it out loud to make sure you aren't embarrassing yourself before you post it, and if there is a machine that does this for you within casual friend gatherings, I will give you all my money to pick one up for me and leave it on the back deck and go the fuck away.

I just wanna Gchat about the hidden messages buried in the 160 misspelled characters that new dude you're dating just texted you, not rub a palmful of almond oil into my skin at the end of the evening to loosen up all the silicones I piled on my enlarged nasal pores so you wouldn't know the toll thirty-six tumultuous years on this earth actually take on a human face after you make me talk about it at a restaurant. I just want to fast-forward to the part of the relationship when I don't have to buy fancy bottled water in an attempt to trick you into thinking I really care about myself or peel my body out of the overpriced underwear with an extra panel I bought to make this poorly chosen sweater dress look more appealing. At what point in this nascent friendship can I let my eyebrows grow back in and admit that I regularly cry to the animated version of *Beauty and the Beast*? Forget figuring out how many dates until it's appropriate to have sex—I want to know how many we have to get through before it's acceptable to stop.

I don't wanna talk on the phone, I just want you to text me. That way I can look at it and answer your question when my show is over. I once dated an asshole who, every single time I called, would immediately text, "Are you in a burning building?" Um, no? If I were, and I still had the ability to breathe and see the numbers on my phone while choking to death on smoke, my first call would most certainly not be to a dude who says LIE-BARRY and is afraid to try artichokes.

There was a brief period in the mid- to late nineties when all I ever wanted to do was call people on the phone. But, like the periwinkle stirrup leggings and snap-crotch bodysuits I preferred at the time, dialing a person's telephone number in an attempt to have an actual conversation with him is now horribly outdated. I will never harass your ears with a list of the mundaneness of my day, nor will I expect you to pause *The Walking Dead* to try to string an interesting sentence together for my benefit. Before we were able to bore each other in person every day, Mavis used to call me at the end of each night. I would break out in a cold sweat trying to come up with a way to make Wednesday distinguishable from Tuesday; it was the hardest thing I've ever had to do in my life. I mean, I just don't do that many *things*. I was living the same unremarkable life every single day, and trying to put a new outfit on Friday when it was exactly the same as Thursday was exhausting. How many times can I say "Brooke and I ordered hot dogs for lunch, and I read another chapter of [enter the title of any John Grisham novel] on the toilet"?

And I don't wanna talk face-to-face, either—that might even be worse. I can't play games on my phone if you are watching me. Tell me, when was the last time you had some soul-draining emotional talk with someone and came away from it feeling happy and secure and wanting to spend more time with the person who just berated you for forty-five minutes about something you couldn't give a fuck about? Wait, scratch that. When was the last time someone came at you suggesting a "talk" and it turned out to be anything other than forty-five minutes of being berated about something you couldn't give a fuck about?!

I have never, in any of my interpersonal relationships, with women or men, proposed to sit down somewhere and have a talk. No one ever wants to sit you down and talk about something good, like how he or she should buy you more stuff; people want to trap you in an uncomfortable chair so they can go through the laundry list of your perceived crimes. And all you can do is sit there like a scolded child, nodding sadly in agreement that yes, you are the literal worst.

I'm not doing any of that. You'd have to trick me into a talk. If I was lucky enough to get a warning text, you would never see me again in your life. That is not a joke. The minute you say, "Hey, Irby, we need to have a talk later," you can guarantee that my phone number will be changed by the end of the business day. Send me a follow-up e-mail to reiterate that a conversation must absolutely take place and I will be in witness protection by the end of the week. Can't I just apologize before you work yourself into a lather and save us all a bunch of nervous sweating? I swear to God, I'm really sorry for that thing I did, and I promise I will never ever do that thing again as long as you promise not to leave me any more anxiety-inducing voice mails.

I'm depressed, man! Please don't ever leave me a voice mail! Lexapro has yet to cure the existentialist horror that is modern telecommunications! I see the voice mail notification pop up and am instantly consumed by dread. I mean, I didn't pick up, so you should know I'm not emotionally prepared to say words into a phone right now. Why make it worse by saying "Dude, call me back" without specifying why or whether this is time-sensitive information?! Like, literally, someone better be dead, or even better, the caller better be dead and calling from the grave to give me the info I'll need to collect that insurance. THIS IS HOW MURDERERS ARE MADE.

I am a simple person. Kind of. I mean, I don't really have any dreams beyond comfortable pants and unlimited sparkling water. When I was little, I was never brave enough to declare what I wanted to be or what I wanted to do, because I grew up in the kind of situation where you just wanted to make it to the end of the week, or the next school day, or to graduation, or to work, or to the next paycheck, or to Red Lobster every once in a while to celebrate. I don't like to think more than a few weeks ahead; I just ride the least choppy wave and see where it takes me. I like to sit at home in mild terror as the world rages outside without me, hoping that no one is going to drop by and expect me to come up with a humorous anecdote or ask me to have an opinion on something. I like to get in the car and turn some funeral music up real loud (King Krule, Mazzy Star, anything dark and brooding) and drive around looking at all the nature I don't want to get on me. I want to go to Walgreens and have the cashier pretend I wasn't just in there yesterday, buying the same exact shit. All I want is for the self-checkout at Target to be open—is that a crime? I also just want to pay whatever the fuck things cost, without question, even if I think it might be wrong and especially if there's a line form-ing behind me, because arguing with someone who can smell you is embarrassing. I can feel my organs shutting down when-ever I'm forced to stand behind a woman demanding forty cents off a bottle of ketchup despite the fact that she forgot her coupon at home. As if she is red-faced and raging at Mr. Heinz himself, rather than Jonathan, who has to ride his bike home and write a book report after this.

I will never be snappy with a waitress or lose my mind on

the phone with customer support or make small talk with someone else's kid, because, honest to God, I would rather eat my own teeth than suffer any more humiliating human contact. I promise you that I will never ask the woman at the wine shop about her shiny new engagement ring or wonder aloud about whether the pizza delivery man caught that flu that's been going around. I will smile politely at people walking their dogs, but I will never grab them by the arm and say, "Hey, what breed is that?" while they struggle to decide how to courteously answer my question with a steaming bag of shit in their hands. While I do appreciate a succinct elevator pitch, I am balls at delivering one effectively. Joanna, who owns the indie bookstore down the street from our crib, asked me the other day to give her the name of a good book I'd read recently, and because I value her opinion, I stood in front of her for, like, three real minutes cycling through every book I've rated on Goodreads in the last three months trying to determine which one would be the most impressive. I just stood there with my ears on fire wondering if I should just say *A Little Life* because no one would think you were dumb if you made it all the way through a seven-hundred-plus-page book. And I didn't; I did not make it through that book, because a quarter of the way in, this other book about teenagers in love that I wanted to read came out, so I abandoned the smart shit to spend an afternoon sobbing over a story about children I could have given birth to having sex.

I went to a book lecture earlier tonight, and it took me forty-five minutes of bewildering indecision to figure out what to wear just to sit in an audience in an indie bookstore next to your aunt Jill and her second husband, Craig. Craig took copious notes the entire time, filling his battered Moleskine with scribbles about how to structure a piece of short fiction, while I squirmed in a folding chair and wondered if the leave-in conditioner I'd used made my hair look dusty. Or was it too crunchy? I have a very specific textured look that I hope to achieve whenever I let my hair grow out, and maybe this new stuff I tried isn't working right, but now I'm stuck in a place where pulling out a mirror would definitely draw an inescapable number of eyes. Plus, it wouldn't be appropriate, and I pride myself on knowing things like when and when not to use the reverse camera in your phone to make sure your curls are poppin' (but not poppin' too much, because you're going for a natural kind of thing). Frankly, none of the middle-aged white people in this room could explain what a C4 curl pattern is, but when you spend your life in a near-constant state of unease, details like that don't matter.

This is the particular prison my anxiety has created: I can go and do the thing, and say the other things, but I gotta spend an hour wrecked because the only clean daytime pajamas I have available to me are the ones that don't do enough to conceal that crease in the upper arm fat under which my triceps are buried. Or trying to preemptively answer any question I might be asked, by anyone. Or worrying that this is the kind of place where you have to actually interact with a person to get the key to the bathroom. A person who will be counting the minutes it takes for you to return with that key, a person with whom, once you cross the six-minute mark, you will definitely have to construct an awkward joke to deflect from the fact that you just took a shit in their bathroom. My mind is a never-ending series of shame spirals. Do I have to go to that? And if I do agree to go to that, who else is going? In what capacity do these people know me? As an Internet joke person, or as a sad real-life person who sometimes makes jokes? Sad people make not-sad people uncomfortable, so I better think about smiling. Or will that be off-putting? If someone asks me a question while I have food in my mouth, how am I going to deal with that? Should I answer and cover my mouth and gross everybody out, or sit there chewing for an eternity while they expectantly wait? Are the chairs sturdy at the restaurant? I better look the place up on Google images. If they don't look sturdy, how do I tactfully suggest someplace else? OMG, remember that time I broke a chair? I wonder if anyone who was there still thinks about that time I broke a chair? When they get together, and no one is paying attention to how much is on their plates because they are thin, do they ever bring up that time they got to watch as a cartoon fat person had to get up from the floor after she— I'm not going. I'm just not going to go. My nice clothes are not nice enough for this place and I'm not sure whether there is enough money in my bank account to cover a dinner this extravagant and what if my card gets declined? What if my card is rejected because I never signed up for overdraft protection? I thought you had to pay more and I'm sure one of these people with good credit will cover it, but how will I be able to get up and walk out of that fancy restaurant since my face will be melted down the front of my shirt? Why do I feel so embarrassed all the time, and why can't I figure out how to not do the things that embarrass me? Like pick good shirts I actually like and sign up for overdraft protection and look people in the eye when I talk to them and just get over whatever is holding me back and *ask* the lady at the M•A•C counter in the mall how to correctly use concealer instead of walking around looking like a trash panda?!

We are never meeting in real life.

acknowledgments

My undying devotion to my family and my friends and my heroes. Thank you to everyone who has made me laugh and helped take care of my rotten heart + brain, especially my chosen family: Laura Daener, Anna Galland, Caitlin Pinsof, Carl Cowan, Jessie Mae Martinson, Keila Miranda, Giancarlo Olvera, Lara Crock, Emily Barish, Vanessa Robinson, Keith Ecker and Mario Calhoun, Kate Packard, Dolores and Jeff Strom, Damon Young, Kiese Laymon, Kaitlyn Greenidge, Chris Terry, Akilah Scott, Julia Goldberg, Brian Sweeney, Kirsten West Savali, Erika Nicole Kendall, Julia Borcherts, Sarah Hollenbeck, Kate Slagoski and Erin Kahoa, Fred Owens, Zachary Jones, Laura Munroe and Mark de la Vergne, Megan Stielstra and Christopher Jobson, Brooke Allen, Melissa Fisher, Jared Honn, Jeremy Owens and Andy Fine, Mariyam Hussain, Carly Oishi, Luvvie Ajayi, Danielle Hahn Chaet, Debbie Pressman, Ian Belknap, Torean Wilson, Christine Wolf, Roxane Gay, Keely Jones, Angie Frank, Katy Maher, Cara Brigandi and Ted Beranis, Marina Hayes, Mel Winer, Lindy West,

Samantha Bailey, Pauline Vassiliadis, Mya Seals, Amy and Ryan Warren, Amelia Tomlinson, Mark Bose, Danielle Henderson, Regina Burris, John Sundholm, Issa Rae, Megan Reynolds and Sarah Hill, Jenny Lawson, Kelly Knabb, Jason Van Fosson and Tell Williams, Alex Hardy, Allen Makere, Joanna Parzakonis, and James E. Hagedorn.

I would like to thank Crissle and Kid Fury for making the brilliant podcast *The Read,* the only thing I consistently have to look forward to other than television courtroom dramas. Thank you to Ben Affleck for making *The Accountant* so good and punchy, and God bless Forest Whitaker for existing. Plus, big thanks to my imaginary friends and various Internet communities. I would not be alive if not for your hilarious memes.

Actually, without Drs. Lori Jackson and Manoj Mehta I would definitely be dead? Thanks for humoring my awkward jokes and not making fun of my disgusting body while prescribing many things to keep it alive. Dr. Mehta, who has looked in my gross, gaping butthole so many goddamn times and never recoiled in horror, deserves some kind of award.

It feels so weird and pretentious to, like, *have an agent* but who am I kidding: without them I would be handing out photo-copies of this trash I make on whatever street corner is closest to my house, because I am very lazy. Anyway, all my love (and a portion of my earnings) to Jason Richman and Kent D. Wolf, especially Kent, who is the exact same amount of horrible I am, thus making this the greatest working partnership of all time. And, holy shit, I couldn't have done any of this without my editor, Andrea Robinson, who didn't seem disappointed with me during any part of this process even though she absolutely should have been.

THANK YOU, WIFE. YOU ARE PROBABLY THE BEST PERSON I HAVE EVER MET.